Hello, Stranger

Hello, Stranger

How We Find Connection
in a Disconnected World

Will Buckingham

GRANTA

Granta Publications, 12 Addison Avenue, London W11 4QR
First published in Great Britain by Granta Books, 2021

A CIP catalogue record for this book is available from the British Library.

1 3 5 7 9 10 8 6 4 2

ISBN 978 1 78378 564 3 (hardback)
ISBN 978 1 78378 565 0 (ebook)

Typeset by Avon DataSet Ltd, 4 Arden Court, Arden Road, Alcester,
Warwickshire B49 6HN

Printed and bound by CPI Group (UK) Ltd, Croydon, CR0 4YY

www.granta.com

In memory of Elee Kirk (1977–2016)

'To have friends coming from afar, is this not a joy?'

– Confucius

Contents

Contents

Introduction

It was mid-morning, an overcast day at the beginning of August. I let myself into the house and called out for the cat, who came padding over, mewling in greeting. I reached down to stroke him. For the past week, he'd been neglected. I had spent the last seven days in the hospice by Elee's bed, returning home only occasionally to top up the cat's food. I felt bad for my neglect. Shutting the front door behind me, I went into the kitchen. The cat padded after me, curious and hungry.

On the kitchen work surface was a large plastic tub filled with vegetarian kedgeree, left by a friend who had keys to the house. Back then, so many friends had keys, I had lost count. There was a handwritten note on the lid: *In case you can't be bothered to cook.*

I looked out into the back garden, where the sun was doing its best to break through the cloud. I thought of how Elee had left the home we shared so suddenly, just over a week ago, without time to pack. We imagined it would be a brief hospital visit, that she'd be back after a few hours. We thought we would have more days, weeks even, before the end. But when we arrived, they took her straight to the acute ward, and from the ward they took her to the hospice, and Elee never came home.

I was ragged from my week in the hospice, sleeping in the chair by Elee's bed, holding her hand, watching her mind drift and fade, waiting for the end. And now she was gone, and I was back, and the house was empty. I was too exhausted to cry. I needed sleep. Thirteen years of shared life, and now this emptiness. I was not yet familiar with grief, with the gusts and tides of it. I was waiting to see what it did to me, how it would remake me.

That afternoon, I contacted friends and family. I passed on the news. I posted on Facebook about Elee's death. The messages came rolling in: from friends, from strangers. I was grateful for the kindness, but it was too much. I replied to a few messages, then I closed the laptop, and I wondered what to do with myself.

In grief, the poet Naja Marie Aidt writes, 'We have no hope for the future, we can neither imagine nor sense the future anymore. We can't see an hour, a quarter of an hour, a minute ahead. We cannot make plans. We find ourselves in a futureless time.'[1] Grief is a paralysis; it is a loss of the future. What do you do, when the world is broken? My first instinct was to hide. To curl up with my grief like a wounded animal. To not show it to the world, as if this grief was unique, exceptional, something to be treasured – mine and mine alone. I wanted to coil in on myself, to withdraw into the shell of loss.

In the evening, I cooked. I wondered if I should get drunk. On the sideboard was half a bottle of single malt that would do the job. But when it came to it, I didn't feel up to drinking. I made a glass of hot milk and went to bed. The cat came and snuggled into me. In the early hours of the morning, annoyed by my sobbing and my restlessness, he went back downstairs.

The following day, after a bad night's sleep, I sat again at the dining-room table. I thought of the homes Elee and I had shared over the years, our many visitors, the strangers and friends we had hosted. I thought of the way people came and went, the way our home had always seemed so porous, the way it had *breathed*.

'My house is diaphanous, but not of glass,' the poet Georges Spyridaki writes. 'It is more of the nature of vapour. Its walls contract and expand as I desire. At times, I draw them close about me like protective armour . . . But at others, I let the walls of my house blossom out in their own space, which is infinitely extensible.'[2]

I needed breathing space. Now more than ever. To draw the walls around me, then to let them open out. The in-breath and out-breath of living.

I opened my laptop, went online, posted a short message. I was bruised, I wrote. And I was hurting. But I didn't want to hide away. I wanted to be with others, to connect and reconnect.

Come on over, I said. I'll cook.

Loss tears a hole in the world. It exposes us, leaves open a rent, a gap. It is disorientating, puts the compass points of our lives in disarray. Loss makes the future impossible, because it refers only to the past. But loss is never total. And sometimes into that gap, that rent, the breeze of newness can blow; and in the acknowledgement of our brokenness – in the softness of it – a stranger reaches out to embrace us, and in this embrace is a bridge to something new. The relationship to the stranger, the philosopher Emmanuel Levinas once wrote, is a relationship with the future.[3]

Several days after Elee's death, I was walking down the high street. My bike had just been stolen from outside the station and I was raging inwardly at the thief's inconsiderate timing ('To the thief who stole my bike,' I posted on Facebook, 'you could have chosen a better time. You could have chosen a better bike.')

In the street, I was stopped by a stranger – a charity fundraiser. She was in her twenties and had an open, optimistic face. 'Hi,' she said. 'You look like a friendly person. Can you spare a minute?'

I hesitated. I saw the logo on her tabard. She was fundraising for breast cancer research.

'Do you know much about breast cancer?' she asked.

I could have lied. I could have brushed her off. I felt a constriction in my throat. But then I thought I might as well tell the truth. 'Yes,' I said. 'My partner died in the hospice, earlier this week.'

The stranger paused to take this in. 'What was her name?' she asked.

The question surprised me. It was the simplest of questions, and it seemed like a gift. 'Elee,' I told her.

She smiled and reached out to touch my arm. 'You need a hug,' she said. Then she put her arms round me and squeezed me hard, her plastic tabard crackling. A hug of solidarity; a shared acknowledgement of the difficulty of living.

'Thank you,' I said, crying into her shoulder, utterly overwhelmed. 'Thank you so much.'

INTRODUCTION

*

I needed many things in the days and weeks after Elee's death. I
needed solitude. I needed friends; the people who were closest to
me, who shared in the same loss. I needed to draw the four walls
of my home around me like protective armour. And I needed to
let them extend outward, to invite people in. But I was surprised
by the extent to which I also needed strangers – people who knew
nothing of Elee, who knew nothing of the particularities of my
grief. For much of my life, without realising it, I have sought out
strangers, strange ideas and strange situations. I have opened up
my home to people I've never before met, and spent time in the
homes of others. My life has been shaped again and again by
these encounters; but it was only after Elee died that I realised
how connecting with strangers can act as a powerful antidote
to the paralysis of grief. The person serving me in the coffee
shop who asked how I was (I lied, of course). The fruit sellers at
the market ('How are you, m'duck?'). The conspiratorial looks
exchanged with fellow passengers at the train station when the
display board flashed up the message that the train was cancelled.
The men who came to varnish the floor – we'd booked them in
weeks before. These were all small things. But in those days and
weeks and months after Elee's death, in my encounters with
strangers, I was reassured that the world still went on, that grief
was not everything.

The stranger, the sociologist Georg Simmel writes, is both
nearby and remote. This combination of proximity and remote-
ness, he adds with some optimism, is 'of course a completely
positive relation'. Simmel obviously never had his bike stolen by
a stranger at the worst possible time. And while there is no

relation, anywhere, that is completely positive – everything has its upsides and downsides – in those days after Elee's death I realised that there is also something freeing about strangers, about the possibilities they bring. Strangers are unentangled in our worlds and lives, and this lack can lighten our own burdens. This is why strangers sometimes unexpectedly become confidants; with them, Simmel says, we trade, 'the most surprising revelations and confidences, at times reminiscent of a confessional'.[4]

When the stranger who was raising funds for cancer research hugged me in the street, I felt myself become lighter. Like one of the faithful after leaving the confessional, I was restored to the knowledge that even when the world is torn, when it is broken, it can be remade.

This book is about strangers. It is about the hope for newness that strangers bring with them and the fear of harm they provoke in us. It is about how, when the world seems to be at its darkest, it can help to allow our homes and our worlds to breathe more deeply, to become porous. The human brain is equipped to keep track of 150 people, give or take a few. These 150 are the people we can claim to know, the people with whom we have ongoing connections. They are the people who wouldn't find it weird if, when we bumped into them in the street, we suggested going for a drink – or sent them a message from our locked-down apartment, suggesting a chat on Zoom. They are the people about whom we imagine we have some kind of insight, some sense of their inner world, of what makes them tick.[5]

For most of the human past, this was the circle of our belonging: the people closest to us; our kin, our friends, our associates. These were the people with whom we lived out our lives, endured our everyday struggles, took our greatest pleasures. They were the small huddle of others with whom we shared our corner of the world. This is how our brains are designed: our neocortex can only take so much before it loses the thread of all those lives.

Back in the day, when our ancestors lived together in small hunter-gatherer bands, more or less everybody in the community was kin. And if a stranger turned up – somebody astonishing and new – they either went on their way or, if they stuck around, they were soon absorbed into these kinship networks. 'Those who come into the community (with the possible exception of the lonely anthropologist),' Robin Dunbar writes, 'soon become embedded into that web of relatedness because they marry and have children with members of the community.'[6] In the Tanimbar islands of east Indonesia in the mid-1990s, when I was carrying out anthropological fieldwork, my host, Ibu Lin, told me I should think of myself as her adoptive son. As such, she said, it was her duty to find me a wife. Kinship is not so much about descent as about sharing this common interest in future generations. Marry me off and I become part of this future too, part of a network of belonging.

Until around 1800, most of us lived in small face-to-face communities like this. We were surrounded by kin, neighbours and friends, and strangers were few and worthy of comment.[7] But the Industrial Revolution changed everything, setting in motion a one-way ratchet of urbanisation that is still under way. And as we continue to crowd into conurbations of millions upon millions of strangers, it is no surprise that we start to feel the strain.

*

When set against the eight billion or so with whom we share our planet, our small circle of 150 intimates dwindles almost to nothing. However assiduously we weave and reweave a sense of home in concentric circles of belonging, these circles soon blur off into the bewildering masses of humanity who are unknown to us. How can we even make sense of all this dizzying strangeness, all this unknowability, all these multitudes?

Our responses to strangers are always double – a quiver of anxiety and possibility, excitement and fear. Strangers are hard to read, hard to pin down.[8] We don't know what they are thinking, what they are up to. We don't know what they are capable of, whether they might harbour violence or strange disease. Strangers are beyond our grasp, beyond our power and our comprehension. And there are so very many of them. This fear of strangers is a fear of many things. It is the fear of what strangers might do. It is the fear that our hands are already full, that we have enough people to care for already. It is the fear that our fragile circles of belonging will be broken and that this multitude will overwhelm us. It is the fear of change, of the new things, both good and bad, strangers may bring into our lives.

The fear of strangers – literally 'xenophobia' – runs deep through us. We are accustomed to thinking of xenophobia as a vice. But before it calcifies into hatred or into hostility, xenophobia has its roots in the sheer unknowability of strangers, in a justified anxiety at the risks unknowability poses. When we think of our own softness, our vulnerability, and when we think of the hardness of the world, a shudder runs through us. This tremor is felt in some of the world's earliest texts. It is there in the *Odyssey* – a text obsessed by the doubleness of promise and threat posed by strangers, by the thin line between hospitality and hostility, welcome and violence. It is there in the Bible too, as it is in the *Epic of Gilgamesh*, and in the ancient texts of China and India: books written at exactly the time when people were beginning to crowd together into cities, when the problems posed by strangers were multiplying, and when people asked more urgently what it means to live in a world where most of those who surround us are unknown to us.

But the fear of strangers is only part of the story; strangers also intrigue us. They promise unthought-of possibilities, futures we can't yet imagine. Xenophobia has its counterpart, its not-quite-opposite, in a fascination with newness, in the sheer curiosity we have in the face of the strange and the unfamiliar. The Greeks call this friendship with the strange, this desire to connect with strangers, 'philoxenia'. The word has its roots in the New Testament. 'Do not be forgetful of philoxenia,' Hebrews 13:2 says, 'for through this, some have entertained angels unawares.' Although humanity's most ancient texts are alive to the risks posed by strangers, they also pulse with the electric thrill, the sheer potential, that comes from opening up our lives to difference. They testify to the human desire to reach out, to connect with the unknown.

Every encounter with newness is a complex web of curiosity and fear, philoxenia and xenophobia, hospitality and hostility. This admixture of fear and fascination lurks in language itself: the English words 'host', 'guest', 'hospitality', 'hostility' and 'hostage' (not to mention 'hotel', 'hostel' and 'hospital') share a common root. Following linguist Émile Benveniste, the philosopher Jacques Derrida traces the origins of all these concepts to the ancient root *hosti-pet* (the asterisk indicates that this word is a reconstruction).[9] The reconstructed root has two parts: the first, *hosti*, means 'stranger'; and the second, *pet*, means 'potential' or 'power'. Strangers have always presented us with uncertainty: angel or devil? Possibility or threat? There is power in these questions. There is the potential to change things, for better or for worse.

There is something about living in this world of strangers that deepens our isolation and our aloneness. We are social mammals, living on top of each other, crammed into tower blocks and underground trains, jostling for room on the crowded pavements. But still we struggle to connect. Urbanisation provides fuel for loneliness; and in urban centres, we live increasingly solitary lives.[10] The last two centuries have seen a global shift in how we live. Once, most of us lived in agrarian societies, where multiple generations shared the same household, where social mobility was low and long-distance travel was rare. Back then, it was easy to know who our tribe was, the huddle to which we belonged. Now, our lives are more atomised: we are more mobile; many of us live alone; our relationships are more transitory and fleeting.[11] And, as a result, the ache of loneliness runs through us. We hunger for connection, for a sense of what it might mean to live out our lives in the company of others, but this connection is too often elusive. 'We don't have a word for the opposite of loneliness,' Marina Keegan wrote. 'It's not quite love and it's not quite community; it's just this feeling that there are people, an abundance of people, who are in this together.'[12] The paradox of urban living is that we have access to a greater abundance of people than ever before, but what we lack – what we crave – is this sense of togetherness. And this creeping, spreading loneliness has devastating consequences. It affects our mental and physical well-being. It severely depresses the immune system.[13] It impacts our health. It is a truth repeated so often that it has become a cliché: we are surrounded by countless others, milling around right here in the midst of our worlds and our lives, but nevertheless we are disconnected and alone.

In this book, I explore how to tackle both these problems: the problem of living in a world of strangers and the problem of loneliness. I am interested in opening the door a little wider and finding ways of reconnecting, so that we can overcome our isolation to live more expansively, more hospitably, more open to the promise that strangers bring. In seeking out ways to free ourselves from the big, unwieldy problems of isolation and xeno-phobia, I cut across cultures, disciplines and historical periods, weaving together stories from philosophy, literature, history and anthropology. Because if these problems can seem unmanageably vast, human ingenuity is bottomless, and sometimes the solutions we seek can be found in surprising places.

In the first part of this book, I explore the intimacies of our interpersonal lives. I ask about our homes – how they breathe, and how they hold their breath. I ask about how it feels to welcome strangers, or to be welcomed in turn. I explore the subtle dance of ritual as we cross the thresholds of each other's lives, the codes of honour that bind us and divide us in equal measure, the shared pleasures between hosts and guests, the things that can go wrong, the inevitable moment of departure, and the moment when we ourselves become strangers to the living, slipping over the threshold from life into death.

Then, in the second half, I expand the circle outwards, to ask questions not just about our homes and the intimate circles of our lives, but about how we can contribute to building the kinds of societies that are worth living in. Part Two is about the journeys made by travellers and migrants as they navigate difficult borders and thresholds. It is about the doubleness of cities and crowds: the hurly-burly of collective delight and the ache of loneliness. It is about how we can get on better with the neighbours. And it is about what community could mean, in a world in motion, a world where strangeness is the norm.

The strangers who surrounded us, who outnumber us, are not going to go away. So we have a choice. We can retreat and claim indifference, asking what business it is of ours what these other people get up to, saying that their lives are no concern of ours. We can let xenophobia get the upper hand, and put ourselves on a war-footing, seeking to drive out the strangers in our midst, to control them, to denigrate them. But neither indifference nor hostility offers a reliable path to a shared future worth living in. In this book, I explore the third option, one that is more difficult, but ultimately more rewarding: the challenge of opening up the door to the strangers in our midst, alive to the knowledge of how afraid we are and of how easily we can be wounded. The task of opening up the door, to say, 'Hello, stranger,' and to embrace the strangeness of others – so that, together, we can find better, more creative ways of living.

Part One

I

Welcome Home

It was 58 BCE and the great Roman orator Marcus Tullius Cicero was far from home. Exiled to Thessaloniki, he sat out the sweltering summer on the shores of the Aegean. Exile was an agony for Cicero. Surrounded by strangers, he sank into a deep depression. With nothing else to occupy him, overwhelmed by homesickness, he busied himself sending letters home, a chronicle of anger, misery and loneliness. Uprooted from those closest to him, he wrote to his brother Quintus that he was reduced to 'merely a ghost of a living corpse'.[1] No one, he claimed, had ever experienced such wretchedness, such misery. Stripped of his citizenship, unable to return to the city he loved, separated from his kin, from his native land, he felt his sense of self crumble away. 'I miss not only my possessions and my family,' he wrote, 'but also my former self, for what am I now?'[2]

Any of us could ask the same: what are we, without the tenuous connection we have with home, the ties that connect us to a place, a community, a small corner of the world where we have gained a foothold, where we are not a stranger? Home is a sacred space, a place of protection against the many uncertainties of the world. Home is who we are. And if we want to better understand what it means to be a stranger, first we need to understand what it means to be at home.

The Roman statesman was sent into exile in the wake of a long-running feud with his rival Publius Clodius Pulcher. Four years before Cicero's exile, Clodius had caused a scandal when he was caught dressed as a female lute player, infiltrating the rites of the goddess of chastity, Bona Dea. The sacred rites were restricted to women and were presided over by the Vestal Virgins – priestesses of the hearth goddess, Vesta. The ceremonies were conducted in the utmost secrecy in the house of Julius Caesar, hosted by Caesar's wife, Pompeia. According to Plutarch's account, Clodius was in love with Pompeia; and, for her part, 'she was not unwilling'.[3] Clodius disguised himself and snuck in to seduce Caesar's wife. He passed as a female musician – he was, Plutarch tells us, naturally beardless – only to give himself away when he fell into conversation with a slave girl. Horrified by his deep voice and seeing through his costume, she raised the alarm.

It was almost the perfect scandal: a seething cauldron of religion and politics, power and desire, gender taboos, sacredness and violation. Clodius was prosecuted on charges of impiety, the maximum sentence for which was death. In court, it was Cicero who testified against him.[4] The trial took two years, but at last Clodius was acquitted. This might have been the end of it had Clodius not been appointed people's tribune – the representative of the people – in 58 BCE. He was a brashly populist politician and he stirred up violent mobs to support his growing power.

Then he went for Cicero. He proposed a new bill that held culpable any official who had put citizens to death without due legal process. Crucially, the bill was retrospective. Five years before, Cicero had suppressed the Catiline conspiracy that sought to overthrow the Roman Republic. Cicero had declared martial law to put the conspiracy down and ordered the summary execution of the main five conspirators. In forcing through his bill, Clodius had Cicero in his sights; and when the bill passed, Cicero was charged and found guilty.

The punishment imposed upon Cicero was *aquae et ignis interdictio*, or 'interdiction from water and fire'. The interdiction was a form of social exclusion that made it illegal for anybody to offer him hospitality – a drink of water or a shared hearth. Removed from all normal social intercourse, Cicero had no option other than to flee into exile – renouncing all claims to his property, to citizenship, to a permanent place of residence. It was the loss of everything he knew as home.[5]

Cicero would not have been unaware of the bitter irony. The story began with Clodius violating the rites of the Vestal Virgins, the priestesses of the hearth. It ended with his expulsion from his own hearth, and from the hearths of all those close to him.

In exile, Cicero went into decline. He lost weight. He contemplated suicide. He couldn't stop crying. The interdiction from water and fire, the forced absence from his home, was almost too painful to bear.[6] He raged and sobbed and paced. But as his exile went on, Cicero's anger, his homesickness and depression hardened into the determination to return. His letters home became more strident, more argumentative. He sent petitions to the powerful, arguing that the interdiction was unlawful, that it should be rendered null and void. He pressed for Clodius's law to be withdrawn and he argued for his own reprieve. Meanwhile, in Rome the political tide was turning. There were calls for Cicero to be reinstated. Clodius responded by raising violent mobs to back up his authority. The factions friendly to Cicero raised their own mobs and there were pitched battles in the street.

When Clodius's term as tribune came to an end, the allies of Cicero were in the ascendant again. The exiled statesman, receiving letters from home saying the mood in Rome was turning in his favour, moved from Thessaloniki to Durrës on the Adriatic coast, to take advantage of the prevailing political winds. From there he could return at short notice, when the political situation allowed it.

Back in Rome, in an attempt to make sure Cicero had nowhere to return to, Clodius razed the statesman's home to the ground. On the site, he erected a shrine consecrated to Libertas, the goddess of liberty. But events were moving quickly: on 4 August 57 BCE, the Senate met to pass a bill that permitted Cicero to return, and the exiled politician sailed back to Brindisi in Italy.[7] From there he travelled to Rome. On his arrival, he was feted. Pretty much everybody in Rome was sick of Clodius. The great and the good of Rome came out to embrace the returned exile; and, as Cicero later wrote to his friend Atticus, 'the steps of the temples were thronged with the lowest members of society, who offered their congratulations with tumultuous applause.'[8]

*

Cicero was back where he belonged. But he was not yet home. He might have had his land restored into his ownership, but the shrine to Libertas still stood. And it presented him with a problem. Cicero had two choices. He could rebuild his home next to the statue and live out his days in the shadow of this monument to his humiliation. Or he could get rid of the statue altogether. But the latter course was not easy. You couldn't go around in Republican Rome tearing down statues. Charges of impiety, as Cicero well knew, could easily lead to death.

On 29 September, Cicero put his case to the highest religious body in Rome, the Collegium Pontificum or College of Pontiffs. His speech, *De domo sua* – 'On His Home' – was a masterpiece of savage rhetoric. Cicero argued on two fronts. First, he said, the original consecration of the land was invalid: Clodius had not followed the proper process; and, besides, he was an impious scoundrel. What can you expect of a man who goes sneaking around forbidden rites in women's clothing? Simultaneously, Cicero argued that the *domus*, the home, was itself a sacred unit. 'What is more sacred, more closely guarded by religious safeguards, than the home of each and every citizen?' Cicero asked. 'Here are the altars, the hearths, the household Gods; here are focused the family rites, observances, and ceremonies. The home is an asylum held sacred by all; to tear any man away from his home is a sacrilege.'⁹

Cicero's double-pronged strategy was successful. The College of Pontiffs ruled in his favour. Clodius was humiliated. The statesman got his land back. He removed the statue and rebuilt his house at public expense.

*

The human need for a place to call home goes deep. So too does the sickness that comes from being away from home. But we are not the only creatures who fashion and refashion homes in which to live. Many animals adapt their environment to make a more secure refuge, remodelling the world in which they find themselves. The animal kingdom is filled with burrows, nests, webs, warrens and hives. Weaver birds craft architectural marvels. Beavers remodel whole ecosystems to their liking. Chimpanzees select the best wood to make sleeping platforms, looking for the sweet spot where springiness and stability are perfectly balanced; then they doze in safety, high above the forest floor.[10] Swallows piece together their nests out of mud. Bower birds, frivolous and dandyish, are ostentatious architects: they build follies purely for display, faux-homes to attract mates. Termites pile up great ziggurats of earth. Hermit crabs are squatters, living in the homes others have vacated. On the riverbed, caddisfly larvae glue together tubes of stone and sand with silk, and take up residence inside. As a child, I plucked them from the water, fascinated that something so small could nevertheless build.

The specifically human desire for somewhere to call home is rooted in our animal vulnerability, in the softness of our bodies, the need we have for nooks into which we can curl ourselves and feel safe. There are, as philosopher Martha Nussbaum writes, 'some forms of vulnerability that human life contains for all: bodily frailty and disease, pain, wounds, death'.[11] We cannot escape these things, but we can ameliorate them by building a protective shell around ourselves, and by seeking comfort within the place that we have built.

But if the human idea of home is continuous with these animal attempts to manage our vulnerability, it is vastly more complex than a weaver bird's nest, the sleeping platform of a chimpanzee or the calcified tube of a caddis fly. Because home for us is not just a place: a territory, a range, a corner of the world. It is, as anthropologist John S. Allen says, 'not simply a location on the landscape where a person lives'. Instead, for human beings, home 'has a privileged place in our cognition'.[12] It is this cognitive dimension, the sheer emotional force of the idea of home, that separates out human home-building from the homes built elsewhere in the animal kingdom. Home is – at one and the same time – a place, a community and a fiercely burning tangle of feeling and imagination. We feel intensely about our homes. We relish the homeliness of being where we belong. We ache with the homesickness of being away. And all of this is why Cicero's claims about the sacredness of home seem anything but hyperbolic. Because home is not just where we happen to live. Nor is it just the people to whom we feel we belong, the circle of our kin and our intimates. It is also a deep sense of *being at home*. It is the insouciance we have when we know this place is *ours*, cognitively and emotionally set apart from the strangeness of the world in which it is immersed. It is the way we care about the housekeeping; it is how we order the spaces in which we live. It is the desire to nest, to snuggle, to curl up with our intimates, to huddle together and spin a sense of belonging. Home is, as Verlyn Klinkenborg writes, 'a place we can never see with a stranger's eyes for more than a moment';[13] it is a place where you never need to be asked to 'make yourself at home', because there is nothing to make, because home is where you already are.

*

Even for those of us who consider ourselves to be wholly secular, a sense of sanctity hovers around the idea of home. Some of humankind's earliest gods were gods of the hearth. The oldest of all Indian religious texts, the *Rig Veda*, contains over 200 hymns to Agni, the god of the sacred hearth fire. 'Let us have a good fire and be beloved,' one hymn reads. 'For when the gods have a good fire, they bring us what we wish for. Let us pray with a good fire.'[14] Agni has his counterpart in the Greek Hestia and the Roman Vesta – whose name comes from a proto-Indo-European root meaning 'to dwell' or 'to spend the night',[15] and whom Cicero called 'the guardian of our most private lives'.[16] While other gods had a statue, in Vesta's shrine in ancient Rome there was instead a sacred fire. It was this fire that was tended by the Vestal Virgins – whose number Clodius tried, with such little success, to infiltrate. In Rome, there were also gods of the domestic hearth, the *penates*, who by Cicero's time were already regarded as unfathomably ancient. Meanwhile, in China the stove god Zaoshen still presides over kitchens, keeping his eye on family business, returning to heaven every year to report to the Jade Emperor on how things are going.

We cannot know how far back into prehistory these ancient hearth gods go. And yet, given that human beings have always been preoccupied with gods, and that fire is so hard to manage – so seemingly possessed of its own mind, its own will – it would not be surprising if they went back to our first attempts at controlling fire. But however far into our shared past these fire gods reach, one thing is clear: the invention of the hearth was the thing that made home possible.

*

If home begins with the control of fire, archaeologists still argue over how to date this turning point.[17] But whenever it was that our ancestors first built a hearth, and first fashioned a shared sense of belonging as they stared into the flames, some of the best early evidence of human-like homes comes not from the settlements of *Homo sapiens*, but instead from the hearth fires of our cousins the Neanderthals. It is in Neanderthal settlements that it is possible to see the emergence of the rich cognitive brew that characterises the human sense of home: the layering of social meanings, the coming together of place and community, the sense of home as somewhere that is constantly *remade*, so that it can provide permanence in a changing world. As Laura Spinney in the *New Scientist* puts it, 'Neanderthals may have been the original home-bodies.'[18] As a community, they ate and slept in the same small locations. They organised their domestic spaces and, in doing so, they organised their shared lives.

If you go down to the Abric Romaní rock shelter near Barcelona, you can see the remnants of the hearth fires where generations of Neanderthals lived, ate and died. Abric Romaní was inhabited for seventy millennia, from 110,000 to 40,000 years ago. Archaeologists have unearthed multiple hearths at the site, surrounded by animal bones. According to researcher María Gema Chacón, in the places archaeologists have dug deep into the soil, revealing these ancient hearths, it is still possible to smell the scent of roasted deer. Here, for generation after generation, a fluctuating community of between ten and twenty individuals lived together, more or less full-time. And this shared home offered protection in a dangerous world. It was a circle of care, where these early human communities could deal with the hazards posed by wild animals, illness, disease, exposure to the elements, natural disasters and, latterly, those troublesome *Homo sapiens* – who may have had a larger or smaller part to play in the Neanderthals' eventual extinction.[19]

Human beings are social animals; their best hope of protection has always been through cooperation, clustering together into groups of mutual support. And these networks of mutual support often extend outwards from the home to encompass neighbours and outsiders. The site at Abric Romaní is set in a naturally defensive position; but its organisation is as much domestic as defensive.[20] It speaks of the mutual security that comes from shared lives. Around the cooking hearths is evidence of collective feasting. Neanderthal cuisine was surprisingly complex: roasted deer, bones that were boiled for stock, smoked meat and flavouring provided by wild herbs. But our Neanderthal kin did not just feast in small family groups, they also had people over for dinner: the number of those eating by the hearth often far exceeded the number of those in the community. There is no better way of strengthening alliances with outsiders than by holding a party.[21] Then, as you sit around the flickering hearth fire, chewing on hunks of deer fragrant with herbs and smoke, you can settle into the social warmth of belonging, knowing that someone has your back.

Home gives us a foothold in a world. When looking for a place to call home, our ancestors favoured places of shelter and verdancy, places where there was fresh running water, where prey animals were abundant and predators few. They liked low hills and semi-open spaces – good for visibility, but also for hiding when necessary. Places like Abric Romaní, in naturally defensive positions, but open to the world, were close to ideal. These preferences recur in the dreams of paradise that are found throughout the world's artistic and religious traditions: the cool caves to shelter from the heat of the sun, from the driving rain and from the dangers of the outside world; the low hills; the copses and shady groves; the trees hanging heavy with fruit; the rivers abundant with fish; the deer that come to drink, unafraid of human contact. According to the scholar of religion Jani Närhi, 'Paradise representations reflect the evolutionary ideal, although it is unreachable in this world.'[22] But the dream of paradise is not just a dream of a particular kind of environment, but also one of a particular kind of community: a community at peace with itself. Paradise for social animals like ourselves is social: it is living together harmoniously, having fun, hanging out in the cool caves, the pavilions and the huts that dot the landscape. Evolutionarily speaking, this dreamed-of paradise – a place of abundance, where as a community we together live and flourish – is the optimum environment to support our flourishing. And if the world sometimes falls short, as it inevitably will, together we try to fashion the world to our will; we make the best of things. We are, after all, an ingenious species, finding hospitality in places that seem most inhospitable, turning even deserts of ice and sand into places of abundance.

Human understandings of home have always been flexible, adaptable. The interplay between place, community and imagination has led, throughout history, to a bewildering variety of human habitations: palaces and cave houses; nomad tents and longhouses; suburban homes and communes. And the ways in which our fellow humans have organised their households socially is no less diverse. 'Home is not merely a place,' writes the anthropologist Fran Barone, 'it is a *lived experience*, bound with space, proximity, love, togetherness, doing and making.'[23] And the ways in which this doing and making play out differ from place to place. In many parts of northern Europe, homes are typically quiet and private, housing nuclear families, having few visitors, the boundaries between inside and outside firmly drawn. In other places, home is more rambunctious and sprawling. In some cultures, homes may have dedicated spaces for sleeping and entertaining guests. Elsewhere, as in some Iranian homes, pretty much any room, other than the kitchen and bathroom, might find itself repurposed in any way whatsoever.[24] For some, home is a fixed place, the place where your family has lived for generations. For others, it is movable, as in nomadic communities; and in such communities, homesickness may be less the longing for a single location and more the desire for movement itself, for paths and trajectories instead of places.[25]

But if home can be many things, it is also something we can reimagine and reshape; and in a world of increasing isolation, and increasing fear of strangers, we have never needed this reimagining more. In my early thirties, I was living in Birmingham. Strapped for cash, I took a job as a researcher on a Europe-wide project, interviewing old people about their levels of happiness. It was not a glamorous role: I tramped the streets, knocking on strangers' doors, and if there were old people at home, I arranged to interview them about their well-being. For the first few weeks, I was working in the suburb of Aston. It was a place known for its deprivation and poverty. It was also at the time one of the epicentres of the seemingly unending cycle of violence between Birmingham's two biggest gangs, the Johnson Crew and the Burger Bar Boys. When I was assigned to work in Aston, my boss told me to take care, but from the first it was a place where I felt welcomed and at home. The doors of the terraced houses hung open on their hinges. People sat out on the steps and chatted. Kids played in the street, kicking footballs around. Their parents hailed me from the doorsteps, called me over to chat. The old folks were welcoming: they invited me in, and as I went through the survey's interminable questions, they plied me with tea, coffee, cakes and the odd glass of rum.

After finishing up in Aston, I was relocated to a quiet, private estate on the other side of town. The detached houses were set back from the road behind iron gates. They bristled with security cameras. The streets were leafy, but silent. Nobody walked the tree-lined boulevards, unless they had a dog as an alibi. No kids played out. These were homes standing on the defensive, barricaded against outside threat. I walked up and down the streets, pressing on the buzzers beside the iron gates. Mostly there was no reply. The residents had already seen me on camera, identified me as an outsider, made their decision. Only sometimes did the speakerphone crackle with the tinny voice of an invisible resident, afraid of what I wanted, angry at the intrusion.

I spent several days walking those streets, but I was never invited in. Not even once. Nobody called out in greeting. Nobody offered me cake, or tea, or rum. Nobody wanted to chat. And after a week, I got fed up. It was a thankless task. I couldn't bear it any longer. I quit the job.

Throughout history, human homemaking has been enormously diverse; but in our contemporary, urban societies, there has been a drift towards a very specific idea of home – the idea of home, above all else, as a fortress built to keep out strangers, a securely defended realm shored up against the dangers of the outside world. The idea that there is, or should be, something fortress-like about our homes goes back to the Elizabethan lawyer Sir Edward Coke. 'The house of every one,' Coke wrote in his *Institutes of the Lawes of England*, 'is to him as his Castle and Fortress as well for defence against injury and violence, as for his repose.'[26] The lawyer took this idea, in turn, from Cicero, whom he paraphrased when he wrote in Latin '*et domus sua cuique est tutissimum refugiam*' – 'and each person's home is their true refuge'.

The context for Coke's assertion was a tricky legal case involving a plaintiff called Peter Semayne. On New Year's Day in 1604, Semayne went to the civil court to try to reclaim a debt from George Beresford, who owed him a substantial sum of money. The problem Semayne faced was this: Beresford was dead. But there was hope. Beresford had shared a house in Blackfriars with a certain Richard Gresham and, after Beresford's death, Gresham had inherited all his housemate's property. The sheriff's men went to reclaim Semayne's debt by seizing the property. But when they called on Gresham, the householder wouldn't let them in. There was a stand-off at the threshold, the sheriff's men withdrew and ultimately Semayne and Gresham ended up arguing the toss in court.

The issue that preoccupied the court was not that of the ownership of the property. It was a larger issue: did the sheriff's men even have the right to break down the door and enter Gresham's home? After some deliberation, the court ruled they did not. If they were not invited, they had no right of admission. 'Gresham,' the court concluded, 'has done nothing wrong but what he may lawfully justify, *viz.* shut his own doors.'[27]

For Coke, this was important as it established the principle that the threshold of the home put a limit on the power of the state. A century later, Pitt the Elder defined home in terms of the ability to refuse entry: 'The poorest man may in his cottage bid defiance to all the forces of the crown. It may be frail; its roof may shake; the wind may blow through it; the storms may enter, the rain may enter – but the King of England cannot enter.'[28] Home is where strangers have no jurisdiction, even if the monarch himself comes calling.

Today, in many cultures, this idea that the home is a fortress of sorts, barricaded against the world, is seen as so unexceptional that it is taken for granted. It is an idea fuelled by the growth of high-tech home security regimes that aim to watch, monitor and protect the sovereign territory of our homes twenty-four hours a day. But more often than not, our fortress homes do not make us more secure. Instead, the reverse is true; and the proliferation of the machineries of defence risks leading to a heightened sense of living in a world of amorphous, omnipresent threat.

The anthropologist Setha Low, who has spent her life studying gated communities and documenting our obsession with domestic security, writes that the precautions we take to secure our home, 'actually may increase rather than reduce a person's fear of crime'. When we erect high fences, put up cameras and pull down our blinds, when we see strangers as a threat to our well-being, then we withdraw ourselves from the broader social fabric. Our connections with the world beyond our walls begin to fray, and this in turn leads to a heightened sense of vulnerability and threat. There is a vicious circle here: feeling more vulnerable, we take 'even greater precautions . . . thus becoming even more isolated socially'.[29]

Research from across the world shows how this enhanced concern with security reinforces class and racial divisions. These divisions then fuel the fires of mistrust and fear.[30] In her interviews with largely white middle-class homeowners in the United States, Low writes how despite all the machineries of security and defence, the things that dominate among these privileged communities are 'fear, insecurity, worry, paranoia and anxiety'.[31] One of Low's interviewees, a woman called Helen, explained to the anthropologist why she lived in a gated community. She had a white friend, she said, who lived near Washington, DC. One day, a stranger turned up at her friend's door, selling goods, 'and she was very intimidated because she was white, and he was black, and you didn't get many blacks in her neighborhood'. The householder was 'scared as hell' by this situation. She bought something from the trader, but only to get him away from her door as quickly as possible. 'That's terrible to be put in that situation,' Helen concluded her story. 'I like the idea of having security.'[32]

Where, then, does true security lie? Among the Manggarai, an ethnic group from western Flores in Indonesia, what makes a home a place of safety is not the endless building of walls and fortifications, but instead the shared social warmth of being alongside others. The anthropologist Catherine Allerton, who carried out fieldwork among the Manggarai, says that in these communities, as with many communities in Indonesia, what makes a home a place of safety is that it is *ramai*. The Indonesian word *ramai* means something like 'lively' or 'rambunctious'. A *ramai* home is a home that bustles with life and visitors, with the sharing of food, cigarettes, jokes and conversation; it is a home that fizzes with the 'protective, effervescent, social buzz' that comes from being together.[33]

Traditional Manggarai homes are as far from fortresses as it is possible to be. They are communal places, 'defined and animated by the rhythmic thud of women pounding coffee and foodstuffs, the seesawing scrape of men sharpening their machetes, and what people call the *tok tok* sound that is made as women bang their weaving swords onto textiles on the back-strap looms'.[34] Built of wood or bamboo, traditional Manggarai houses are often home to multiple families and are characterised above all by their continual sense of life. Noise seeps in and out; people yell through the walls, calling jokes and greetings to their friends and family. Manggarai homes are so permeable – to sounds, to smells, to life – it is possible to sit at home and keep track on what the neighbours are up to in nearby houses (saying, 'Ai, that boy doesn't stop crying . . . never mind, that's called the sound of the village,' or 'Weee, that house is really lively'). In the world of the Manggarai, noisy neighbours are not an irritant, but a reassuring sign of being all in it together. And if your neighbours' house becomes too silent in the evening, it is quite normal to try to redress the issue by shouting out, 'Don't go to sleep too early.'

Not only is there what Allerton calls a 'cheerful conviviality' within and between houses, but there is a lot of coming and going. Dogs and chickens wander in and out. People turn up unexpectedly, hang around and then wander off. Guests and visitors – whether friends or strange anthropologists – are a normal part of daily life. And people in the community may be fully at home in a number of different dwellings, each of which they refer to as 'my own house', so that any household has more members than those who eat and sleep there daily. All this *ramai* liveliness is not only said to 'make life "feel delicious"', preventing a house from succumbing to sadness, but it also has 'important protective qualities'.[35] The true source of protection and security in Manggarai homes is not to be found in the flimsy walls of wood or bamboo, but in the lively warmth of the community: eating together, inviting people in to talk and drink coffee, hanging out in a big huddle, teasing, storytelling, exchanging jokes. Because the Manggarai know that the best refuge from the difficulties and dangers of life is to be found not in castles, but in cooking up community with others.

I have stayed in many places like this in my time in Indonesia: houses that are permeable to guests, to chickens and dogs, to spiders and lizards, to anthropologists, sounds, smells and noises from outside. Further to the east of Flores, in the province of Maluku, my friends Paay and Tin invited me to spend New Year with them. Paay was from Ambon and his wife, Tin, from the neighbouring island of Saparua. They built their own home in the forest outside Ambon, a small house made of wooden boards. It was a perfect spot. Around the house, they planted pineapples. The stream at the foot of the hill served as a bathroom for washing. The forest was abundant with fruit trees: rambutan, mango and *gandaria* – a sweet mango-like fruit the size of an apricot. I moved in, and all day we hung around, gorged on fruit, read books, chatted, washed in the stream, shared food and played interminable games of chess with members of Paay and Tin's extended family. Neighbours, friends and family members popped by unannounced, trekking through the forest to say hello; when they did, they were invited in for coffee, because visitors are always a good way to generate liveliness, with mutual fun, joking and chatting. At New Year, Paay and Tin held a party. They invited people over and we drank hard Indonesian liquor. I cooked courgette cake on a box oven that was balanced precariously on top of a paraffin stove. And as the fireworks blossomed far in the distance, I heard the ships in the harbour blowing their horns to herald the New Year and life was indeed delicious.[36]

There was something familiar to me in this way of living. My first home was a vicarage in rural Norfolk, a place closer to the *ramai* liveliness of Indonesia than to Coke's fortress or castle. I was the son of the local priest, my dad the last in an unbroken line of Anglican ministers stretching back for five generations. The house was draughty and porous. Heat seeped out through the walls; damp seeped in. Spiders, silverfish and woodlice scuttled in dark corners. When the winter came, we huddled for warmth by the open fire and crammed draught excluders under the ill-fitting doors. But in the summer, the house was a refuge. It was cool and smelled of dust, mouldering rugs and furniture polish.

Our vicarage was a 'tied house'. Owned by the church, it was both our home and not fully ours. It occupied a halfway position between family home and community gathering place, neither entirely public nor wholly private. None of us had an absolute claim on the space. People came for meetings or to discuss parish business. Passers-by dropped in to say hello. Strangers turned up because they had nowhere else to go, because they thought that in a vicarage they might find comfort or assistance. 'Gentlemen of the road' – as rural homeless men were delicately known back then – knocked at the door. My parents gave them cheese sandwiches, cups of tea and some money to keep them going.

At any time of day or night, we learned to expect a knock. We were turfed out of the sitting room to make space for meetings. When overnight guests turned up, we were shifted from our bedrooms so they had somewhere to sleep. And when we were not hosting other people, we were providing refuge to a succession of rescue animals. Once we found a kestrel lying in the snow, stunned from colliding with power lines. We took it home and warmed it in a shoebox on top of the kitchen boiler. Mum wore gardening gloves and fed it hunks of fresh meat. We marvelled at its pink-blue plumage. The following day, we took it into the countryside, where we released it. It soared up into the flat winter sky and was gone.

The vicarage was not so much a retreat from the world as its own microcosm. Sometimes it was hard to deal with the hubbub of people coming and going. But there was also a sense of being safe because of being in society with others, a freedom from fear, a feeling that here was a place that was made secure precisely because it was porous and open to the world. Of course, we had locks on the doors – sometimes we even remembered to lock them. At times we withdrew and huddled by the fire, just the four of us. Sometimes you need to hunker down, let the world fade into the background. But this never lasted long, and soon there would be a knock on the door, a stranger turning up, another meeting or event, and things would open up again.

Security – as our predecessors and close cousins the Neanderthals knew – is about more than defence. It takes more than walls and locks and doors to make a home secure. If we really want to manage our vulnerability, our best hope lies not in ever more elaborate technologies, but instead in each other. It lies in seeking out the protective warmth that comes from sharing our lives. It comes from inviting outsiders to sit by our hearth fires, and from venturing out to sit by the hearth fires of those who would otherwise be strangers. And then we see that we are not alone in facing the challenges of the world; and we know that there is always somebody looking out for us.

It sounds counter-intuitive, even dangerous. But sometimes, when our fears are at their greatest, the best way to secure our homes is by opening up the doors.

2

A Stranger at the Door

It is the year 1990 and I am in the backwoods of Pakistan, a teenager travelling alone. It is the first time I have been away from home for an extended period and I am learning to relish the freedom and the insecurity of finding myself a stranger among strangers.

For my first six months in Pakistan, I have been teaching English in a school in Lahore. But now the teaching position has come to an end and I have cut loose to travel the country. I am heading to Katas in the Salt Range, a line of salt-rich hills that extends along the northernmost bank of the River Jhelum. It is the last leg of a journey that has taken most of the day and I am on the back of a motorbike, having cadged a lift in nearby Choa Saidan Shah. The sun is setting as we speed into the valley. 'Katas,' the driver says. He stops the motorbike and drops me off by the side of the road. Then he says goodbye, wishes me luck and roars off into the distance.

It is six in the evening and Katas is deserted. Down at the

bottom of the valley, the waters of the lake reflect the sky. Despite the salt rocks, the water is fresh, fed by underground springs. According to legend, the lake was made from Siva's pooled teardrops, as he sobbed in mourning for the death of his wife Sati. Or as he sobbed in mourning for the death of his horse. Accounts differ. There are many reasons a god might weep.

Clustered around the lake is a raggedy collection of broken-down temples. Legend has it that these are the temples in the Hindu epic the *Mahabharata* where the Pandava brothers spent four years of their exile. Once Katas was a place of pilgrimage, a university where, in the eleventh century, the Arabic scholar Al-Biruni learned Sanskrit and wrote his famous history of India. But now, in Islamic Pakistan, it is almost deserted.

In theory, there are lodgings available. That is what my out-of-date and unreliable guidebook has told me. But when I arrive at the traveller's hostel halfway up the hill, I look through the dusty windows to find it empty of life and of furniture. I walk around, calling out, 'Hello.' Soon the chowkidar, the watchman, appears. He is shocked to see me, this pale, white figure in a salwar kameez. There is nowhere to stay, he says. I should leave, head back into Chao Saidan Shah; but I don't want to leave, and eventually he agrees to take me to the bottom of the valley, where part of the ancient temple complex has been converted into a home.

I follow the chowkidar down the hill to where the ruins are clustered. There is a figure standing outside them, an old man. He is upright, with a grey beard and a beautifully embroidered dressing gown. When we reach him, he greets me. His English is impeccable, with a polite lilt. He invites me into a courtyard.

Inside there are several kids running around, good-naturedly hitting things with sticks. My host offers me tea.

I accept. He smiles and asks why I have come to Katas. I say I am here to see the ancient temples. 'Where are you going to stay?' he asks. I hesitate. 'You would be welcome to stay with me,' he says, 'but as you can see, all my grandchildren are visiting from Rawalpindi, so you will not have any peace.'

A friend of my host turns up, a local teacher called Tanveer. He suggests I stay in the local school, then changes his mind. 'It won't be comfortable,' he says. But there is, he adds, a hut on the hillside. It has everything I could possibly need. Would I like to stay there?

'Yes,' I say. 'Thank you.'

I finish my tea and I say goodbye to my host. He tells me to come back later for dinner. 'I have two other guests,' he says. 'They are both archaeologists. You will find it interesting.'

Tanveer leads me along the side of the lake of Siva's tears and up the hillside to a small hut. He unlocks the door. It has a bed, a table, two chairs, and a view out across the salt hills. It is perfect. He leaves me to unpack.

That evening, I sit in the ruins of the old fort with my host and his two guests. The three men talk about archaeology and politics and history, slipping easily between Urdu and English. They are courteous and try to include me, but I don't really have much to add. I zone in and out. Tanveer turns up to rescue me. 'Come and see a film,' he says.

I thank my host and leave. Tanveer takes me to his home on his motorbike. We eat snacks and listen to covers of Madonna and Michael Jackson, Bollywood style. Then we sit through all

170 minutes of *Paap Ki Duniya*, a Bollywood movie about a jailer, a master criminal and a love triangle.

When the film comes to an end, it is already late. The moon is high over the valley, reflected in the water of the lake. Tanveer delivers me back to my hillside hut. He wishes me goodnight. I lie in bed, looking at the moonlit hills. Somewhere not far off, I can hear the yelps of jackals.

I fall asleep, knowing that here, far from home, I am safe.

Over the last few decades, travel has changed. Even in the most remote areas, there are people with mobile phones and internet access. You can check out where to stay online, weigh up your options, study reviews, look at photographs, book in advance. Even where there are no hotels or guest houses, you can call ahead, speak to your hosts, make yourself known. But when I turned up in the Salt Range – appearing at the door of a stranger, hoping for kindness, warmth, shelter and safety – I was travelling as people have done since before the beginning of human history: turning up from out of nowhere, unannounced, wandering around, calling out, 'Hello,' and knocking on doors until somebody responded.

From birth, we have been a migratory species. 'Evolution,' Bruce Chatwin writes, 'intended us to be travellers.'[1] And if evolution, in reality, didn't intend anything at all – that's not how evolution works – Chatwin is right in his diagnosis of the depth of our restlessness. The first migrations of the genus *Homo* out of Africa began around two million years ago. And from 60,000 years ago, *Homo sapiens*, our own species, embarked on a series of migrations from Africa until they occupied almost every corner of the globe. These were people like us. They had language and culture. They told stories. They made art. And they travelled, taking their stories and their art with them.

Migration is nothing new: driven by need, by climate change, by the hope of a better life elsewhere, by sheer curiosity, our ancestors spread out across the earth. Human migration was made possible by our ability to innovate. Our brains, our capacity for language and the malleability of our cultures 'almost certainly played a critical role in the rapid expansion of modern humans out of Africa and into a wide range of habitats and climate zones'.[2] And the causality goes both ways: our ability to innovate drove our migration, while our migration fuelled this creativity and flexibility.

Back before all recorded history, this is an encounter that must have been repeated a thousand thousand times: a stranger appears, speaking a language only partially comprehensible, if it is comprehensible at all, bringing the promise of newness – new possibilities, new innovations – and the frisson of danger.

The world's cultures are full of stories about strangers, braidings of philoxenia and xenophilia, advising us that we should treat the outsiders in our midst well and that things can go badly wrong. You find the figure of the stranger standing on the threshold – uncanny, exciting, full of promise and threat – in the very earliest recorded documents. Chinese bronzes, dating from around 1500 BCE, bear the character for *bin*, or guest. The etymology of the word is pictographic: above there is a roof and under the roof a person bearing seashell money. The stranger is the one who sojourns under your roof, who brings with them value and riches. Several centuries later, one of the earliest of all the Chinese poems recorded in the *Shijing* or *The Classic of Poetry*, which dates to between the ninth and eighth centuries BCE, talks of the auspiciousness of guests, how they bring blessings in their wake and are worthy of hospitality. 'I have good liquor,' one poem reads, 'to honour and gladden the hearts of my auspicious guests.'[3]

Sometimes in the texts of the ancient world guests are not only auspicious, they are divine. In the sixth century BCE, the Old Testament book of Exodus tells the story of how three visitors turned up at the tent of the patriarch Abraham. It was a hot day and Abraham was sitting at the door of the tent. He gave the strangers water and washed their feet. His wife, Sarah, kneaded bread-cakes out of fine meal. And together they served up a feast of bread, milk, curds and a 'tender good calf'.

The strangers turned out to be angels. In return for Abraham's hospitality, they predicted that Sarah, although elderly, would bear a child. Sarah laughed at the prophecy. But the angels knew what they were about: Sarah became pregnant. After the child was born, he was called Isaac, meaning 'He will laugh'. No wonder the New Testament reminds us not to forget philoxenia, because strangers might be angels in disguise.

If ancient ideas of home can be traced back to the gods of the hearth, then there is something sacred too about thresholds and strangers. The Greeks called it *theoxenia*, the welcome extended to a stranger (*xenos*) who is a god (*theos*) in disguise. In a story told by the Roman poet Ovid, one night in the town of Tyana, two footsore travellers turned up looking for food and shelter. Household after household refused them entry. Then an impoverished old married couple, Baucis and Philemon, opened up their door. They offered the travellers a meal of old bacon softened in boiled water, cabbage leaves, eggs, curdled milk, radishes, endives, pickles and sweet wine. But as she topped up the wine, Baucis noticed that it was not running out. Only then did the old-timers realise that something strange was going on. Their guests were not human travellers, but Zeus and Hermes in disguise. In honour of the passing gods, the old couple offered to serve up their goose, 'the trusty guardian / of their minute domain'. Zeus demurred: this was a step too far. He praised them for their hospitality and, as a reward, transformed their cottage into a much more beautiful, but possibly rather less practical, temple.[4]

When I think about the complexities of our relationships with strangers, I find myself returning over and over to the troubling tales in Homer's *Odyssey*. The book is a treatise on the nature of home, of travel and of *xenia*, 'guest friendship', or the code of honour between guests and hosts. Translator Emily Wilson writes of how Homeric Greece was a place where guests were expected to be treated with hospitality: 'When a bedraggled stranger in need shows up at your door, you must – before even asking his name – ask him inside, offer him a warm bath and a clean change of clothes, give him food, wine, and a seat by the fire, and let him listen to your resident poet or singer, if you are lucky enough to have one.'[5] Before the existence of 'money, hotels or public transportation', Wilson writes in the introduction to her translation of Homer's text, travellers were forced to rely upon the munificence of strangers.[6]

This, at least, was the ideal. In reality, things could always go awry. In the *Odyssey*, the hero Odysseus, a 'complicated man', wants to get home from the Trojan War. He is on fire with *nostos*, the longing for home. But at every point, his desire to return is thwarted. And as he is buffeted around the Mediterranean basin by the fickle whims of the gods, and the winds of misfortune, he finds himself both the beneficiary and the victim of the complex Greek codes of guest friendship. Throughout the book, Odysseus perpetually shape-shifts, from honoured guest to hostage to parasite: the code of *xenia* may be the ideal, but not everybody lives up to it, not even Odysseus himself. When Odysseus and his men stay with the Cyclops Polyphemus, son of Poseidon, instead of feeding his guests, Polyphemus chooses to eat them. Odysseus pleads with the monster, asking him to respect the ways of the gods: 'And Zeus is on our side, since he takes care / of visitors, guest-friends, and those in need.'

The Cyclops is having none of it. He calls Odysseus a fool, slanders Zeus and says that his only duty is to himself, so he must 'do the bidding / of my own heart'.[7]

Odysseus escapes by turning the tables on Polyphemus, offering him wine and getting him drunk. He then blinds the Cyclops and makes the passage from unfortunate hostage to vengeful guest. He escapes with his life, but only just. However, you don't mess with the code of *xenia*, even if your life is at stake; later Poseidon punishes him for treating the monster so poorly.

In the *Odyssey*, the code of *xenia* serves to protect both guest and host; but it also has a darker side. Hovering, Wilson writes, 'in an uneasy space between ethics and etiquette', it harbours the possibility of violence and of brutality. The same code that offers

protection can also be used 'as imaginative justification for rob-
bing, killing, enslaving, or colonising those who are reluctant to
welcome a group of possible bandits or pirates into their home'.[8]
Or it can be used as an excuse for putting out the single eye of a
one-eyed giant.

Things don't always go right with *xenia*. The *Odyssey* is testimony
to the tangle of fear, hope, danger and naked human need that
lurks in all encounters with strangers. But the stories of the
Odyssey are also rooted in a deep awareness of the contingency of
human life, the knowledge that you too could one day find
yourself a stranger. This sense of contingency appears in other
ancient texts also. 'Thou shalt neither vex a stranger, nor oppress
him,' it says in the Old Testament, 'for ye were strangers in the
land of Egypt.'

Settled communities have always feared the strangers who
turned up at their doors. But at least when a stranger comes
calling you are on home ground. When the roles are reversed
and, like Cicero, you find that you yourself are the stranger – far
from your own hearth, exposed, isolated and alone – then the
stakes are even higher. Relying on the kindness of others is
difficult. Sometimes it is terrifying.

To accept the offerings of strangers requires trust. And trust
is hard. When I first arrived in Pakistan, the culture shock was
severe. I did my best to fit in. I started to make inroads into learning Urdu. I dressed in salwar kameez. I borrowed a bicycle from
the school where I was working and took myself off exploring.

One day, in the first few weeks far from home, I found
myself in a crowded bazaar. I was locking up my bike when a man

emerged from a tea shop. He was in his thirties or early forties, dressed like me in salwar kameez. He stood with his hands on his hips, watching me fiddling with the lock. When I was done, he came over to me.

'Hello, my friend,' he said. He shook my hand. 'Where are you from?'

'England,' I told him.

He beamed. 'Welcome. Come drink tea with me.'

I hesitated. In my limited life experience, strangers never offered tea to strangers without some ulterior motive. I defaulted to suspicion. I wondered what malign intent lurked beneath his friendly smile. 'Sorry,' I said. 'I'm in a hurry.'

The man was insistent. 'Come,' he said. And he led me by the arm into the tea shop.

I sat down in the semi-darkness, my shoulders hunched and tense. My host gestured to the tea-shop owner. The *chai wallah* brought over a cup of hot, sweet tea for each of us. 'Please,' said my host. And he smiled.

I had been warned: lurid, unsubstantiated tales of foreigners who accepted drugged tea and woke up without passports, money or clothes.

I must have made for an ungratifying guest. Edgy and uncomfortable, I drank the tea too quickly, quivering with mistrust. It scalded my tongue. My host asked polite questions. I answered tersely. When I finished the tea, I offered to settle the bill.

My host put out his hand to push the money away. 'Let me,' he said.

I insisted, angry now. No, I told him. I will pay myself.

For the first time, my host looked irritated by my behaviour. But still he refused to let me pay. He paid the *chai wallah*, then turned to face me. 'It has been good to meet you,' he said. He put out his hand.

We shook hands stiffly and said goodbye. I left the tea shop and walked away.

I had no more appetite for exploring. I just wanted to escape. I unlocked my bike and pedalled out of the bazaar. And as I did so, I realised how furious I was. I was blazing with anger at this stranger's kindness.

Later that night, when I sat down to write my diary, I tussled with this anger, wondering where it had sprung from. 'I hate this sense of obligation,' I wrote. 'I hate being in debt to strangers. I hate not being free.'

Anger, Martha Nussbaum says, is almost always tied up with our helplessness, with our knowledge of our vulnerability. When the world overwhelms us, when we feel that we are no longer in control of our lives or our destiny, that is when anger kicks in. 'Anger aims at restoring lost control,' Nussbaum writes, 'and often achieves at least an illusion of it.'[9] When I think back to my fury as I pushed my bike away from the bazaar, I am ashamed at my mistrust. But if I cannot excuse it, at least I can understand it. I was angry because I was afraid; and I was afraid because I was vulnerable and exposed.

This was one thing, above all else, that I learned in Pakistan: that it takes courage to face up to our dependency upon strangers. And this courage is not always rewarded. Malcolm Gladwell has argued that a tendency to default to trust in our relationships with strangers can be perilous. Odysseus trusted the Cyclops and in reward he found himself on the menu. In Pakistan, I was luckier than Odysseus, but I might not have been. Strangers always present us with risks. They are hard to know. They are hard to understand. It is difficult to be sure what they are going to do next. So it pays to be on our guard.

And yet, as Gladwell says, 'the alternative – to abandon trust as a defence against predation and deception – is worse'.[10] The longer I spent in Pakistan, the more I settled in to the experience of being a stranger far from home, the more I recognised that often trust, although it never came without risk, was the best hope that I had for getting by. Writing to his friend Lucilius, the Roman statesman and philosopher Seneca claimed that, 'Trusting everyone is as much a fault as trusting no one (though I should call the first the worthier and the second the safer behaviour).'[11] But Seneca was wrong: there is nothing that makes you more exposed, more cut off and at risk, than generalised mistrust.

The word 'trust' has its roots in the Old Norse *treysta*, which means 'to secure', 'to rely on' or 'to make safe and strong'. Trust is like those gossamer bridges you find in legends – bridges that only appear if you believe in them and if you are willing to take the first step. There are no guarantees that the bridge will be there beneath your trembling feet. So you have to stay alert; you have to watch your step. The philosopher Onora O'Neill, in her 2002 Reith Lectures, argued that trust is called for, 'not because everything is wholly predictable, let alone wholly guaranteed, but on the contrary because life has to be led without guarantees'.[12] This makes the art of knowing how and when to trust a delicate one. But the refusal to trust, the refusal of all possible connections, leaves you alone in your vulnerability. And so, without guarantees, your body trembling, you take a step onto the gossamer bridge; and if all goes well, you don't go plummeting into the abyss but find yourself in a world that is a little more secure than it was before.

There is nothing irrational about xenophobia, the fear of strangers. It trembles through our every encounter with somebody new. It is there on a first date, in a job interview, when we find ourselves somewhere without a map. Condemning xenophobia as a vice to be eradicated does nothing to address the fundamental fear we have of strangers, and of how they may transform our world, for better or worse. And this fear of strangers is much more deeply rooted, and less amenable to antidotes, than we might hope. Some scientists have suggested that xenophobia may be adaptive, in that it may help to protect against infectious disease. And who has not, faced by the recent pandemic, trembled at the sight of a crowd on the street, knowing that beyond our closest, most intimate circles, contact with strangers might mean infection, perhaps even death?[13] Other researchers have suggested that this fear of strangers helps mitigate the risks of outsiders coming in and breaking with the close fabric of cooperation on which small groups depend.[14]

Whatever the evolutionary origins of xenophobia, research with young children suggests that the fear of strangers kicks in at an early age. Before they can even walk or crawl, children in all cultures distinguish between members of the in-group and members of out-groups. They respond differently to familiar and unfamiliar faces.[15] For infants, the world is divided into 'us' – close kin and household members – and 'them' – strangers and non-kin. By the time children begin to be independent explorers of their own worlds, they tend to exhibit a more marked fear of strangers. This happens across cultures, and it continues until between eighteen months and two years, when it begins to tail off, without ever being eradicated.[16]

But for infants, not all strangers are equal. Context matters. Infants are wily, astute at picking up on signs. If nobody around them is spooked, they are less likely to be spooked themselves. If children are at home, they find strangers in general less frightening than if they are in unknown territory. The evidence suggests that gender matters too: fear of strangers is more pronounced in relation to men than women. Strange, adult males – particularly strange, adult males who are free of any reassuring context – are what children fear the most.[17] And no wonder: both contemporary statistics and the historical record show that among human beings, as for many other primate species, the greatest risk of violence towards infants is from fully grown, male adult strangers. If this is the world we live in, it pays not to be too trusting.

And yet fear is not the only response that infants have to strangers. While they are often afraid of strange men, they are often far less afraid of strange women, and intensely curious about other strange children. They may shrink away from lumbering males, but when they see other children, there is an urge to connect, to poke and prod, to say hello. Children too are a cocktail of fear and curiosity, xenophobia and philoxenia.

*

Xenophobia is an inescapable part of what it means to be human, part of a complex brew of emotions we experience in our encounters with strangers. But too often, it calcifies into prejudice and hate. In the United States, in the wake of Donald Trump's inauguration, there was a surge in racist hate crimes. Trump's election campaign had been often openly Islamophobic. Life for minority communities in the States – and for Muslims in particular – became increasingly hard. The surge in hate crimes that followed from Trump's election was concentrated in those regions and counties where Trump won by larger margins.

When faced by irrational hatred, the temptation is always to harden your own borders and thresholds. But this hardening is not inevitable. Once Trump was sworn in, seeing the growing hatred directed towards her community, one teenager in California came up with an audaciously creative response. Yusra Rafeeqi was a shy, quiet fifteen-year-old. Her family were of Pakistani heritage. They were active members of the local community and practising Muslims. Like many families, the Rafeeqis were worried by the changes going on around them. In public, Yusra's mum, Khalida, wore a hijab and abaya, a long, loose-fitting robe. Before the election campaign, nobody paid her much attention. But now, her Islamic dress increasingly drew suspicion and hostility. At school, Yusra was accused by her peers of being a terrorist. Yusra's sister, Samrah, faced abuse when she went to the park with her one-year-old.[18]

One night over dinner, Yusra's family talked about the situation and what, if anything, could be done. Yusra proposed they should have a campaign – a campaign that crossed between public protest and the private sphere, an idea that was both out there and intimate. They would go to the busiest intersection in town, once a week, and they would invite strangers to dinner.

Yusra and her father made some signs. Samrah volunteered to be campaign manager. Her brother was appointed official photographer. And just before four o'clock on a Thursday afternoon in May 2017, they drove out to the intersection of El Camino Real and Embarcadero Road in Palo Alto. In the car, Yusra was nervous. They arrived, parked, got out of the car and held up signs that read 'Have Dinner with a Muslim Family' and 'Fight Islamophobia. Dine with my Muslim Family!'

At first, Yusra found the embarrassment excruciating. She stood awkwardly by the side of the road, not sure if the campaign was a good idea after all. Her brother took photographs. But then a car swished past and the driver gave a thumbs up and sounded the horn in support. 'After I got that first honk of appreciation and that thumbs up,' Yusra said, 'I felt a lot less out of place.'

It was the opening phase in a campaign that was to last for a year, and that saw Yusra's family host more than fifty feasts in their house, inviting in complete strangers to eat and chat. The ritual of sharing food is a simple one. But it runs deep in Pakistani culture, as it does in all the cultures of Islam. According to the philosopher Al-Ghazālī, who was active around the turn of the twelfth century, the Prophet once asked rhetorically, 'What is faith?' And he went on, 'The giving of food and the exchange of greetings.'[19]

Every subsequent Thursday, Yusra and her dad went out to invite strangers to dinner. Some approached them at the intersection – occasionally curious, sometimes hostile, frequently

puzzled, often cautious, they came up to talk. After a little conversation, and reassurance that there were no ulterior motives,
they exchanged contact details and set a time to eat. Others heard
about the campaign online. They sent Yusra and her family
emails, asking if they could come over. However they made the
connection, for weeks and months, the Rafeeqis hosted armies of
strangers, who arrived on their doorstep to share friendship,
conversation and good home-cooked Pakistani food.

Yusra's mother and sometimes her aunt cooked: fresh naan,
fragrant spiced biryani, chicken tikka masala, slow-cooked beef
nihari and sweet kheer rice pudding, washed down with cups of
masala tea. At the beginning of the meals, the guests were often
awkward. They all ate snacks and made small talk. But usually,
by the time everyone had started on the main course, things were
more relaxed. The conversation turned to more substantial
matters. Talk about anything, Yusra's dad said. So they did:
Islam, Christianity, politics, violence, terrorism, history, culture,
what the Quran really said, what it was like growing up Muslim
in America, favourite foods, popular culture, how it was possible
to make a better world. By dessert, conversation drifted to other
matters – lighter and sweeter. No longer strangers, the Rafeeqi
family and their guests cracked jokes and shared confidences.
And when the guests left at the end of the evening, it was with
gratitude, expressions of kindness, return invitations and promises
to keep in touch.

I called up Yusra and Samrah on Skype because I wanted to find
out about their campaign, about this extraordinary display of trust
in the face of hatred. It seemed remarkable, this opening up of

their home just at the point at which many would think of closing the doors and windows, and pulling down the blinds.

'Why now?' I asked them. 'And why dinner?'

'Trump specifically targeted my group of people,' Yusra told me. 'I was hurt by that. I wanted to let people know I was a part of their community too. And I thought dinner would be the best time to do this . . .'

But it seemed unfair to me that the Rafeeqis were having to make the first move. Weren't they the ones under threat? Weren't they the object of fear, hatred and misunderstanding? Why should the responsibility to act be theirs, I asked, when none of this was their fault?

Samrah responded first: 'If we want to do something, we have to do it ourselves and make sure we are being represented truthfully. We hate how people misconstrue us, but as much as it annoys us, our focus is on changing people's misconceptions. As soon as you communicate, you see that change in people in front of you. You see that light.'

And Yusra added, 'When people are hostile, treating them with kindness helps them come to the realisation that we are just humans. People come up to us super-defensive, but when we treat each other as neighbours, and as friends even, it helps them overcome this defensiveness.'

Samrah agreed. It is when we enter into this state of vulnerability, she said, that we can begin to change.

I thought of Al-Ghazālī's idea of faith as exchanging greetings and giving food, and of the immense kindness I had met in Pakistan. 'Is this Islamic hospitality, or maybe Pakistani hospitality?' I asked the sisters. 'Or is it something more broadly human?'

'Human nature is good,' Samrah said. 'The point of religion is to nurture that goodness.'

And then Yusra said, should I ever find myself in Palo Alto, I should let her know, and come round to have dinner with the family. With that invitation, we ended the call.

Back when I was a teenager myself, living in Pakistan, I grappled with the boundaries between trust and mistrust, with my fears of vulnerability and my knowledge that only in connecting with strangers could I really be safe. After the incident in the bazaar, once the anger had subsided, it left behind a feeling of awkwardness, embarrassment even. I was ashamed of myself, of my own hostility. The next time I was offered tea by a stranger, I kept my anxieties in check, and I made for a better guest.

As time went on, I became used to the kindness and solicitude of strangers in Pakistan. And I found that Pakistan was the most hospitable of countries. In Nawabshah, a small city in the province of Sindh, a hotel owner put me up for free for several days, fed me in his restaurant, introduced me to his family and showed me around the town, sending me on my way with a new salwar kameez and a bus ticket to my next destination. In the Thar Desert in the south, when I fell sick, the owner of a cheap restaurant I had eaten in several times tracked me down. He knew I was staying for a while longer, and when I had not been to his restaurant for a day or two, he got worried. He asked around and found me shivering with fever in a cheap hotel where the walls were made of plasterboard. He took me to a doctor on the back of his motorbike and paid for my medicine. In a town on the North-West Frontier, I shared a meal with strangers in a fortified compound. They piled their Kalashnikov rifles by the door and we sat in a circle on the ground, dipping cardamom-fragrant *sheermal* bread into thick, spiced stew.

And when I returned from Pakistan, I was a different person from the one I had been when I set out. I was more liable to trust than to distrust. I was less alone. I was more aware of my indebtedness to others, and more comfortable with this awareness. And I was more open to strangers and the promise that they might bring.

Because, as Yusra and her sister reminded me, this is one way that change happens and trust is forged: with the exchange of greetings and the sharing of food; with the offering of a simple cup of tea; and with the coming together of strangers around a table laden with fragrant, steaming pots of curry.

3

Come on in

When a stranger enters the warm, intimate circle of the household, everyone is on their guard. Something new has arrived in the world and nobody yet knows what it is. While the gossamer bridge of trust is still fragile, everything depends on how you take your first steps, on those crucial moments of first encounter when everybody is sussing each other out, trying to decide what they are dealing with. 'Come on in,' we say, and the guest smiles and steps through the door. But underneath the warmth, there is a wariness, a tremble of uncertainty. Because from now on in, anything could happen.

In 1923, the young Russian geologist Andrej Simukov set off on his first expedition to Mongolia. He travelled on foot, on horseback, by motor vehicle. It was the beginning of a long love affair. Simukov returned many times throughout the 1920s and 1930s, immersing himself in the study of Mongolian language, culture, history, geography, ethnography, geology and natural history. By the mid-1930s, he had journeyed over 50,000

kilometres.[1] He wrote that it was possible to travel the length and
breadth of Mongolia, armed with nothing more than a pouch of
tobacco and a knowledge of Mongolian language and customs.
With these things in hand, he said, you could be certain you
would never want for food to eat or somewhere to lay your head.

In the rural Mongolia of Simukov's day, there were no hotels
or lodging houses to put up weary travellers. Instead, those on the
road had to depend on the hospitality of others. And when far
from home, travelling among strangers, there are two things
above all else that guarantee you safe passage: knowledge of the
appropriate rituals and the giving of gifts – in Simukov's case, a
pouch of tobacco.

In Mongolia, the customs that regulated the relationships
between hosts and guests were codified in a set of oral maxims
known collectively as the *yos*. For guests and hosts alike, the *yos*
provided a common reference point, a set of ritualised gestures
and actions that helped to build a more secure bridge between
strangers meeting for the first time. When travellers turned up out
of the blue, crossed the threshold and made themselves at home,
the *yos* were a way of ensuring that everything went well. The
demands of the *yos* were extensive and exacting. There were rules
about what you should do if your guest's horse is taken by wolves
(you should say, 'The mountain god took your horse,' and offer
another as a replacement). There were rules about not exposing
your thighs in the *ger* – the Mongolian yurt, or felt tent – of your
host. There were rules about how the tea should swirl in the bowl
when the host offered it to the guest (clockwise). There were
rules about how guests should eat their first mouthful of meat (it
should be a small chunk, chewed in an extravagant fashion, to

suggest it is large and generous). There were rules about not singing in bed in your host's house ('Though you may be very happy, don't sing in bed,' the saying went. 'Though you are very sad, don't cry in bed'). And there were rules about how older people should admonish their talkative younger companions (by telling them, 'A bad person's noise is great; a donkey's groin is great'[2]).

Today, a century after Simukov first set out for Mongolia, the *yos* no longer have quite the same power they once had. Nevertheless, Mongolian hospitality, and the ways in which visitors manage the difficult transition from stranger to guest, are still governed by shared understandings that derive from the *yos*.[3] And while the *yos* cover a wide range of situations, they are particularly exacting when it comes to crossing the threshold from the outside to the inside. The anthropologist Caroline Humphrey lived in the Mongolian grasslands in the 1980s and recorded these rules in detail. On turning up unannounced, you must stop your horse and call out, 'Mind the dog!' On hearing the visitor calling, the women and children of the household should come out to restrain the dog. Only then should the visitor dismount and approach the threshold. After this, the newly arrived visitor should stop in front of the threshold, clearing their throat to announce their arrival. Before entering the *ger*, they should disarm, leaving guns, whips and other weapons outside. If the visitor has a knife hanging from their belt – useful for eating and for cutting up food – they should not touch the hilt.

The rules go on. The visitor should enter the *ger* with their right foot forward, without treading on the threshold. On entering, the visitor should make sure their clothing is all in order:

their coat buttoned up, their cuffs pulled down and their hat on.[4] Mongolian men – and solitary travellers in Mongolia were largely men – have traditionally taken their hats seriously. A man's hat, through long use, is said to 'hold on' to a part of his soul: mess with a man's hat and you mess with his soul.[5] Once inside, the visitor should greet the host. 'What is there that is strange and beautiful – what is the news?' the host should ask. And the visitor, now settling down into their role as a guest, should reply, 'Nothing at all – fair and peaceful.' Then the guest will be served food and drink.

The complexity of these rules shows how maddeningly understated was Simukov's 'nothing more than a knowledge of Mongolian language and customs'. It takes time to learn Mongolian, or any other language. But it takes even longer to become fluent in a culture. If Simukov thrived in Mongolia with only a pouch of tobacco in his pocket, crossing and recrossing the thresholds of strangers, it was thanks to his understanding of the complex codes of behaviour that transformed strangers into guests, binding them in the mutual relationships of obligation and care that allowed them to thrive in this difficult environment.[6]

Thresholds quiver with possibility and danger. The Romans understood this; they knew that the passage from the outside world to the sacred realm of the *domus* was always fraught, never straightforward. In ancient Rome, the threshold – in Latin, the *limen* – was a place of such importance that the Romans invented their own god to watch over it. Janus, god of doorways, has no Greek equivalent; he is a purely Roman invention, associated with anywhere there is a crossing. He presides over the doorway of the house, the gates of the city, the borderlands between communities. With two faces, he looks out and looks in, keeping an eye on who comes and who goes. Cicero claims his Latin name, *Ianus*, derives from the verb *ire*: 'to go', 'to pass', 'to flow'. Janus – with his emblems, the key and the cudgel – is the god who manages the inflows and outflows between different worlds. He unlocks new futures, and he threatens violence. In Rome, he was associated with war as much as with peace, with hostility as much as with hospitality. All sacred rites in Rome began with the invocation of Janus, the god of the threshold. They all ended with the invocation of Vesta, the goddess of the hearth. 'As in everything,' Cicero writes, 'it is the beginning and the end which are most important.'[7]

Between threshold and hearth, this is where everything happens.

The exacting ritual codes of the Mongolian grasslands, with their precise stipulations about how to cross the threshold, amount, says Humphrey, to a 'craft of allaying suspicion'.[8]

The first thing a visitor must do is disarm. This requirement that guests should disarm as they cross the threshold is not quite a universal rule across cultures, but it is widespread. In that fortified compound in Pakistan, my fellow guests piled up their automatic rifles outside the door before they came to eat stew and *sheermal*. Archaeological evidence shows the mead-halls of the Anglo-Saxon world had antechambers where visitors left their weapons before they went in to feast.[9] In the Old English epic poem *Beowulf*, the hero turns up with a bunch of heavily armed men and makes his way to the Heorot, the mead-hall of Hrothgar, king of Denmark. The king's herald, Wulfgar, asks what is to be done with these dangerous outsiders. The old, grey-headed king says that they should be invited in and permitted to wear their battledress, but their shields and spears should be left at the door.[10] In the *Odyssey*, Athena visits Odysseus's son, Telemachus, disguised as Mentes, the king of Taphos and an old friend of Odysseus. She is decked out in armour and carries a bronze spear. Telemachus, ever the good host, welcomes her at the door. 'Good evening, stranger,' he says, 'and welcome. Be our guest, come share / our dinner, and then tell us what you need.'[11] Then he takes her spear, courteously stows it in a polished stand just inside the door, and invites her to sit down and to eat.

It is a bad guest who insists on remaining fully armed. An armed guest is not just a risk; they are also an insult. A guest who comes to your house and sits on the sofa holding an assault rifle ('just in case') is not just a threat, but also an affront, their refusal to disarm a sign of their lack of faith in your ability to act as host and protector.

Not all guests are willing to give up their arms so easily. In 2013 the United States division of the coffee-shop chain Starbucks caused consternation among its loyal customers from the pro-gun lobby. Previously, Starbucks had an 'open carry' policy in place, permitting customers to carry unconcealed weapons in US states where this was permissible. But when a number of pro-gun Facebook groups, including one called I Love Guns and Coffee (their logo is a Starbucks mermaid holding two pistols) decided to hold a series of Bring Your Gun to Starbucks events, the company took action. The photos from the events show smiling men and women holding pistols or AK-47 assault rifles, posing for the camera and slurping milky, oversized coffees through green straws.[12] Starbucks could have responded by banning firearms altogether in their stores. But instead, they took a different line. In an open letter to customers, Starbucks CEO Howard Schultz 'respectfully requested' customers leave their weapons at home before coming to sup on their skinny lattes. He wrote about how Starbucks was a 'third place', somewhere between home and work, between public and private, a place given over to peace, community, pleasure and coffee. 'Our values,' he wrote, 'have always centered on building community rather than dividing people, and our stores exist to give every customer a safe and comfortable respite from the concerns of daily life.'[13]

It was a masterful, but ultimately unsuccessful, response. Schulz's letter attempted to cultivate a tone of welcome, expressed in the language not of rules and obligations, but of hospitality, of invitation. Instead of leading to a de-escalation in tension, though, the letter provoked protests and boycotts. The guests refused the demands of the host; Starbucks's gun-toting customers, unwilling to leave their weapons at home, switched their loyalties to rival chains.

As the disarmed stranger settles into a place between the threshold and the hearth, they find themselves neither at home nor unwelcome, neither fully belonging nor not belonging: a guest. The anthropologist Victor Turner talks about this ambiguous place as one that is 'betwixt and between', or 'neither here nor there'.[14] The guest is still under the watchful eye of Janus, the god of the *limen*.[15] In this liminal space – where everything is up for grabs and anything could happen – we navigate the complexities of our interpersonal relationships through ritual.

When we think about ritual, we often see it as something reserved for special occasions: weddings, funerals, birthdays, the opening of shopping centres or the launching of ships. But more subtle, everyday rituals underlie almost every aspect of our lives, giving them shape, providing a shared music that helps us get along. Ritual is there when we knock on someone's door (a jaunty knock-knock-a-knock-knock for people we know well, a friendly but brisker knock-knock for those who are less close to us). It is there in the studied casualness with which we treat close friends, and in the formality with which we treat strangers. It is there when we offer tea to drink or food to eat, knowing our guest is neither thirsty nor hungry. It is there when we stand a round of drinks in an English pub, or toast fellow diners with *baijiu* sorghum liquor around a table in China. It is there in the stock condolences offered at funerals, in the congratulations to the happy couple at weddings, in the good wishes at birthdays and the expressions of regret at farewell parties. In fact, ritual is pretty much everywhere, acting as a powerful social glue, as a means of helping us elegantly navigate the demands of shared living.[16]

For all its power, ritual has also often had a bad press. The sixteenth-century Protestants decried it as a form of idolatry and superstition.[17] And today many people still regard ritual with suspicion. We talk of 'empty' ritual or 'mere' ritual. We suspect that ritual sucks the life blood from things, that it gets in the way of naturalness, that it is a matter of solemn processions and dusty liturgies, grave faces and ridiculous hats.

But ritual is inescapable. It is something that runs through our shared life; and it is particularly urgent when we meet with strangers, and when the stakes are at their highest.

In all of history, there is perhaps nobody who understood ritual better – its omnipresence and its importance – than Confucius, the Chinese philosopher-sage. The China of Confucius's time, the sixth and fifth centuries BCE, was in a state of upheaval. The area that is now north-east China was split into a multitude of smaller states, each struggling with the others for power and supremacy. Confucius was a government official, a functionary who spent the first five decades of his life in the state of Lu. He was preoccupied by the chaos. He looked back nostalgically to former times, and to the greatness of the Western Zhou dynasty, between the eleventh and eighth centuries BCE, which he imagined as a lost time of order and virtuous rule. In an attempt to re-establish the virtues of earlier times, he proposed a series of reforms to the ruler of Lu. Perhaps he would have succeeded had the ruler of the nearby state of Qi not intervened. According to the first-century-BCE *Records of the Grand Historian* by Sima Qian, the ruler of Qi was anxious that Confucius's reforms would make Lu too powerful. So he sent the duke of Lu eighty courtesans and a hundred horses as a distraction. The duke – his head easily turned – shut himself away with the women and gave himself over to pleasure.[18] Disgusted by the duke's neglect of his responsibilities, Confucius left, choosing self-imposed exile over a dissolute employer.

For the next two decades, Confucius wandered the fragmented political landscape of north-east China. He went from state to state, a perpetual stranger, in an unsuccessful attempt to encourage those in power to take an interest in virtue. He became practised in the art of gracefully crossing the thresholds between cultures. In the *Analects*, his recorded teachings, Confucius says, 'If your words are faithful and trustworthy, your conduct earnest and respectful, then even if in the barbarian lands, you will get by.'[19]

The Chinese term for ritual is *li*. The character in Chinese depicts a ritual vessel presented before an ancestral altar, and initially referred to the gestures and acts prescribed by religious rites. But Confucius saw that ritual had a much wider scope. His own understanding of *li* was all-encompassing: there was no aspect of life that was untouched by it. And it is particularly when we are far from home, or among strangers – in the barbarian lands of which Confucius spoke – that we need ritual to help ease the difficult task of connecting.

The *Analects* are full of accounts of how Confucius sought to adapt to the contexts in which he found himself: how he would hold himself when meeting those who were grieving; how he would accept and offer gifts; how he would moderate his posture according to the occasion, moving comfortably and fluidly from high formality to relaxed ease. 'When undertaking ritual,' Confucius said in the *Analects*, 'take harmony as what is most valuable.'[20] This concern with harmony, and with attuning ourselves to others, is why Confucius sees ritual as being closely allied with music. Because once you have learned how to play along, this shared music of finely calibrated gesture, speech and act can become something beautiful – a conduit for feeling, for pleasure, a way of connecting ever more deeply, a means of cooking up togetherness. In Mongolia, Humphrey writes, parents tell their children that when they visit the homes of others, they should 'take account of the tone' of their hosts.[21] They should be mindful of the musicality of the world they are entering, so they can seek out ways of harmonising with this new world. To be skilled in ritual is to have a heightened attentiveness to the music of our being together.

It takes time to overcome the cultural suspicion of ritual. In their brilliant study *Ritual and Its Consequences*, Adam Seligman and his colleagues write about the tension between ritual and sincerity. Rituals, they argue, stand at the opposite pole to sincerity. At a wedding, we might sit through the ceremony thinking the happy couple to be wildly unmatched. We might be party to knowledge that suggests the marriage will be short-lived. But we still might find ourselves acting as if this is a match made in heaven and will endure for all eternity. Similarly, if invited to dinner by somebody who we know is a terrible cook, we might eat our host's appalling food and suppress a grimace, smiling and complimenting them on their cooking, with every appearance of enjoying ourselves.

This tension between sincerity and ritual is the fodder for endless domestic comedies. But ritual reminds us that sometimes sincerity is not the only thing that matters; at times, ritual 'encompasses the ambiguity of life much better than sincerity can'.[22] Instead of unpacking the chaos of our inner lives for everyone to see, ritual contains this chaos, in favour of a shared world where we act 'as if' things were smooth and harmonious, 'as if' all were fair and peaceful. The performance of ritual, Seligman and his colleagues argue, is not so much insincere as *subjunctive*.[23] Ritual acts are acts 'as if' the world were other than it is. And there is something astonishingly powerful about this subjunctive 'as if': because if we all play along, in the betwixt-and-between space of ritual, we can bring into being a new shared reality, a new music and a new sense of connection. We can usher this 'as if' world into being.

When meeting with strangers, the carefulness of ritual is often accompanied by something lighter: the leavening agent of playfulness, the willingness to joke around. When we sit down together to try and work each other out, it is not only exaggerated high formality. The host may bring coffee, or pour wine, or conjure up something from the kitchen with a kind of flourish. But alongside these solemn ritual gestures, there is often also a large dose of joking and teasing. Ritual reinforces the boundary between us; but playfulness and joking, as Seligman and his colleagues put it, 'tickle the boundary'; they push at the boundary to see what gives.[24] The anthropologist Julian Pitt-Rivers says that both joking and the ritualised gestures of hospitality are means of managing potential conflict when crossing boundaries: 'whereas the joking relationship suppresses the conflict by the prohibition to take offence, hospitality achieves the same end by the prohibition to give offence.'[25]

This combination of ritual and play is not restricted to human beings. Researchers at the University of Pisa studied a community of lemurs, and how they related to incomer lemurs who were strangers to them. When they are hanging out with friends, lemurs like to groom. But grooming requires mutual trust, and trust doesn't arise out of nowhere. When lemurs encounter strangers, they don't immediately extend trust. But neither do they default to mistrust. They respond, as we ourselves do, with a cocktail of fear and aggression, curiosity and fascination.

It is on this boundary between trust and mistrust that ritualised play comes into its own. To test out strangers, lemurs pod and poke. They gently slap each other, they turn cartwheels, they engage in rough and tumble, they play-bite each other's genitals. This is behaviour that is specifically reserved for dealing with strangers: adult lemurs don't play with their friends. But when, through play, everybody has got the measure of each other, when it is clear that nobody means any actual harm – when you know that you have had your genitals in somebody else's mouth and they haven't done anything untoward – then you can get on with the serious business of mutual grooming. Strangers become allies, allies become friends.[26]

In the human realm too, ritual and play can build bridges, allowing strangers to sound each other out, test boundaries and make connections. In 2013, the Muslim community in York heard some disturbing news. The far-right English Defence League, a virulently Islamophobic group, announced that they were planning a protest outside the York Mosque. When news of the protest reached the mosque, the community set about coming up with a response. Mohamed El-Gomati, a professor of electronics at

York University and one of the mosque's elders, gave the problem some thought, then proposed a solution. 'We'll have a party,' he said. 'That should be our response. It's our tradition, and it would be the Islamic way of dealing with something like this.'

The worshippers at the mosque mobilised quickly. They arranged an open day to coincide with the protest. They made a banner reading, 'York Mosque welcomes anyone who condemns extremist violence.' They prepared food and refreshments, and invited over 150 friends and supporters, to provide safety in numbers.

When the EDL arrived, the protest was smaller than promised. There were six people in all: three men and three women, with red and white St George's flags, chanting slogans in the street. The first thing the mosque community did was to put on the kettle and go out to offer trays of tea and biscuits. Later, *The Times* newspaper called El-Gomati's approach 'Custard Cream Diplomacy'; but it was more than diplomacy. It was a kind of faith, a belief in the 'as if' power of ritually drinking tea together, in the idea that through the giving of food and the exchange of greetings there were points of connection, meeting places to be found. 'We all think of sitting down with a cup of tea as something quintessentially English,' El-Gomati wrote later, 'so we thought that offering a cup of good old-fashioned Yorkshire tea and hospitality would be a start.'[27]

At first, the protesters were suspicious, as I was suspicious in the bazaars of Lahore. It takes courage to accept tea from a stranger. But before long they gave in – in Yorkshire, no ritual is more powerful than that of offering and accepting tea. The protesters accepted the offered food and drink, and started to talk.

The women from the EDL fell into conversation with the women from the mosque. They cracked jokes together. Somebody from the mosque proposed a game of football. Somebody else fetched a ball from inside. And the day ended with a friendly kick-about in the mosque grounds.

Ritual, play, joking, offerings of food and drink: this is the craft of building trust.

'A generous host is sure to be remembered,' the *Odyssey* says, 'as long as his guests live.'[28] In the *Odyssey*, once guests are disarmed, their hosts ply them with gifts. The code of *xenia* obliges the host to offer 'food, drink, baths, clothing, and shelter for the duration of the guest's visit, as well as guest-gifts and transportation at the time of departure'.[29] Hosts give gifts in the hope of gaining a glorious reputation, or *kleos*: honour or renown rooted in 'how one is viewed and talked of by one's peers'.[30] Once their guests have eaten their fill, they reciprocate the generosity and protection of their hosts by telling stories that act as counter-gifts. When Odysseus is washed up naked on the island of the Phaeacians in Hyperia (a 'land of dancing'), he is taken in by the princess Nausicaa, because 'all beggars come from Zeus / and any act of kindness is a blessing'.[31] Nausicaa escorts him to the palace, where he is given food and drink. When he is sated, the queen, Arete, asks him where he is from. Then Odysseus takes a deep breath and starts to tell his tale. 'It would be difficult, Your Majesty,' he says, 'to tell it all . . .'[32] And the gift exchange does not stop there: when he eventually leaves, he is swept back home to Ithaca on a magical ship, a gift from the Phaeacians, heavily laden with presents from his former hosts.

This exchange of gifts, both tangible and intangible, sets up enduring connections between guests and hosts. Centuries after the *Odyssey*, far to the north-west, when the warrior Beowulf has defeated both the monster Grendel and Grendel's mother, he makes clear his intention to return home. He praises Hrothgar for his hospitality and generosity. 'You have dealt well with us,' he says.[33] And Hrothgar responds by saying, 'so long as I rule / this broad kingdom / we shall give treasures, / and many shall greet / each other with gifts / across the gannet's bath.' Because gifts, Hrothgar says, are 'the strongest tokens'.[34]

Shortly after Elee and I first got together, we moved into a terraced house to the west of Birmingham, and we set about working out what it meant to share our lives. Elee had a job in a museum, where she ran education projects. I was working part-time, teaching classes in creative writing and philosophy to adults across the city, trying to make ends meet while I got my PhD finished. We settled into our new home quickly and life was good. We tended the garden. I grew lopsided vegetables. We read books. I cooked up things in the kitchen. We met friends. We attended the weekly quiz in the local bar. We had a cat.

But there was something missing. Elee, like me, was an atheist child of the clergy – her stepfather was a Methodist minister. She had spent at least half of her childhood and youth in a house noisy with siblings, step-siblings and half-siblings, with guests, friends and strangers. Soon, the quietness of our life began to unsettle us both. After a few months, we came to the uneasy realisation that we were bored. Not with each other, but with the shape of our life. The house was too quiet. It called out to be peopled. So we signed up with Couchsurfing, the American-run hospitality website that was still in its infancy; and we offered our guest room – which doubled as a study – to passing strangers, free of charge.

Many friends and family members were horrified. Why would we do such a thing? they asked. Wasn't it dangerous? Wouldn't we live to regret it? They imagined the worst. We would be robbed. We would be taken advantage of. It would disrupt our routines. It would mess with the orderliness of our lives. At best, it would be an irritation; at worst, we would end up dead, murdered in our beds. You are asking for trouble, they said.[35] And they were right: we had everything we needed in our lives except trouble.

So over the years that followed, we hosted something over a hundred guests. They came from everywhere: the Americas, Europe, Africa, Asia, Australasia. They slept in the spare room, in the shadow of shelf-loads of philosophy books. We shared our table, we cooked together, we exchanged stories. And as they crossed the threshold of our home, our guests came bearing strange and wonderful gifts. Bottles of bitter Unicum, the potent medicinal alcoholic drink from Hungary. Hunks of home-made Parmesan cheese from a family farm in Italy. Household ornaments. Once, we hosted a Syrian pancake chef. He set up his hotplate in our kitchen and prepared a feast of crêpes and galettes. Another time, an Austrian transgender artist, attending a conference at a nearby university, gave us a small treasure: a hand-made book. The artist identified as a tree sprite; the book contained drawings, poems and photos of them looking spritely and naked, high up in the branches.

*

There is nothing that smooths our passage over the threshold better than a well-chosen gift. Confucius knew this: according to the later Confucian philosopher Mencius, when Confucius was travelling far from home, he always knew the appropriate gift to bring his hosts.[36] The anthropological fascination with gift-giving goes back to at least 1925, when Marcel Mauss published his *Essai sur le don*, translated into English as *The Gift*.[37] Mauss was a man whose own gifts were prodigious. The nephew of the great sociologist Émile Durkheim, he started life as a philosopher. But his omnivorous intellectual interests mushroomed to include the study of anthropology, Sanskrit, Indian religions and the Māori language. Mauss was a skilled amateur boxer, a charismatic teacher, a storyteller who could spin tales – it was said, 'as if he were Scheherazade'[38] – and a committed socialist. His interests were so broad, so widely divergent, he found it hard to finish anything. On his death he left a bewildering array of book-length projects incomplete: books about prayer, about nationalism, about money.

At the heart of Mauss's influential argument in *The Gift* is the idea that, although we give gifts 'as if' they are given out of free generosity, gift exchange is part of a strict accounting system. Gift-giving is, he writes, an 'intricate mingling of symmetrical and contrary rights and duties'.[39] These rights and duties break down into a threefold obligation: the obligation to give, the obligation to receive and the obligation to reciprocate. Failing to meet these obligations is always perilous: it can lead to social disapproval, to exclusion or even to violence. In Mauss's view, gift-giving, being a ritualised act, is inherently insincere; it is 'polite fiction, formalism, and social deceit . . . when really there is economic obligation and economic self-interest'.[40]

But Mauss's views on the gift, for all their influence, are too harshly exacting. What he misses is the spirit, the music, of the gift. If gift-giving is itself a kind of ritual, it might be better to see it not as wholly insincere, but as something that shares with other rituals that not-quite-sincere subjunctive world of the 'as if' – the world of hope for a future in which everybody stands to gain, and nobody to lose. Reciprocity suits no one: anybody who has ever turned up at somebody's door bearing a gift, or who has sent a guest away laden with presents, knows that strict reciprocity is not the point. To reduce the subtle nuances of gift and counter-gift to a cover for a ruthless concern with parity is to miss what is most crucial about gift-giving: that what we want in the giving of gifts is *a*symmetry.[41] The anthropologist Roy Wagner, who carried out fieldwork in Papua New Guinea, writes that among the Daribi-speaking peoples, symmetry in gift-giving is explicitly forbidden, because an obsession with symmetry is the very thing that risks killing dead the rich dynamism that is the very reason for gift exchange.[42] Of course, appropriateness matters. If I turn up at a friend's house for dinner and I offer them a half-empty bottle of wine, there is something lacking in my gift. The half-empty bottle – half-full for the optimists – suggests that I am careless, that I lack the proper sense of nuance. Equally, if I go the other way and turn up for a casual meal bearing a crate of expensive wine and a baby ocelot, my gifts might be judged to be unnecessarily ostentatious (and troublesome too: what do you feed an ocelot?). But appropriateness is not the same as symmetry; and to insist on complete parity, on exact exchange, misses the point – and the fun – of gift-giving.

There is a Burmese proverb that says, 'For the morsel of rice and curry you have enjoyed with satisfaction and relish, you can never reciprocate or pay back in full.'[43] You can, if you like, invite the person back for another morsel of rice and curry; but the two gifts will not cancel each other out. Gift-giving is not a zero-sum game. Instead you have two gifts, *both* of which can never be reciprocated in full. Gift-giving doesn't work by cancelling out but by amplifying our connections, and by augmenting the pleasure and significance of these connections. The giving of gifts sets up a complex web of asymmetries where both parties win, and where each is in debt to the other with a debt of gratitude that can never be discharged.[44]

In the Tanimbar islands of east Indonesia, there was once a complex system of ritualised gift exchange that extended throughout the islands, a cycle of gift and counter-gift of which Beowulf and Hrothgar might have approved. In this great cycle of gift exchange – called the *lolat ila'a* or 'great row' – noble households from different villages travelled long distances by sea to ritually exchange gifts. When the anthropologist Susan McKinnon asked why they went to such trouble and took such risks to make these exchanges, her Tanimbarese hosts said that the purpose was not to 'look for profit', but instead to 'look for relation'.[45] You give and receive gifts, because giving and receiving gifts is, in the Fordatan language of Tanimbar, *manminak* – 'tasty', 'sweet' or 'good'. Gifts forge relationships full of pungency, flavour and sweetness. There is something gratuitous about the giving of gifts. It is a kind of grace, something 'over and above what is due, economically, legally, or morally', something that is 'neither foreseeable, predictable by reason, nor subject to guarantee'.[46] Because this is where the true tastiness of gift-giving lies: in the power that gifts have to open up new futures.

The writer Lewis Hyde has argued that creative works are gifts.[47] But the reverse is also true. Gifts are creative works. They create trust between strangers. They create new possibilities, and new futures.

When we meet with strangers at the thresholds of our lives, both the risks and the rewards are great. We have no guarantees that things will go well. But we don't turn up empty-handed. If we come equipped, as Simukov did, with a knowledge of the customs of the place and with gifts to exchange, the chances are that things will go well. Exchanging gifts, attuning ourselves to each other's music, probing and tickling at the boundaries through play and fun, we begin to connect, and the wakeful god Janus relaxes his vigilance. He puts down his cudgel and he sets about unlocking the doors to the future.

But there are no guarantees; things can always go wrong – through misreading the signs, through a joke that goes awry, through a gift ill-considered and ill-made. Then Janus reaches again for his club and, in a cycle of offence, dishonour and disgrace, things spiral out of control.

4

Codes of Honour

A friend and I were travelling by car through central Bulgaria. We were on our way from the capital city, Sofia, to Varna on the Black Sea coast. It was a long journey, so my friend suggested we stop midway for lunch in the town of Omurtag. She had a friend there to whom she wanted to introduce me. His name was Hasan Yakub Hasan, a local scholar, polyglot, historian, folklorist and farmer. My friend called ahead to say she was bringing an English visitor. Hasan immediately invited us for lunch.

Hasan was a small, neat man in a pinstripe suit and a black hairnet. An eccentric autodidact, when he was not farming, he wrote on the history of Bulgarian place names. Alongside Bulgarian, Greek, Turkish and Esperanto, he spoke idiosyncratic English. He was famous in Omurtag for two things: for the fierce home-brew *rakiya* he made (but, being a Muslim, didn't drink); and for having created a special harness for his horse-drawn plough. With this harness, he could attach a book to the plough, allowing him to both study and work at the same time.

We sat together talking in his sitting room. Soon various dishes appeared from the kitchen, brought by Hasan's wife: salad, some pastries, and *tarhana* – a stew made of fermented goat's milk and cracked wheat. Hasan urged us to eat. The *tarhana* was good, and it was a long time since breakfast. I ate a bowlful, then put the bowl down. 'Would you like more?' Hasan asked. I said I was full.

Hasan looked disappointed. 'You have not eaten enough,' he said.

I insisted that I couldn't eat any more. 'Let me tell you a story,' Hasan said. Then he told me the following tale.

It happened in some village or other. Who knows which one? There are so many villages, so many stories, it is hard to keep track. But in this village lived a poor family, and although they were poor, they often accepted guests for the night. When travellers passed by at dusk, the family welcomed them in and invited them to stay. The following morning, when the guests took their leave, the other villagers watched the family waving their guests off, wishing them well for the road. But occasionally, something strange happened. The neighbours were woken by the sound of the guests being driven from the house, pursued by their host, who would be swinging a large cudgel.

Nobody could understand why some guests left on good terms, while others were sent on their way with beatings and curses. So the village council – all old men who wore the white beards of wisdom and experience – asked the host what he was up to. And the host explained.

He offered his guests all that he could, he said: the finest food he could afford, the best sleeping-spot on the furs by the fire, the tastiest *tarhana* for breakfast. And the family made room. They gave up the toastiest sleeping-space. They ate only cracked wheat without goat's milk. They didn't share in the evening meal.

Some guests accepted all this generosity without complaint. But others refused. 'You are poor,' they said. 'We cannot accept your food.' Or when their host spread the furs out before the fire, they protested, 'I will not sleep on the furs. Your family will be uncomfortable.' And at breakfast time, they said to their hosts, 'Please, eat the *tarhana* with goat's milk yourselves. I will be fine with cracked wheat.'

When the guests refused the hospitality of their host, the children protested, 'Father! What is so wrong with our house that our guest does not eat our *tarhana*, or sleep on our furs or accept food in the evening?' And this made the host ashamed. So he took up a big cudgel from the corner of the room and beat the offending guests, until they ran, yelping in pain, from the house.[1]

Hasan finished telling me this story. Then he asked me again: are you sure you wouldn't like more *tarhana*?

I hesitated. The scholar grinned. 'I have a big cudgel in the next room,' he said. 'Now will you eat more?' He pointed at my empty bowl.

I glanced through the open door, into the other room. Just in case.

Janus, with his cudgel and key, reminds us that in crossing the threshold of others' lives, the line between hospitality and hostility, welcome and violence, is often very thinly drawn.

Close to lunchtime, the air in the Seroy Shahzoda money exchange market in Kabul is filled with a high-pitched background hissing. It is the sound of cooking *shurba*, a soup of meat, potatoes and beans. Traditionally, *shurba* is slow-cooked and served with fresh naan bread. But to cut cooking time down to a more manageable couple of hours, many Afghans use a pressure cooker, a *deg-i bukhar* – literally 'cauldron of steam'. The anthropologist Magnus Marsden describes how, in the mornings, you can see men going to work, carrying a *deg* that they will use to make lunch to offer to friends and strangers.[2] By noon you can hear the hissing of multiple *degs* and smell the fragrance of the stew. As a symbol of hospitality, the *deg* has strong religious overtones. In Sufi shrines across the Islamic world, volunteers cook up stew to feed worshippers and the needy in large cauldrons. These cauldrons, big brothers to the marketplace pressure cookers, represent what Marsden calls the 'boundless and uncalculated generosity' of the Sufi saints.[3] But as a symbol, the *deg* is ambivalent. One Afghan trader told Marsden, 'The *deg* essentially is a bomb.' Used well, it makes good, rich stew; but if not managed with sufficient skill, these rickety hotpots are liable to explode, sending shards of jagged metal as far as 250 metres.[4]

The ambiguity was not lost on Marsden's Afghan hosts. Welcoming strangers involves both tastiness and danger. Things can always explode, when you are least expecting it. Encounters between strangers are often tangled up with elaborate codes of honour, where a single misstep can lead to offence, and to a spiralling cycle of outrage and anger. As Martha Nussbaum argues, real or imagined status-injury is one of the deepest triggers for anger, violence and discord. When our guest refuses the good *tarhana*, or refuses to sleep in the place by the fire, we feel ourselves down-ranked. We are caught up in an overwhelming rush of hot passion.[5] Injured and insulted, our gift refused, we reach for the cudgel, as if only violence could purge the dishonour and re-establish the proper order of the world. As if this explosion of violence were not only justifiable, but *called for*.

In all of literature, one of the most troubling stories about guests and strangers, honour and status, hospitality and violence, is the story at the end of the *Odyssey*. Odysseus is struggling to make his way back to Ithaca from the Trojan War, held up again and yet again by various adventures. At home, his wife, Penelope, unsure whether he is dead or alive, weaves his funeral shroud. Meanwhile, the palace at Ithaca is overrun by 108 hangers-on, all eager to marry Penelope and inherit the throne.

These suitors are parasites: they live off the abundance of the palace. They slaughter the fattest of the royal cattle and turn their skins into sitting-mats. They drink the best wine. They idle around all day. They give nothing back. But we shouldn't be so hard on them. As Emily Wilson points out, they are little more than boys or teenagers. And everybody knows how much teenagers eat. We should give them a break. They're just doing what teenagers do.

Penelope shuts herself away, weaving. Years pass without news of Odysseus. She settles into the discomfort of not knowing what has become of him. He is a missing person, neither dead nor alive. Uncertain of everything, Penelope stalls for time. She plays the suitors off against each other, hoping Odysseus will eventually turn up and sort everything out. She 'sends notes to each', keeping them hanging on, keeping their hopes up; 'but all the while her mind moves somewhere else'.[6] She promises the boys that she will choose one of them after the funeral shroud is finished. And at the end of every day of weaving, under cover of darkness, she unravels her work.

If the suitors don't press the issue too hard, it is because they are not really interested in Penelope. What they want, more than anything else, is to extend the feast. They want to go on eating and eating and eating, without thinking too hard about tomorrow, or about Odysseus, or about the consequences of their actions. They boast and brag and argue and drink and play checkers. And when Athena comes calling, Telemachus, the son of Odysseus and Penelope, does not recognise her. Instead he complains to her that, 'these men are only interested in music – / a life of ease. They make no contribution. / This food belongs to someone else, a man / whose white bones may be lying in the rain / or sunk beneath the waves.'[7]

Then Odysseus appears, fixed up by Athena in his homeless beggar's disguise. The suitors don't recognise him and they treat him badly. Long-term guests themselves, they don't extend him even the minimum of courtesy. Instead, they mock him. Antinous is the cockiest, the most swaggering and rude. He sneers at Odysseus, and tells him that they will drive him out, and ship him off to take his chances with Echetus, a king renowned for his cruelty to beggars.[8]

Odysseus holds back a little longer. But when the retribution comes, it is brutal and merciless. The pressure cooker explodes. The *deg* of hospitality goes off. Odysseus reveals himself as the true ruler of Ithaca and sets about slaughtering the parasitic kids. Antinous gets an arrow through the neck. Others are speared by Odysseus's allies. Still others are bound in ropes and hung from the rafters to die. Homer writes that 'Screaming filled the hall, / as skulls were cracked; the whole floor ran with blood.'[9]

Before long, the hall is littered with corpses.

'It is justice which is at issue here, not sentiment,' says Julian Pitt-Rivers. 'The world turns the right way up once more. Order and peace are restored.'[10] The *kleos* or renown that comes from giving gifts and welcoming strangers has a dark side. In a world where reputation is all, there is something dishonouring about being taken advantage of; and lost honour must be restored.

This restoration of order and peace – making the world right again through the violence that recovers lost status – is not limited to ancient Greece. One night, when Caroline Humphrey was carrying out her fieldwork in Mongolia, a guest turned up at the *ger* where she was staying. He parked his car outside. He didn't call out, 'Mind the dog!' Nor did he step over the threshold with his right foot, or pull down his cuffs as a sign of respect for the dignity of his hosts. He simply marched into the house where he called out in greeting, not to the host, but to the anthropologist. Having down-ranked the status of the host, he then invited the anthropologist to dinner. The host intervened, insisting that the unruly guest stay and eat in the *ger*. Reluctantly, and with bad grace, the guest agreed.

When the meal was ready, the host raised his glass and toasted the guest. Then he toasted him again, and again, and again. As the host repeatedly toasted the guest, the traditional compliments that, as host, he was required to pay to the guest became more and more insulting. The atmosphere in the tent crackled with hostility as the host clawed back his lost status and repeatedly put down the visitor. As for the guest, now effectively a hostage, he drank glass after glass until he was blind drunk. He attempted, too late, to pay honour to the host, offering to bow before him: an honour that the host refused. When he was unable to bear it any longer, the unfortunate guest stumbled outside. Once he had passed the threshold, he was no longer a guest. He was, Humphrey writes, now 'fair game'. The host sent a group of men to beat him up as reparation for the harms the guest had caused to his status and his honour.[11]

Of all the codes of honour that human beings have invented – whether formal or informal – few are as exacting as the Kanun of northern Albania. This ancient code is said to reach back 3,000 years – to the time of the writing of the *Odyssey*. Perhaps it reaches back further still, to the age of Odysseus himself. In its contemporary form, it is traced back to Prince Lekë Dukagjini (1410–81), who is said to have systematised these Albanian traditions of oral tribal law. But it was only in the twentieth century that an enterprising Franciscan monk and folklorist called Shtjefën Gjeçovi decided to write the whole thing down, in twelve volumes.[12]

84

The Kanun rests on three pillars: honour; hospitality; and *besa*, an all but untranslatable word that is 'a mélange between a sworn oath, a binding promise, protection and faith'.[13] This threefold obsession runs through Albanian culture. As Ismail Kadare writes in his novel *Broken April*, 'The Kanun was stronger than it seemed. Its power reached everywhere, covering lands, the boundaries of fields. It made its way into the foundations of houses, into tombs, to churches, to roads, to markets, to weddings.'[14] The early-twentieth-century writer Edith Durham, who fell in love with Albania and is still honoured in the country today, wrote that in Albania 'all else is subservient' to these codes of honour.[15]

Durham first travelled to the Balkans just after the turn of the twentieth century. A trained artist, already in her late thirties, she had spent much of the previous decade caring for her sick mother. Feeling trapped in a future that offered no more than 'endless years of grey monotony', she was on the brink of a nervous breakdown.[16] Edith's doctor recommended she rest, and suggested that travel might do her good. Edith negotiated with her family: she would take two months out of every twelve for travelling; the rest of the time, she would look after her mother. Her family agreed and Edith caught a steamer to the Dalmatian coast. It was here that her long love affair with the Balkans began.

Over the years that followed, Edith spent as much time as she could there. When her mother died in 1906, she travelled to the mountains of Albania. After the stultifying boredom of life in London, the high mountain passes suited her. She was proud of her own fearlessness and stamina, disdainful of those who could not match her. She fell in love with the landscape, the culture, the language, the generosity of her hosts. Compared with the lukewarm British, she wrote, 'for open-handed generosity and hospitality, the Albanian ranks incomparably higher'.[17] One day on the road, she stopped by a house and asked for water. The householder brought out a cup. Edith swigged the water and handed him back the cup. As she turned to go, the man told her 'that I now ranked as his guest, and that he should be bound by his honour to avenge me should anything happen to me before I had received hospitality from another'.[18]

In its obsession with hospitality, the Kanun sets the bar high for hosts. The house of the Albanian, the Kanun says, belongs to God and the guest. Or as one Albanian friend told me, 'If a guest is staying over, it is the host who takes the sofa, always. Guests should have nice and crisp bedsheets and be offered the best of what's in the home.' They should be given all the good, sweet things in the house; and if they refuse them, their hosts will beg them to eat until they relent.[19]

But in the Kanun, for all the pleasures of this extravagant hospitality, violence is never far away. There are, according to the Kanun, two justifications for a man killing his wife: infidelity and a failure to provide hospitality.[20] In the past, the parents of women who were to be married gave their in-laws a bullet with which to kill their daughter if she violated either rule.[21] The Kanun is a reminder of how the codes of honour that regulate the relationships between strangers, between guests and hosts, are frequently gendered; and how the burden falls disproportionately on women. A woman, the Kanun says, is 'a sack for carrying things'.[22]

The Kanun also provides the justification for Albania's

tradition of blood feuds. According to the Kanun, slights to status or to honour are to be avenged by blood. The code sets out in precise detail the calculus of violence: this insult, this slight, is worth this many deaths.[23] And the obligations are reciprocal: blood must in turn be avenged with blood, and the feud continues on. Even today, the tradition continues. It is hard to establish precise data, but estimates are that the families still caught in blood feuds, passed down from generation to generation, number in the hundreds. Within these families are children who are unable to leave their homes, because they are 'in blood' to other families, and if they dare to step outside, they risk being murdered.[24]

The Kanun perpetuates violence: vengeance rebalances the moral scales, as it did in the time of the *Odyssey*. This is justice, not sentiment. But the law code that has trapped so many in these never-ending cycles of violence also puts the brakes on the worst excesses of feuding; and the demands of hospitality in the Kanun trump the sacred demands of bloodletting. 'If a guest enters your house, even though he may be in blood with you,' the Kanun says, 'you must welcome him.' One night in Albania, Edith Durham stayed in a roadside inn. Two of her fellow guests were blood foes who had accidentally found themselves lodging together. 'Being with friends and meeting under one roof,' she wrote, 'it was not etiquette to shoot. They drank coffee together and became so friendly they swore peace for six weeks. The company thought this was an excellent joke and laughed heartily.'[25]

Codes of honour put a burden on both guests and hosts. 'To invite a person to your house,' according to Victorian food writer Isabella Beeton in her epic *Book of Household Management*, 'is to take charge of his happiness so long as he is beneath your roof.'[26] And this taking charge of guests is no small task. Beeton opens her book with a quote from the Book of Proverbs 35:21–28, about the virtues of a good wife: 'Strength and honour are her clothing; and she shall rejoice in time to come . . . she looketh well to the ways of the household; and eateth not the bread of idleness.' The stakes are high. The hostess is responsible for staving off the social risks of slighted honour, while providing the greatest possible pleasure for her guests. She should, Beeton says, take care 'in the selection of the invited guests, that they should be suited to each other'. She should make sure there is a suitable mixture of 'talkers and listeners, the grave and the gay', to provide the optimum conversation. After the guests have all arrived, the half-hour before dinner commences – that gap of anticipation, when the small talk is awkward – is 'the great ordeal through which the mistress . . . will either pass with flying colours, or lose many of her laurels'. The hostess has to attend to the arriving guests, while also making sure that the cook and domestic staff are all doing as they should. As well as juggling all this, she must also 'display no kind of agitation', but instead 'show her tact in suggesting light and cheerful subjects of conversation'. However much trouble she is going to, Beeton writes, she should maintain an untroubled demeanour.

When dinner is called and the guests are seated, the ordeal is not over. The hostess must continue to serve, cajole and chat, while all the time being aware that her 'behaviour will set the tone to all the ladies present'. Then, after the meal is over, she should be attentive to the moment at which there is a lull in the conversation, and then she should rise, giving the signal for the ladies to depart, before the men become 'unfit to conduct themselves with that decorum which is essential in the presence of ladies'.[27]

Sometimes the demands that these codes of honour place upon hosts are so great, they can be ruinous. Sandwiched between Ukraine and Romania, Moldova is one of the least-visited countries in Europe. As in many nations in east and south-east Europe, in Moldova hospitality is a matter of both personal and national pride. Hosting strangers and guests brings social status and increases your moral standing in the community. But the honour bestowed by guests comes at a cost. The anthropologist Jennifer Cash writes that the task of hosting strangers in Moldova is often 'exhausting and thankless'. The codes of honour that demand hospitality put a burden on the household, not only in terms of time and labour, but also financially. It is not uncommon for people to take out loans to fulfil these demands. 'We live badly,' one Moldovan woman explained to the anthropologist, 'but we make very lavish feasts because they represent our goodness, the hospitality of the Moldovans . . . It is our tradition to make rich feasts, even if we have nothing, for birthdays, holidays, Easter, Christmas, and even when we visit someone. Even if you have nothing, you go and borrow the money to put on a better feast, because that is our nature.'[28] This puts not only hosts, but also potential guests in a difficult position. Do you eat the food your Moldovan hosts have provided? Do you hold out your bowl for another serving? How do you choose between dishonouring your hosts and causing them material distress?

As an anthropologist in Indonesia, I was perpetually aware

of the burdens my presence put upon my hosts. I was an exasperating guest. I misunderstood things. I asked stupid questions. I lumbered around with clueless goodwill, causing offence and getting things wrong. Ibu Lin, my host in the village of Alusi Krawain, proclaimed herself practised in the art of hosting anthropologists. She had put up previous visitors to the islands and was proud of her knowledge of this strange breed. She took charge of me, managing me like she would any other unwieldy project. She schooled me in local customs. She filled me in on all the gossip from the village. She managed whom I could and could not speak with. She fed me copiously. She pinched my cheeks and told me she was fattening me up because when I arrived I was too skinny. She stood over me to make sure I ate everything on my plate.

I often fretted over the abundance of food she forced upon me. It was more than I could eat and I worried about the expense. I knew I was taking up most of her time and effort. I suspected that Ibu Lin could ill afford the indulgences she offered me. I knew I was trouble. I just hoped I was trouble worth having. Because for all the downsides, for Ibu Lin there was a pay-off. My presence in her house elevated her status. It put her on a different footing in the village. It gave her an international reach. One day, she said, I would write a book, and I would put her name in it, and then everybody would know who she was. And if this meant she had to suffer the temporary inconvenience of my presence in her home, it was a deal that, as far as she was concerned, was worth making.

When it comes to the complexities of our human relationships, questions of honour and status are inescapable: they are a part of what it means to be a social being. However much we disavow these concerns, or treat them with suspicion, it is difficult, as Alain de Botton argues, 'to imagine a good life entirely free' of status anxiety.[29] And the less status we have, the more it matters. For those who have little, status and dignity are a part of keeping hold of what it means to be human. It is only those who are secure in their status who have the luxury of professing themselves free from status concern.

I met Rahim around three years ago. He was attending a writing class for refugees I was running in the city of Leicester. Back in Iran, Rahim had been a doctor.[30] A critic of the regime, he had fled the country under threat of imprisonment, and eventually he found his way to the UK, where he applied for asylum. He was a shy, quiet man, thoughtful and intelligent, and desperate to improve his English. But the Byzantine machinery of the asylum process was moving slowly and since arriving in the UK Rahim had been caught in interminable limbo. Until his case was decided on, he was living on the meagre welfare provided by the British government: just over five pounds a day, loaded onto a pre-paid card that could be used only in designated supermarkets. He had no other income, nor was he allowed any.

Rahim and I got on well, but when the class ended we didn't keep in touch. Then one morning several months later, I ran into him on the street. It turned out that we are almost neighbours: he lived just a street away from me.

'You must come to visit,' he said. 'Later today.'

I thanked him for his invitation. 'I'm free,' I said. 'I'll come over.'

Rahim wrote down his address.

That afternoon, I went to knock on his door. He looked out of the window, waved and called out, 'Wait a minute!' I heard him moving around the furniture. A minute later, he opened the door. 'Come in,' he said.

On the table Rahim had laid out plates of nuts, biscuits and chocolate. 'Tea or coffee?' he asked. I said I would have tea.

Rahim went into the kitchen. I heard the kettle boiling. He came back with two steaming cups of tea. We drank tea and he urged me to eat. I knew he could barely afford to offer me this food. But I also knew how much it meant to host me. I nibbled at a biscuit, ate a square of chocolate, picked at the nuts. But I also held back, knowing the more I ate, the more I risked Rahim not eating later that week.

Rahim, seeing my hesitancy, smiled and pushed me to eat more. Sovereignty, the anthropologist Andrew Shryock writes, 'is manifest in the ability to act as host'. So, afraid that to hold back would cause offence, I thanked him, and helped myself to more – a handful of nuts, a few more squares of chocolate, a biscuit. Because perhaps for Rahim, lost in the horror of the UK asylum system, the ability to act as host may have helped him salvage a sense of his own humanity and agency in the face of the inhumane world.[31] And as the poet Alicia Stallings says about her work with refugee writers in the anarchist squats of Athens, 'Human dignity seems to be about what you can offer others. Even if it is just a cup of tea, it is important that it is offered and accepted.'[32]

If the ways in which the dance of honour and dishonour between guests and hosts play out can seem endlessly complex, the things that go wrong remain remarkably consistent across cultures. Julian Pitt-Rivers talks about a law of hospitality with 'universal validity'.[33] A guest infringes this universal law by showing rivalry, by usurping their host through violating the rules of the household, or by refusing the hospitality offered them, as the unfortunate Bulgarian guests refused the *tarhana*. Conversely, a host insults their guest by allowing rivalry to run unchecked, by failing to protect the guest's person and their honour, and by failing to adequately meet their needs.

Nevertheless, if this pattern is universal, in different contexts there are endless variations on this simple theme. In some places, the consequences of misreading the signs and violating these codes of honour might result in mild disapproval, or the quiet severing of future relations. But in other settings, breaking with these codes can lead to the most unexpected, horrific violence. Somewhere in Mongolia, a bad guest stumbles drunkenly out of a tent and is beaten to a pulp. In a palace on the island-kingdom of Ithaca, a returning king visits unimaginable bloodshed on a bunch of kids. In Bulgaria, a guest is driven from the home where they are lodging, beaten with a heavy stick, having committed the sin of solicitude towards his hosts.

The earliest audiences of the *Odyssey* would have understood that the violence that exploded in the hall at Ithaca was not just a matter of earthly justice. This moral rebalancing of the books was about the discharging of a sacred obligation. In the world of the *Odyssey*, the code of *xenia* is less a set of shared understandings about how to get by in the world, and more a religious duty underpinned by the threat, and the very real possibility, of violence. And so when things go wrong, the demands for retribution take on the air of a ritual purging. Even Odysseus hesitates before he unleashes his vengeance on the unruly kids. He really isn't particularly into it. He would prefer a more measured solution. It takes an immortal, the goddess Athena, disguised as Odysseus's old friend Mentor, to goad him on to slaughter. 'Now you are home at last,' Athena asks, 'how can you flinch / from being brave and using proper force . . . ?' Then, having set the sacred violence in motion, the goddess flies 'like a swallow through the smoke'. She nestles serenely in the rafters and there she watches the horror unfold.[34]

We all know the sting of an insult, the hot rush of anger when we are taken for granted, the pain of not receiving what we think is due to us. These things matter even when we negotiate our relationships with those close to us; when we are trying to work out how to get along with strangers, all the time managing our underlying fear, the stakes become so much higher. When things go wrong in our relationships with strangers, when we perceive that someone has behaved badly in the sacred space of our home, it is easy to feel violated. Offence is real. For social beings like ourselves, status matters; and even trivial, accidental slights can wound us deeply.

But if status is inescapable, when we transmute our natural concern with status into notions of *kleos*, or sacred honour, everybody stands to lose. Pitt-Rivers reminds us that the law of hospitality, although universal, is not a 'divine law'; instead, it is merely a 'sociological necessity'. It is good to remember this in the heat of the moment, when we arrive home to find 108 suitors living off the abundance of our household. If we can strip our status concerns of their sacred clothing, if we can pause before picking up the cudgel of divine retribution, then the path is opened to another way forward. When we hold back, for all our indignation and our outrage, then the goddess Athena, knowing there is nothing more to see, soon gets bored and flies out from the rafters to find another place to lodge. Then, the possibility of sacred violence forestalled, we are left instead to fumble around for the right key that might unlock a way forward, seeking solutions to this ordinary human mess, free of the interference of the gods.

Martha Nussbaum writes about 'transition-anger' – the stab of outrage that comes from being slighted, before it hardens into the desire for payback, or the desperate attempt to reclaim lost status.[35] Transition-anger thinks, 'How outrageous'; but then it asks how we can find a better response to this outrage, how we can avoid the cooking pot of our shared lives blowing up in our faces. Because the clumsiest and most difficult of interactions can be salvaged if we approach them with sufficient wisdom and good humour, with an eye on the kind of future that is worth holding out for. Then, if somebody stumbles into our tent in the wilds of Mongolia without observing the proper rituals, we might find a way to laugh off their boorishness. If our feasting-hall is unexpectedly filled with parasitic teenagers, rather than resorting to all-out slaughter, we might send the unruly kids away with stern notes for their mums. And if a visitor to our house somewhere in the mountains of Bulgaria refuses our *tarhana*, we might simply shrug, sigh lightly and sit our guest down to explain just how hurt we are.

Someone who understood the value of de-escalation was the

Stoic philosopher Seneca. One evening, in the status-obsessed city of ancient Rome, he was slighted by his hosts. At a dinner party, finding himself seated in a place of low rank, the philosopher was furious. He seethed at the insult. He resented his host, he resented the other guests, he resented the people who had been placed in more favourable positions.

But then, in a moment of Stoic clarity, he realised the fruitlessness of it all. 'Madman,' he said to himself, with a healthy edge of self-mockery, 'what difference does it make what part of a couch you plant your weight on?'[36]

5

Feasts

It was the early 1980s and we were on our first family holiday abroad, driving south through France in an old, battered Renault 4. Up front, Mum and Dad took turns driving and map-reading. In the back seat, my sister and I took turns being travel-sick or fractious. I looked out of the window at the signs written in French, at the passing cars, at the houses and fields that were almost but not quite the same as back at home, and everything seemed strange and unfamiliar and exotic.

By evening, we were exhausted and behind schedule. In the back seat, my sister and I were becoming unmanageable. To the right of the *autoroute*, the sun was beginning to sink in the sky. The plan had been to break our journey halfway, finding a cheap hotel, before heading further south to the *gîte* Mum had bravely booked over the telephone in her broken, heavily accented French.

Just before dusk fell, the engine started to make grinding noises. We pulled off the road onto the hard shoulder just as the engine spluttered and died. Dad flicked on the hazard lights. We got out and sat on the verge. Mum and Dad had urgent, whispered conversations.

The sun set and the air became cool. Mum and Dad waved at passing cars. Eventually, one of the cars stopped. The hazards went on, flashing orange, and a thin, pale man got out. He was in a black and white striped shirt and stonewashed jeans. The back of his car was covered in bumper stickers in French proclaiming the love of Christ: 'Jesus loves you! How do I know? I talked to him this morning!' The stranger must have seen the 'GB' sticker on the back of our car, because he addressed us in English. 'Can I help you?'

Yes, Mum and Dad told him. We had broken down.

The stranger said it was no problem. We could spend the night with his family. There was a garage in the village and his friend was the mechanic. He would get the car fixed and we could continue on our way. The stranger smiled. 'I do this in the love of Christ,' he said.

Dad usually reserved overt religious talk for the pulpit, if then. Always uneasy when people were too demonstrative in their faith, he gave a tight smile of thanks.

The stranger set about improvising a way of towing the car. Mum took us to one side. It was probably safe, she said, but not all strangers are to be trusted. If she shouted 'run', we should run. We said we would, even though I was not sure where to.

The stranger hitched the Renault 4 to his car. We piled in and he towed us back to his village. We parked up at his house and he invited us in. It was a dark, rambling place with a large balcony overhung by a vine, heavy with ripening grapes. Our host introduced us to his extended family: wife, children, parents, grandparents, cousins, friends. Then he showed my sister and me to our room – a four-poster bed, heavy velvet drapes, dark wood panelling that exuded the smell of polish. Mum flustered around, anxious. Dad looked strained.

Later that night we sat on the terrace underneath the vine with our host and his family. Crickets chirred in the night. There was a smell of honeysuckle, of jasmine, of creeping, fragrant things. Our host's mother cooked up an omelette. When it arrived, our host announced it contained twenty eggs. He set about dividing it up. We ate omelette and French bread, and salad, and cheese. Mum and Dad drank wine and chatted in English, with occasional lapses into French for the sake of making an effort. We drank fruit juice and stayed up past our bedtime. When the meal was over, Mum took us to bed. She reassured us we were safe, although she didn't sound sure. My sister and I slept in the four-poster, a bolster between us so we didn't argue.

The following day, we had breakfast on the terrace. Our host went off with Dad to get the car looked at. We were lucky it was a Renault 4, as every small-town mechanic in France had spare parts. The mechanic fixed the car at cost. Our host insisted on paying. By lunchtime, we were packed up and ready to head on our way south. Our host waved us off. We pulled out onto the country road and made our way to the *autoroute*. We never saw him again.

An hour or two later, I was leaning out of the window of the car again, feverish and pale. But even the sickness couldn't take away from the lingering sense I had been involved in something miraculous.

Twenty eggs! I had never known an omelette like it.

*

One tenth of a twenty-egg omelette, cooked for a collective feast, is always going to taste better than a two-egg omelette eaten alone. According to the nineteenth-century French lawyer and gourmand Jean Anthelme Brillat-Savarin, the enjoyment of food is a social pleasure. In his *Physiology of Taste*, Brillat-Savarin makes a distinction between the pleasure of eating and the pleasures of the table. The pleasure of eating is 'the actual and direct sensation of satisfying a need'. The pleasures of the table are independent both of hunger and of appetite: they are social pleasures. The real delight of feasting, Brillat-Savarin writes, is the togetherness, the conversation, the sense of having no pressing engagements. When we eat together, our brains awaken. We take on colour, our eyes shine and our bodies are suffused with warmth. We become more perceptive. We chat. And as the conversation unfolds, our imagination flowers. We connect. We forge alliances and friendships.[1]

It is not just that eating together is an excuse for the pleasures of friendship. Shared food, if it is good, actually tastes better. Researchers from Yale University have found that the experience of eating pleasant-tasting chocolate is enhanced by the presence of somebody else eating the same chocolate, even if you do not communicate with the other person who is munching on the chocolate alongside you.[2]

But the reverse is also true. When subjects were given unpleasantly bitter chocolate, they judged it more unpleasant when the experience of eating it was shared. What the researchers call the 'amplification hypothesis' suggests that shared experiences are enhanced. Things that are good seem better when they are shared and things that are bad seem worse.

Not only does good food taste better when eating with others, and bad food taste worse, but for decades it has been known that when people are together, they eat more. This heightening of the experience of eating and the increase in quantity eaten is referred to by researchers as the social facilitation of eating. The effect even holds when people eat alone in front of a mirror.[3]

There is, however, a difference between eating with friends and with strangers. In both situations, we eat more, but the social facilitation effect is far less pronounced when dining with those who are unfamiliar to us.[4] When with strangers, we are more on our guard, more circumspect. We watch out for signs and cues from our host. 'A guest sits briefly, but notices a lot,' as they say in Kazakhstan.[5] We want to eat abundantly, to give honour to our hosts, but we don't want to eat so abundantly that we look gluttonous. It is a fine balance to strike.

We eat more in company with others not just out of a competition for resources – the 'big family' syndrome. We also eat more because collective meals are, by their very nature, expansive.[6] It is abundance – of food, of pleasure, of participants, sometimes of goodwill, sometimes of rivalry – that turns a meal into a feast. Feasting is extravagant and shared; it is defined, according to the archaeologist Brian Hayden, as 'the amassing of surpluses to give away as food or gifts, or to put on display to impress guests'.[7] Feasting implies a lack of restraint, even of caution: a timid feast is no feast at all. Whatever the excuse for the feast, the essence of feasting is this excess: whether it is an extra bowl of *tarhana* in Omurtag, a twenty-egg omelette in France, or the chocolate, nuts and biscuits served by an asylum seeker in a terraced house in England.

Human feasting goes back at least as far as the cooking fires of our ancestors in the Palaeolithic era,[8] and to the bones piled up around the Neanderthal hearths. But if feasting reaches back into Palaeolithic times, it only really takes off once human beings begin to settle down and adopt more sedentary lifestyles.[9] In the small Hilazon Tachtit cave tucked into the hills of northern Israel, an archaeological team led by Leore Grosman uncovered the grave of a woman from the Natufian culture. The grave, evidence showed, dated back 12,000 years. Near the woman's grave was evidence of collective feasting, and she was buried with a strange array of things: dozens of tortoise plastrons and carapaces, the bones of several aurochs or wild cattle, a number of mountain gazelles, a severed human foot, the wing of a golden eagle, the skull of a marten and the pelvis of a leopard.[10] Grosman's team concluded that, given the evidence of ritual care and the magnitude of the feast, the buried woman was 'most probably a shaman'.[11]

The Natufians were a community on the cusp of sedentary living, making the transition from hunting and gathering to settled farming. Grosman and her colleagues speculate that collective feasting was a means of managing what archaeologists call the 'scalar stress' of living together in larger numbers. Feasting builds stronger social bonds. It increases solidarity and provides a way of managing what it means to live in larger and larger groups.[12] In this place, one spring day twelve millennia ago, a community gathered to bury one of their most valued members. They fashioned a grave site from heavy stones. They laid out the array of precious things – eagle feathers, tortoise carapaces, parts of leopards and martens. And then, because their grief was great, they cooked up tortoise flesh and wild aurochs, and together they sought out the shared comforts of the living.

Feasting binds us together in circles of shared pleasure and nourishment: not only those close to us, but strangers too. As our ancestors put down roots, archaeologist Martin Jones writes, 'they were creating a fixed human landscape that enabled a new kind of mobility of travellers, over considerable distances'. And with this increased movement of people came 'new kinds of social encounter, sometimes between complete strangers, and new settings for the sharing of food'.[13]

By the time of the first civilisations, cultures of feasting were well established, both as a way of building community and solidarity in the burgeoning cities, and as a way of managing troublesome strangers. In ancient Mesopotamia, feasts consisted of beer, pears, pistachios, pastries, fish roes, gazelles, birds, truffles and locust kebabs.[14] In the world of the *Odyssey* and the *Iliad*, in accordance with the code of *xenia* or guest friendship, newly disarmed strangers were led to the table, where they ate quantities of bread, roast and skewered meat, wine, black puddings, cheese, seafood, honey, olives and an abundance of fruit.[15]

These lists of good things suggest the abundance that is the hallmark of feasting is a matter not just of quantity but also of variety. In the early 1990s, the American anthropologist Paula Michaels was planning her birthday party in Kazakhstan. She was living as a paying guest with a Kazakh family, studying at the university in Almaty. Her host was a divorced Kazakh woman called Saule, who lived with her nine-year-old son. Michaels was about to turn twenty-six. It was an age at which, in Kazakh eyes, she was already a spinster. She decided to celebrate her spinsterhood by holding a traditional American-style birthday party. She took an inventory of the Almaty food stores and came up with a plan to make American pizza out of Kazakh flatbreads, sausage, pasta sauce and local hard cheese. For dessert, she decided to make a cake out of cake mix (imported from Moscow), substituting instant pudding for frosting. She invited three Kazakh guests and three American guests.

When Saule found out about the plan, she was horrified. The menu, she told Michaels, simply would not do. It was an insult to the guests. It made the whole household look bad. It violated the unspoken culinary rule that Michaels calls the 'salad-to-guest ratio'. In Kazakhstan, the rule is this: the greater the number of guests, the more the variety of dishes. It is not enough to just scale up the quantity of the food. You also need to multiply the number of dishes. 'What I had intended to be a fun yet low-key adventure for me in kitchen experimentation,' Michaels writes, 'turned into a stressful struggle between adherents to clashing perspectives on hospitality.'[16]

The culture of Kazakhstan, like that of Mongolia further to the east, is one that puts a high value on welcoming guests. As Michaels writes, 'One cannot help but notice the priority placed by not just Kazakhs, but all Central Asians on what looks to us like quite grandiose displays of hospitality.' A Kazakh home full of guests is considered a blessing. But only if the host and guest perform their proper roles. The American anthropologist, with her meagre offerings of pizza and cake, brought shame on Saule's household. Worse than this, in Kazakh culture, if you don't provide your guests with sufficient abundance, how will they know when it is time to leave? Full stomachs are the best means of sending people on their way. 'If a guest is full,' the Kazakh saying goes, 'then he's ready to think about the road.'[17]

The sheer extravagance of feasting has often drawn criticism. Plato casts a disapproving eye, making a connection between excessive eating at feasts and erotic excess. In the *Republic*, a disapproving Socrates says that one who is under the spell of the tyrant of erotic love 'goes in for feasts, revelries, luxuries, girl-friends, and all that sort of thing'.[18] And those who are preoccupied with feasting, he continues, have lost their way in life. They wander this way and that, never attaining the true pleasures of higher, intellectual virtues. Because the pleasures of feasting, Plato insists, are not true pleasures; and what we take for pleasure in feasting is merely the relief from the physical pains of hunger, or the mental pains of desire.[19] 'Do you think,' Socrates asks the philosopher Simmias in the *Phaedo*, 'it is the part of the philoso-pher to be concerned with so-called pleasures as those of food and drink?' And Simmias obligingly replies, 'By no means.'[20] And yet of all those who feast, only Socrates is able to do so like a true philosopher. In the *Symposium*, Plato writes that although Socrates has no need for food and is willing to endure the pangs of hunger, he can nevertheless eat copiously when presented with a feast; without any appetite for drinking, he can drink everybody under the table and never become drunk.[21]

Rather than rich feasts, Plato recommends more frugal fare

in the *Republic*. Socrates says to Glaucon that the ideal diet consists of wine, bread made from wheat and barley, salt, olives, cheese, boiled roots and vegetables. To follow, he suggests figs, chickpeas and beans. And for snacks, roast myrtle and acorns. Glaucon is outraged by the idea, protesting that this is a diet fit for 'a city of pigs'. In response, Socrates recites the moral and practical harms of excess: poor health, excessive land use, moral decline, warfare and strife.[22]

The Epicurean philosophers sought to redeem pleasure from its critics. Epicurus writes, 'No pleasure is a bad thing in itself. But the things which produce certain pleasures bring troubles many times greater than the pleasures.'[23] The problem with pleasure for the Epicureans is that we are simply not very good at it: many of the pleasures we pursue are self-defeating, leading to pain and trouble. But the answer is not to turn our backs on pleasure. Instead, we need to get wise to the dynamics of pleasure. We need to distinguish between those pleasures that lead to further trouble and those that are simple and uncomplicated.

The Epicureans lived together communally, outside of the city walls of Athens in a community known as the Garden. Above the door hung a sign reading, 'Here, Guest, will you be well entertained: here pleasure is the highest good.'[24] Admitting men and women equally into their community, and putting a high value on shared pleasures, the Epicureans quickly got a reputation for indulgence – as if the Garden was a place of endless, wine-soaked orgies. But a stranger turning up there would not find themselves entering a realm of uninhibited sensuality; instead they would be invited in and offered a plate of porridge and a large goblet of water, and would be asked, 'Is this not a fine welcome?' And Epicurus himself was modest in his appetites. 'Send me a small measure of cheese,' he once wrote to a friend, 'so that when I want to have a feast I shall be able to do so.'[25]

If this looks like frugality, it is a different frugality from that of Plato. Friendship, good cheese, a small glass of wine, a shared garden, the pursuit of philosophy: these were the things to which Epicurus was partial. And when we sift through our pleasures, weeding out the ones that lead to hangovers, to turbulence of the soul, to regret, and keeping the rest, we discover that a plate of porridge well made and a large goblet of water, offered and accepted in the right spirit, shared in a garden with friends all committed to pleasure, can be the greatest of feasts.

The long-standing philosophical suspicion of pleasure, a suspicion that goes all the way back to Plato, skews how we think about what it means to connect with strangers. When philosophers talk about how we negotiate our relationships with strangers, they almost always overlook the pleasure, the live-liness and the delight that strangers bring. Emmanuel Levinas writes that when we encounter a stranger, the 'first word is obligation', an obligation that may be demanding, even traumatic, but rarely pleasurable.[26] Meanwhile, the great Prussian philo-sopher Immanuel Kant writes of hospitality towards strangers as 'the right of a stranger not to be treated in a hostile manner by another upon his arrival on the other's territory'. For Kant, hospitality is not about shared enjoyment; instead it is about the duty, free of any pleasure or satisfaction, that characterises all acts of 'authentic moral worth'.[27]

This is, by any measure, an impoverished account of what hospitality means. Kant says nothing of twenty-egg omelettes.

He ignores the salad-to-guest ratio. He is oblivious to the win-win situation that characterises human gift-giving, a situation in which at best everybody wins, and the flavour of life – its sheer *tastiness* – is enhanced for us all. But worse than this, Kant's dutifulness makes for bad hosts. There can be nothing more depressing than the thought that your host might be going to all this trouble from mere duty. Nothing more insulting than a host who refuses to crack a smile, who resists the playfulness and joking that help build trust, who is determined not to derive any pleasure from your being there and who carries on their grim duties with a look of high-minded solemnity. As the Confucian philosopher Mencius wrote, 'A basket of food, a dollop of bean soup: to have these means life, to not have them means death; but if they are offered with insults, a wayfarer will not accept them.'[28]

The human enthusiasm for shared feasting has never sat comfortably alongside philosophies that cast a suspicious eye on bodily pleasure. And nowhere was that more the case than in the monasteries of medieval Europe. In the sixth-century *Rule of St Benedict*, which is the foundation stone of the Western monastic tradition, the founder of the Benedictine order writes that it is 'with some uneasiness that we make rules as to how much others should eat or drink'. Nevertheless, he swallows his unease and gives the following advice for how the community should eat together to cultivate harmony. There should be two cooked dishes, so that if anybody finds that one does not suit them, they have another option. Fruit or vegetables may be added as a third dish. There should also be bread – no more than a pound a day each. Meanwhile, although wine is not a suitable drink for monks, Benedict is willing to be flexible. As monks 'nowadays cannot be persuaded of this,' he writes, 'let us at least agree to drink sparingly and not to excess, because wine causes even sensible people to behave foolishly'. As for conversation, mealtimes are for the communal reading of scripture, not for chat. While the designated monk is reading, Benedict writes, 'There must be complete silence and no whispering, so that only the reader's voice can be heard in the room. The brothers should supply each other with what they need while they are eating and drinking, so that no one needs to ask for anything.'[29]

But Benedict recognises that all these rules, if they encourage virtue within the community of monks, are inappropriate when it comes to welcoming strangers coming from afar. For welcoming strangers, the monastery should have a separate kitchen and dining area. Guests, after all, may turn up at any time. In the guest dining room, Benedict writes, the abbot should welcome and dine with the visitors. And when they eat together, they should do so more opulently than the rank-and-file monks, because the rules of hospitality require that when there are guests, every meal should take on the excess of the feast. And while the abbot and the visitors eat together, the rule about silence should be waived. Why demand silence and waste the opportunity of the new intelligence that strangers can bring?[30]

Although wine may cause even sensible people to behave fool-ishly, since the earliest times, as they have feasted with strangers, human beings have used intoxicants to oil the wheels. We manage our relationships with guests and with strangers through balancing the buzz of stimulants and the wooziness of depressants. Diners in contemporary China lift glasses of *baijiu*, the fierce grain liquor that brings in its wake such punishing headaches. In Bedouin tents, visitors are offered coffee. Turning up at a friend's house unexpectedly, I find myself greeted by offers of tea, wine or beer. It's a trick as old as literature. In the Babylonian *Epic of Gilgamesh*, the wild-man Enkidu, reeking with an animal stench, is tamed by the comprehensive hospitality of Shamhat. She leads him to a shepherds' camp, gives him bread and ale, takes him to the barber, clothes him, and shares her bed with him over seven days and seven nights.

In the passage dedicated to 'the Meaning of the Feast' in the Confucian book of ritual, the *Li Ji*, it says, 'establishing guests and hosts: this is the ritual of drinking alcohol'.[31] But if intoxicants can make things go more smoothly, they can also raise the stakes and increase the risks of things going awry. They heighten pleasure. They blur social boundaries. They cook up warmth. But this heat can boil over easily into violence. It is no accident that the disastrous scenes in the Mongolian *ger* were preceded with determined, belligerent drinking. And even the high-minded Plato wasn't above such things. At Greek symposia – dedicated to poetry, philosophy and intellectual pursuits – the evening's high-minded entertainments were often rounded off with a *komos*, a ritualised drunken riot.[32] Plato argued, with his usual sobriety, that this drunkenness was an important part of an education in virtue. Through drunkenness we heighten the emotions. We love more fiercely. Our anger burns hotter. This makes collective drinking a place where we can test the virtues of self-control in the company of others.

*

The purpose of a feast – however simple or elaborate – is never just eating and drinking. We feast not to consume as many calories as possible, but to shape and reshape our relationships. The *Li Ji* says, 'The rituals of feasting are for the purposes of expressing human fellowship.'[33] Feasting builds bridges, helping us cook up social warmth together, even among strangers. There is something alchemical about the power of feasting to bring people together in a shared circle of warmth. In his essay on the sociology of the meal, the nineteenth-century sociologist Georg Simmel writes that 'communal eating and drinking ... releases a tremendous socializing power'. We are the only species that gets together in big groups expressly for the purpose of sharing food with strangers.[34] Food-sharing with strangers is not an exclusively human trait – both bonobos and chimpanzees have been recorded as doing the same; but it is this *gathering together* in collective feasts that is distinctively human. And this shared feasting is not just pleasurable, it is also good for the soul. In Kyrgyzstan, there is a tradition of providing freshly fried bread at feasts and parties. When you give people bread, you gain *soop*, or spiritual reward. The cook fries the bread and recites words from the Quran; and then, when the bread is given to guests, the amount of *soop*, the amount of spiritual benefit, the giver receives is in direct proportion to the amount of pleasure the bread gives.[35]

When Elee and I arrived at Helsinki station, our Couchsurfing host, Yasser, was waiting for us. We recognised each other from the photographs on the website. He was a compact, friendly-looking man in his thirties, fluent in English, Finnish, Russian,

French and his native Arabic. Originally from Egypt, he had lived for years in Finland, where he worked as a bus driver; and he loved having guests in his tiny apartment. That was – more or less – all we knew.

It was the first time we had met. Yasser shook our hands. 'I'm still on my shift,' he said. 'I've taken a break to give you these.' He handed over a mobile phone, a hand-drawn map and the keys to his apartment. 'The map tells you where you need to go,' he said. 'Take the lift and let yourselves in. I'll be back when I finish work.'

Then he added, 'Oh, by the way. There are three Russians turning up later. They're driving from St Petersburg. Let them in when they arrive. Use the kitchen to make yourselves something to eat if you are hungry. If you have any problems, call me. There's only one number on the phone and it's mine.'

We found the apartment, a one-bedroom place in a suburb of Helsinki, and we settled in. We made tea, read our books. After a couple of hours, there was a knock on the door. It was the Russians: a husband and wife, still in their early twenties, and their best friend. We introduced ourselves. The Russians were friendly and polite, although only one of them spoke good English and we spoke no Russian. By now, it was getting late, and we were hungry. Elee and I went to the supermarket and brought back things to cook a meal. I made pasta and sauce. All five of us ate, leaving enough for Yasser when he got home.

Yasser returned from his shift after ten. We had already eaten our fill, but Yasser insisted on extending the feast. He opened tins of sardines, carved hunks of bread and cheese, cracked open bottles of beer. We ate for a second time, exchanging jokes and stories. Yasser translated from Russian to English and English to Russian. The jokes were funnier in translation, in both directions. We drank beer and talked until well after midnight. Then Yasser sorted out places to sleep. He offered us his bedroom, saying he was equally comfortable on the couch. The Russians bedded down on a couple of air mattresses. Soon – well fed, slightly drunk, content, in the company of people who were no longer strangers but friends – we all fell asleep.

It is easy to be hard on Kant, what with his endless banging on about duty. His writing, although fascinating, is famously inelegant and difficult. In some contemporary accounts, he appears to be both fastidious and austere. It is said that when he walked the streets of Königsberg, the other citizens could set their watches by the time he passed. But in both his life and his work, sometimes you can get glimpses of a more human, less fully dutiful Kant. In his earlier years, this champion of reason and good order was known for his unreasonable drunkenness, famous for stumbling out of the bars of Königsberg so wasted that he was unable to find his way home.[36] Always the philosopher, he justified this behaviour with the sweet claim that for the sake of good-naturedness, sometimes it is necessary 'to go a bit beyond the borderline of sobriety for a short while'.[37] Even in later years, Kant was not averse to a good party. Despite the dourness of his moral philosophy, when it comes to the practical business of living, he is more forgiving. In his book *Anthropology from a Pragmatic Point of View*, he sets out rules for how to run a good dinner party. Eating alone, he says, is an unhealthy practice for scholars – the solitary diner 'loses his sprightliness' – so we are better off eating with others.[38]

The perfect dinner party, Kant says, should have between three and nine guests, no fewer than the Graces and no more than the Muses. The meal should have a range of dishes, so individual guests can choose according to their preferences. Conversation around the table should be undertaken on the assumption of discretion and confidentiality. The meal should pass through the stages of narration or sharing news, then arguing or discussion, and finally jesting, as long as the laughter is both loud and good-natured. Deep belly laughs, Kant says, help the movement of the intestines and promote physical well-being. Conversation should be undogmatic, and should not jump from topic to topic; instead, each topic should be exhausted before moving on to the next. And finally, music while eating is 'the most tasteless absurdity that revelry has ever contrived'.

Kant's dinner-party rules may not suit everybody. But they redeem him from the charge of being the joyless proponent of duty he can sometimes seem. His rules provide a holding pattern that helps to promote sociability, making the party more *ramai* – livelier and more stimulating. Because even the greatest advocate of pure moral duty knows that – when it comes down to it – the point of getting together is to have fun.

There is no better way of cooking up collective heat and warmth, no better way of making togetherness, than noisily sharing a pot of food. Several years ago, I found myself in Chengdu, in the province of Sichuan. I was newly arrived, starting on a job at Sichuan University, and I was still finding my feet. A few weeks into my stay, my new colleagues invited me out to share *huo guo*, or hotpot. In China, hotpot is a dish that is uniquely good for creating this sense of social connection. Eating hotpot, people say in Chinese, is *renao*, it is 'hot and noisy'. Hot noisiness is the Chinese equivalent of the *ramai* social buzz of Indonesia. It is the effervescence of Chinese New Year, when you cram into a small kitchen in a big, garrulous huddle to stuff and fold dumplings together. It is the fizzing liveliness of a temple festival. It is the collective fun of a big gathering as you eat, drink and joke. And there is no food more *renao* than Chinese hotpot.

First popularised in Chongqing in the 1990s, hotpot became a national and then a global craze. Today, in hotpot restaurants across the Chinese-speaking world, noisy groups of diners sit around shared, steaming pots of broth, and they drop vegetables, meat and seafood in the bubbling liquid. As they do so, they cook up togetherness, that *renao* warmth that is the stuff of life. The hotpot bubbles. The broth thickens. It takes up the flavours of the things the diners drop into it. It becomes thicker, richer, spicier. Fuchsia Dunlop writes, 'There is something about the heat, the communal atmosphere and the diehard recklessness of eating so many chillies on a sweltering evening that is both hilarious and exhilarating.' As one of her Chinese friends says to her, in the seethe and swirl of the bubbling liquid, hotpot 'makes a person forget about their worries and grief'.[39]

Hotpot is not a dish to eat alone: the whole point is that it is shared. With my new colleagues in Chengdu, I got hot and noisy. Clustered round, we fished with our chopsticks in the steaming pot of strange things – congealed blood, lotus roots, young bamboo shoots, unidentifiable animal parts, things plucked from the bottom of the sea. Occasionally, I pulled something mysterious and rubbery from the steaming broth and asked, 'What is this?' One of my new colleagues – a Kant scholar who carried an image of the Prussian philosopher in her purse, and who occasionally took it out to gaze at him in admiration – reprimanded me for my squeamishness, saying, 'It is better not to ask. Better just to eat and to see if it is delicious.' So I did. And it was.

And at the end of the meal, when I reached into my pocket to pay, my new friends said no.

'*Women qing ke*,' they said. We invite you as a guest.

I removed my hand from my pocket and thanked them.

'*Bie keqi*,' they said. Don't take on the airs of a guest.

Several years after this, I was staying with a friend on the coast of Myanmar. We had rented a small hut not far from the beach. One evening, when returning to the hut, we ran into a Chinese woman carrying a cooking pot. She was travelling alone, she said, and staying in the hut next to ours. She was in her late twenties, short and vigorous, delighted to be able to converse in Chinese. We chatted for around ten minutes, then she ran into her hut and came out bearing a gift: a large brick of plastic-wrapped hotpot *diliao* or broth base – just add water. We thanked her. She said that she had a whole bag full of bricks of *diliao*. She was lugging them around Myanmar to give as presents to people she met.

It seemed a weird gift. We took the brick and I stowed it in my bag. The *diliao* was heavy. It passed its fragrance on to everything: my clothes, my books, the bag itself. Within a few hours, everything I owned smelled of hotpot. After our neighbour had gone on her way the following morning, I took the *diliao* out and examined it more closely. Why lug around such heavy stuff to give to strangers? I wondered.

Then, as I sniffed and prodded the brick of oozing paste, the fragrance took me back to Chengdu, to the shared heat and noisiness around the bubbling broth; and it all made sense. Hotpot *diliao* is the essence of future pleasures. It is hot noisiness in condensed form. It is a promise of a happiness, of feasts to come. It is a kind of hope. And what better gift could there be for a stranger than this?

6

Leave-taking

At the beginning of the *Odyssey*, the wily hero Odysseus is in paradise. He has been washed up on the enchanted island Ogygia, and is living with goddess-nymph Calypso. Now that he is here, Calypso doesn't want him to leave. And Odysseus himself is not so sure he wants to go home. He is torn between the desire to return to the place he feels he belongs and the desire to stay. Calypso's island is beautiful, covered with lush forests of cypress, alder and poplar. The air is fragrant with citrus fruit and pine, and is alive with birdsong. There are grapes in abundance. Springs provide fresh water. The meadows are filled with flowers. As for Calypso, her curls are blonde. Her body, she observes with a degree of spite, is better than that of Odysseus's wife, Penelope. She is taller too. And because this is an enchanted island, if Odysseus wishes to stay, sharing Calypso's bed, he will live for ever.

Calypso is the perfect host. Except for one thing. 'Calypso gives her human guest more than enough of everything a visitor could ask for,' Emily Wilson writes, 'except the final crucial ingredient: *pompē* – the ability to get away.'[1]

However lovely Ogygia may be, however solicitous his host, Odysseus suffers from *nostos*, a longing for home. This longing is a kind of pang. The word 'nostalgia' is literally the pain, *algos* or *algia* (from which we get words such as 'neuralgia') associated with this longing for home. This nostalgia or homesickness goes deep. So deep, it can sometimes be fatal. In the seventeenth century, Swiss mercenaries fighting far from their Alpine homes heard sounds resembling cowbells and succumbed to an illness the doctors came to know as *Heimweh*. The physical consequences were severe: lethargy, heart disorders, skin lesions and – in extreme cases – death.[2] Kant attributed the homesickness of the Swiss to the strength of the human imagination. The cure, he said, was simple – all you need to do is return. Then you will realise that Switzerland was never as great as you imagined it to be and your sickness of the imagination will be cured.[3]

This longing, this *nostos*, guarantees the strangeness of the stranger. As they share the hearth of their host, no amount of feeding, no amount of kindness, will eradicate their otherness, the secret intimacy of their longing.

Nostos and *pompē* are often found together; but they are not the same. When, knowing that we have sat by the hearth too long, we get up, make our excuses and leave, it may be out of the desire to return home. But it may equally be the desire to be on the road again. *Nostos* is about the longing for home, for a destination that might put an end to our journeying. With *pompē*, what is at stake is not the destination but the journey itself. And the journey launched by *pompē* may be for our homeland or for a further horizon. It is, Wilson says, simply the ability to keep on moving.

If *pompē* isn't quite the same as *nostos*, nor is it the same as autonomy. It also requires the cooperation of external forces, whether godly or earthly, to convey you onwards – speeded by fate, by human assistance, by the winds and the waves. *Pompē* is about travelling purposefully, but it is also about being sent on your way, attentive to the assistance gods and humans can bring.

If you can pull it off, the *Odyssey* suggests, there is no better way of cutting a passage through the world.[4]

Sometimes, however, getting away is not straightforward. In July 2002, the BBC radio programme *Home Truths* reported the story of Dan O'Connell, a foreigner living in Kazakhstan. Dan was working in Almaty on an energy-efficiency project. After he left the office one evening, he found a driver waiting to take him to his flat. He got into the car. To his surprise, another man got in the back. The car drove off, past Dan's flat and out into the suburbs. When Dan tried to protest that they were going the wrong way, the driver opened his jacket to reveal a gun.

The car stopped outside an apartment block. The man in the back of the car got out and ushered Dan upstairs into a small flat. Inside were a woman and a girl of about nine. The table was laid for dinner. The woman introduced herself as Irina. Dan's captor said his name was Viktor.

Irina and Viktor invited Dan to sit down. Irina served food. Dan was edgy, but his hosts plied him with beer and vodka.

The alcohol helped soothe him. Although Dan spoke some Russian, communication was not easy: his hosts spoke with thick Kazakh accents. Dan asked why he had been kidnapped. His hosts said they'd always wanted to host a foreigner, but didn't know how to ask. Dan allowed himself to relax. He got drunk and, at the end of the evening, he slept in the bed Viktor and Irina had prepared for him.

The following day, Dan asked to leave. His hosts insisted he stay longer. Dan spent most of Sunday getting drunk with Viktor, sleeping in the apartment for a second night. On Monday, Viktor and Irina released him. They had enjoyed his company, they said. They asked him to keep in touch.

Dan continued to visit Viktor and Irina. They drank and ate and joked together. Later on, he asked them why they hadn't just invited him; he would have come, he said. Viktor and Irina explained that they didn't speak good English and they didn't know how to invite him, and anyway he might have come with a translator; they didn't want a translator getting in the way.

On subsequent visits, when Dan was ready to leave he told his hosts, who smiled and let him go.[5]

Sometimes the lines between guest and hostage are so blurred it is hard to tell the two apart. A hostage is a guest without *pompē*. But once they have crossed the threshold, guests are bound in a complex set of rituals that restrict their ability to leave. Even if I visit a good friend with whom I have a long mutual understanding, once they have invited me in and uncorked the wine, I know that I will not be able to escape for a while; I know that, even if I think better of the evening, my options for getting away are few.

On 2 August 1990, the passengers on British Airways flight BA149 were on a stopover in Kuwait, on their way to Kuala Lumpur. The Boeing 747 had taken off late from Heathrow, because of a fault with the power unit. These were twitchy times. Saddam Hussein's forces were massing on the Kuwaiti border. The news reports talked about the possibility of war. Before take-off, the crew checked for clarification on the political situation. The response came back that everything was fine and the flight could go ahead as normal. They took off and headed towards Kuwait. Before landing, they checked again with Kuwaiti air traffic control. Whoever was in the control tower told them there was nothing to worry about. But when the plane landed, it became apparent something spooky was going on. The airport was almost deserted. It was then it dawned upon the passengers and crew: the land invasion of Kuwait had begun. Before the flight could take off again, Iraqi jets flew in and bombed the runway. The aircraft was evacuated and the passengers detained by Iraqi forces.

A few weeks later in Baghdad, the Iraqi president, Saddam Hussein, appeared on television, sitting and chatting with guests, all of them foreigners. There were people from the flight, as well as others who had been working in Kuwait and Iraq, and none of them could now leave. Saddam asked to speak to a young boy whose name was Stuart Lockwood. His father worked in the oil industry and he was five years old. Through his interpreter, Sadoun al-Zubaydi, Saddam asked if Stuart was getting his milk and cornflakes. 'I don't think all Iraqi kids can get cornflakes,' Saddam said.[6] Then he added, 'Please forgive us because we, like you, have our own children . . . but we are trying to prevent a war from happening, and we hope that you as guests . . . your presence as guests here is not going to be for long, too long, because you're not hostages.'[7]

You are not hostages. There are almost no circumstances in which these words are wholly reassuring. Odysseus isn't exactly a hostage on Calypso's island – he could have left earlier, if he wasn't so seduced by her singing, by the promise of immortality, by the nights of sex. If he didn't have *pompē*, it was not entirely Calypso's fault. His plans, Calypso acidly points out when he says that he wants to leave, 'are always changing'. But for Stuart Lockwood, for his family, for the other guests in Baghdad, there was no possibility of departure. There was no *pompē*. The line between guest and hostage was clear, and they were on the wrong side.

The tradition of taking political hostages – of depriving strangers of their *pompē* for political ends – is a long one. In ancient China, rulers sent princes as *shizi*, or hostage-guests, to cement trust between different states. It was a doubly useful strategy. You got rid of troublesome offspring, who could live at the expense of a foreign court. And for the hosts, the *shizi* acted as a guarantee of the rival ruler's good intention. If things turned sour, the *shizi* could be imprisoned or killed. Meanwhile, over in the Roman Empire, hostage-taking was an everyday part of diplomacy. It was a tradition that continued into medieval Europe, where political hostages were referred to by the term *obses*, coming from a root meaning 'to sit beside', or 'to remain near'.[8] The *obses* was usually a son or a close relation of a rival ruler.[9] Their job was to remain near a foreign throne – neither a prisoner nor a guarantor, but a pawn in the game of international politics.

The lives of the medieval *obsides* were often outwardly comfortable. Food, drink, company, free time: all these could be yours. But it was an uncomfortable existence because your life was dependent on the vagaries of politics.

Like Odysseus, the *obsides* of the medieval world had everything except *pompē*. Unlike Odysseus, who on Calypso's island at least had immortality into the bargain, they daily had to contemplate the possibility of their death.

Odysseus is tormented by the desire to see the smoke that rises from his own hearth fire. Ogygia may be lovely, but it is not where he belongs. It takes seven years for him to eventually get his act together and leave. A mere moment in the life of an immortal, but a sizeable chunk of a normal human life. Over these seven years, Calypso tries to break him out of his mooning and brooding, his sickening for home. But in the end she fails. She presses him to stay, tells him all the reasons why he would be better off with her – she has the looks and the sharp wit to match, he will lack for nothing, he will be immortal and free of suffering. But Odysseus still insists on leaving. He does not argue with Calypso's reasoning. He simply says, 'I want to go back home, / and every day I hope that day will come.'[10]

At last the goddess relents and permits him to go. There is more ceremony to Odysseus's departure than there was to his arrival, washed up spluttering on the beach. Calypso gets dressed in her finest goddess garb: a silver robe, a golden belt and a veil. She wants Odysseus to know, to remember, what he will be missing. Then she provides him with a beautifully crafted axe and an adze, and takes him to where the best trees on Ogygia grow.

She supervises his building of a raft. She provides him with fabric so he can make a sail. Again, she doesn't help. She doesn't get involved in the manual labour. If he wants out, he has to make the effort to leave himself. But neither does she stop him.

Odysseus works on his raft for four days. On the fifth day, Calypso strips him, washes him and dresses him in new clothes, fragrant with incense. She gives him provisions for his journey: wine, water and lots of food.

Then Odysseus climbs aboard, sped by gentle breezes conjured by his former lover, and leaves her for good. He navigates by the instructions Calypso has given him. And in this way – consciously uncoupling, as Gwyneth Paltrow would have it – he regains his *pompē*, and continues on his long and difficult journey.

The hostage is a stranger who is not given leave to depart. But there is another way in which leave-taking can go wrong. The mirror image of the hostage is the parasite; the stranger who remains in the midst of the household, who outstays their welcome, who doesn't depart when you expect them to, but instead goes on taking advantage of the kindness of the host.

The lines between hostage and parasite are often more blurred than they may seem at first glance. In Buster Keaton's 1923 film *Our Hospitality*, the hapless but well-intentioned Willie McKay is caught up in an old family blood feud between the McKays and the rival Canfields. One stormy night in 1810, when Willie is still a baby, his father, John McKay, and the Canfield patriarch, James Canfield, murder each other. Terrified of this Kanun-like cycle of violence, Willie's mother takes him away to

New York so he can grow up in safety. Much later, Willie returns home to claim his father's estate, and there he stumbles into a romance with Virginia Canfield, granddaughter of his father's killer. He ends up an unwitting guest in the home of the Canfield family, sharing a table with Virginia's father and her two brothers. The Canfields are still obsessed by the feud and are eager to spill McKay blood. Like the guest in the Mongolian *ger*, this puts Willie in a bind. As long as he remains within the household, he is protected by the rules of hospitality ('Wait, boys!' the father counsels his more hot-headed sons in one of those text cut-scenes they have in old movies. 'Our code of honor prevents us from shooting him while he's a guest – in our house'). But the moment Willie steps outside, he is at risk of a violent death.

Dinner is predictably awkward. After dinner, knowing that to leave would be the end of him, Willie attempts to forestall his departure. Fortunately, it is raining, and when a passing clergyman is pressed to stay the night, Willie invites himself to do the same. The following day he doesn't leave, but instead settles down to being a permanent house guest. By now, it is hard to tell whether Willie is a guest, a hostage or a parasite. Perhaps he is all three.

Our Hospitality is haunted by the ominous spectre of Odyssean violence. But Willie plays the situation with a cunning that might make Odysseus himself envious. At the end of the film, he makes a run from the Canfield home. Virginia and the Canfield men set off in pursuit. Willie manages to hook up with Virginia and they sneak back to the Canfield home. When the men head back, convinced they have lost the trail, they find Willie, clad in a large blanket, brazenly kissing Virginia in their own house.

Willie has broken the spell of hospitality. He is no longer a guest. He has crossed the threshold uninvited and is unmasked – as far as the Canfields are concerned – as a low-life parasite. The Canfields draw their weapons. But then they spot the clergyman and realise he is about to bless Willie and Virginia's union. Just in time, Willie McKay slips over the border between enemy and kin. The brothers give up their weapons and declare the feud over. And Willie – wilier than he looks – throws off his blanket. Underneath he has stashed a whole armoury of weapons, stolen from the Canfield gun cabinet, just in case. He puts pistol after pistol down on the table.

Now they are all disarmed, the priest blesses the wedding. And, with this, the two feuding clans are at last united.

It is an astute person, whether guest or host, who cultivates the art of orchestrating a timely and elegant departure. The *Annals of the Caliphs' Kitchens*, a tenth-century Islamic cookbook, counsels, 'One should not overstay the visit, be importunate when in need of a thing, or spit into the basin while washing the hands or blow the nose. A person who does these things is called *al-mukawkib* (the dissipater).'[11] A guest who overstays dissipates the abundance of the household. The pairing of overstaying and nose-blowing or spitting in the basin is not accidental. An overstaying guest is, to steal a phrase from the anthropologist Mary Douglas, 'matter out of place', like spit in the basin for washing or snot outside of the nose.[12]

For particularly stubborn guests, there is a Jewish text that counsels a phased withdrawal of hospitality: 'On the day a guest arrives, a calf is slaughtered in his honour. The next day, a sheep; the third day, a fowl; and on the fourth day, he is served just beans.'[13] This move from abundance to lack is found in Serbia too. In Serbian villages, guests are welcomed with *slatko*, sweet fruit compote, so the conversation may be sweet. Then they are served with Turkish coffee, to encourage free and easy talking. Guest and host settle into chatting. They exchange news. But when the hosts have done with their guests, they serve them with another coffee, called a *sikteruša* coffee. The final coffee is small and weak. The name literally means 'fuck off coffee'. The wise guest takes the hint and leaves.[14]

The art of leaving is the art of reading the cues, knowing when the guest is becoming agitated and wants to reclaim their *pompē*, knowing when the host is fatigued and wants to return to their everyday life. But when the cues fail, it can help to fall back on rules of thumb.

Often a good sign that it is time to go is the arrival of new guests. Mrs Beeton writes: 'When other visitors are announced, it is well to retire as soon as possible, taking care to let it appear that their arrival is not the cause. When they are quietly seated, and the bustle of their entrance is over, rise from your chair, taking a kind leave of the hostess, and bowing politely to the guests.'[15]

In the absence of other guests turning up, the rule of three is pretty reliable. *Gast und Fisch stinken nach drei Tagen*, they say in Germany: guests and fish stink after three days. In Germany, this three-day rule goes all the way back to Roman times, when, according to customary law, the host became legally responsible for the guest after three days.[16] The aphorism appears in English too. It is often attributed to Benjamin Franklin, who wrote in the January 1736 edition of his *Poor Richard's Almanack*, 'Fish and visitors stink in 3 days.' But it appears earlier than this, in 1578, in poet John Lyly's leaden novel *Euphues: The Anatomy of Wit*: 'Guests and fish, say we in Athens, are ever stale within three days.'[17]

The three-day rule is not quite universal, but it is surprisingly widespread. According to Islamic tradition, 'Hospitality extends for three days. What is beyond that is charity.'[18] In seventh-century Anglo-Saxon England, the laws of kings Hlothere and Eadric stipulate that three nights is the limit for which a guest could expect to be hosted. Later, in the 'Laws of Edward the Confessor' in the mid-twelfth century, the guidance is, 'Two nights a guest, the third night a local.'[19] In medieval Ireland, there was an expectation guests should be permitted to stay for three days and three nights.[20] Among the Rashaayda Bedouin of the eastern Sudan, the same rule applies. Guests are served tea and coffee. An animal is slaughtered for them. They are presented with the bloody knife to confirm the slaughter and later they are given a broth made from the cooked meat. They are treated with all the courtesy and abundance that guests deserve. But after three days, they are no longer a guest and must leave.[21]

In China, this three-act drama of welcome, stay and departure is reflected in common rituals of meeting and parting. First, guests are met or greeted (*jie*). Then they are detained (*liu*) and pressed to stay ('What are you so anxious about?' hosts might ask when the guest looks ready to leave. 'Sit for a while').[22] Detaining guests in China is close to hostage-taking, a joking, goading encouragement to eat more, to continue chatting, to not leave just yet. It is a game of sorts, where guest and host assure each other of their goodwill, with the guest saying that they would simply *love* to stay, but they simply *must* depart, and the host urging them to continue to enjoy the hot, noisy pleasures they are sharing. It is only once the guest has been 'made to feel that a proper amount of detaining is taking place' that they are permitted to leave, and are sent off (*song*). '*Wo song ni*,' people say. I'll send you off.

The rule of three is counted slightly differently in different places – three days and two nights, three days and three nights, and so on – but the recurrence of this three-act drama is striking. In act one, the stranger arrives, passing the ritual threshold from stranger to visitor to guest. In act two, the guest and host navigate the pleasures and the difficulties of coexisting. And, if things go well, in act three – with all appropriate ritual expressions of mutual gratitude and unending friendship – the guest fucks off.

Departure rituals are no less important than rituals of arrival. There is no greater sign of a failed enterprise than the guest who unceremoniously climbs from the window while everyone sleeps and is gone. In China, the business of sending off guests is elevated to an art form. Once the host has signalled the guest is permitted to leave, it is likely an argument will ensue about whether they really need to accompany you to the door, to the end of the street, to the train station or to the airport.[23] This tradition of sending off guests goes back a long way. Parting rituals, often accompanied by copious drinking, are a big theme in Classical Chinese poetry. In the eighth century, Wang Wei wrote a poem about sending off a government official from a guesthouse in Anxi:

In Weicheng, morning rain
    has moistened the fine dust;

by the guesthouse,
    green willows burst with colour;

and I ask you to share
    one further glass of wine:

for west of Yangguan pass,
    there'll be no more old friends.[24]

Classical Chinese poetry is full of these melancholy departures. Today, the moment we have turned the corner, we can send messages to our hosts thanking them for our stay. We can stay in touch, keeping the thread of connection alive. But for most of history, until very recent times, once you were gone, there was the real possibility that you were gone for good. With no way of telling whether a departure would be the final one, every departure was a kind of death. In a world like this, it paid to forestall the inevitable moment, to take your time and drink a final glass of wine before heading over the pass, to be lost among the clouds.

The possibility of not meeting again lends departure rituals a kind of melancholy. And these rituals are often marked by the performance of reluctance. In Russia, there is a tradition of sitting contemplatively near your packed cases. 'Let's sit a while,' the host says. Then host and guest dwell in silence among the luggage, reflecting. Having sat for long enough, the guest sighs and says,

'Well, I'll be off.' Then they pick up the cases and they depart.[25]

The trick is to get the balance right, not hustling the guest out of the door, but not holding on to them for too long. Some cultures deal with this difficult balance with less finesse. For the English, anthropologist Kate Fox writes, departures are often a mess of awkward embarrassment. This too is a ritual of sorts. While leaving your English hosts, Fox says, it is common for there to be at least ten minutes, sometimes twenty or more, from signalling the initial intention to leave to the guests actually getting out of the door. But these ten or twenty minutes will be marked by an awkward dithering in which nobody seems at all clear what they are doing. After some time, 'Those leaving are desperate to get away, and those hovering in the doorway are dying to shut the door on them, but it would be impolite to give any hint of such feelings, so everyone must make a great show of being reluctant to part.' In England, Fox notes, people often talk about 'saying our goodbyes', as if one goodbye is not enough, and politeness demands that goodbyes have to be multiplied ad infinitum.[26] It is not entirely different from what happens in China, except it is laced with great doses of excruciating discomfort that persist until everyone gets free, and the awkwardness eases.

While rituals of welcoming aim to build trust, to forge a bond between strangers who meet on the threshold, the rituals that attend the departure are more Janus-faced. They look both back and forward. A departure ritual says: yes, things have gone well, the worst has not happened, things have, after all, turned out better than we might have hoped. Sometimes even the most difficult of relationships between guest and host can be salvaged by a well-judged send-off: the final shared meal, the expressions of mutual gratitude, accompanied by relief that the worst is over, and the sweetness of knowing everybody has ridden out the troubles. But farewell rituals also look forward, mindful of the fact that a departing guest is both a potential future ally and also a very real liability. Among the Bedouin in Jordan, there is a saying that the host is right to fear the departing guest: 'When he sits [and shares your food], he is company. When he stands [and leaves your house], he is a poet.'[27] Once free, the guest, no longer a guest, regains their *pompē*; and you never know what they will do with their regained freedom, what they will say. They can make your reputation or break it. They can tell tales about your most intimate secrets. So it pays to handle their departure with care and reverence. Whether you are a Jordanian Bedouin or an Airbnb host, a good send-off can be a charm against future slander.

According to the anthropologist Tom Selwyn, 'Hospitality converts: strangers into familiars, enemies into friends, friends into better friends, outsiders into insiders, non-kin into kin.'[28] But hospitality, the business of welcoming strangers into our lives, does not necessarily transform these strangers into familiars, or draw the circle of belonging closer. Once the guest has departed, they may slip away again into strangeness. We may never see them again, and we may even be glad of it. It is impossible to turn everybody we meet into a friend. But even when hospitality doesn't convert strangers into familiars, it does bring about a deeper, more subtle conversion: what hospitality converts most is ourselves. With every departure, every encounter that has passed off without our worst fears being realised, our sense of the world and of the possibilities it contains expands. The boundaries between outside and inside become easier to cross. Our fear of strangers is eroded. Our xenophobia is eased; our philoxenia becomes more intense. The fearful dread we have of being out-numbered is transformed into something more open and more generous.

Nevertheless, sometimes it happens that a guest, once a stranger, does indeed cross the boundary between outsider and insider. The stranger who was at first treated with the deference and caution due to a guest becomes a friend; and the friend becomes a member of the household. They pitch in, help out with washing the dishes and are absorbed into the community. Among Rashaayda Bedouin communities, the traditional requirement is not that guests *must* depart after three days; it is only that after three days they should no longer have the status of guests. They become the ones to offer water, tea and coffee to new visitors and guests as they arrive. They even have the right and the obligation, if their former hosts are away, to take a knife and slaughter a goat or a sheep from the household flocks to offer new arrivals.[29]

What marks the passage from outsider to insider, stranger to intimate, is the possibility of a shared future. This too is a departure of sorts: you leave behind the status of stranger-guest, you leave behind the codes of *xenia*, and you are welcomed into the circle of belonging. However divergent your pasts may be, once your futures are hitched together, you make the passage from 'one of them' to 'one of us'. In the Tanimbar Islands, where I stuck around long enough to be considered an honorary member of the community, two things stood in the way of my belonging.

The first was my refusal to smoke and the second was my refusal to get married to somebody of my host Ibu Lin's choosing. If only I corrected those two flaws, my local friends said, I would no longer be a stranger. Then I would truly belong.

Sometimes this acceptance of strangers can extend across great gulfs of difference. The primatologist Barbara Smuts tells a story of how, when living in a community very different from her own, she made the surprising passage from tolerated outsider to group-member, a stranger no longer. In the 1970s, Smuts was living in Kenya, studying wild olive baboons. When she first arrived, she aimed to be objective and distanced, as a scientist should. She kept herself aloof, made notes in her notebook, saw herself as an outsider. But as the baboons became accustomed to her, they developed their own ideas. The baboons, she writes, 'stubbornly resisted my feeble but sincere attempts to convince them that I was nothing more than a detached observer, a neutral object they could ignore'.

Whatever her views on objectivity, the baboons knew she was a creature not entirely unlike them, a creature with her own thoughts and desires, a social being who was 'vulnerable to the demands and rewards of relationship'. So, slowly, she gave up her unsustainable commitment to distance and entered into the society of baboons.

It is hard to learn the ritual codes of baboon behaviour. Sometimes it is alarming. When a male is about to charge, if you are a cool, unruffled baboon, you will turn your face away but hold your ground. When youngsters get boisterous, you must turn your back. Smuts paid attention to the social cues and after some time, although not yet fully baboon, she found herself 'sharing the being of a baboon because other baboons were treating me like one'.

The baboons knew, no doubt, that Smuts wasn't quite right. Baboons are nobody's fools. But they welcomed her in as the weird not-quite-baboon she was, allowing her to share their siestas as they lay around in the morning sunshine with their feet in the air, grunting and muttering to each other, enjoying the heat of the day.

When she was first in the field, Smuts used this siesta time to make notes and collect data. But increasingly she forgot about her field notes. Instead she lay among the baboons, idling her time away, making the most of the sun. Because she was only part baboon, she didn't hold her feet in the air as she rested, but the baboons – courteous hosts that they were – did not insist upon this. Listening to the contented grunts and sighs, she felt strangely at home.

Then one day, during the baboons' morning siesta, she fell asleep. When she woke, the troop had gone. It's a risky thing to sleep alone in the wilds of Kenya. There are lions, hyenas, passing strangers. But then Smuts realised she was not alone after all: one adolescent baboon had remained behind, waiting for her to wake up. Baboon and scientist blinked at each other, then the young baboon – with considerable solicitousness – got up and ambled off, leading the scientist back to the troop, of which, as far as the baboons were concerned, she was now an integral part.[30]

7

Ghosts

My grandfather was incorrigible to the end. On his deathbed, he flirted with the nurses, and the nurses kindly flirted back. He talked a little, slept a lot. Knowing he didn't have long left, we spent hours sitting by his bed, watching him slip in and out of sleep. Then, one morning, worn out with the waiting, we went for lunch. When we arrived back at the hospital, he was already dead.

'Do you want to see him?' the nurse asked.

We said we did. She led us into the ward, where we stood and looked at his body. It is so ordinary, but so strange: this experience of gazing upon the body of somebody who was, until a moment ago, living and breathing. The sudden absence is so hard to get your head around. A departure with no forwarding address, Emmanuel Levinas called it.[1] A leave-taking for no place in particular. The familiar becoming strange.

The dead do not depart immediately. There are all kinds of threads left hanging. Bureaucracies, unfinished business, stories half-told, secrets, promises unfulfilled. There is no final accounting with the dead. So they stick around. They stay with us, in dreams and memories and imaginings. They fill our conversations. They intrude upon the things we living still share: stories, jokes, reminiscences. We adjust to their absence. But they are still somehow there.

So it was with my grandfather. A couple of days after his death, I went away on a Buddhist retreat. After days of thinking about death, it felt good to be there, enjoying the stillness of meditation. I drank in the silence. I took pleasure from the fact of still being alive. I sat on my meditation cushions, feeling my breath come and go. The ordinary, mysterious business of living.

I kept to myself on that retreat. I got up, meditated, ate breakfast, walked in the gardens, didn't have much to do with anybody. I was not particularly distressed by my grandfather's death. I had known it was coming. But I wanted space to think, to experience what it meant.

On the second or the third night, my grandfather turned up unexpectedly. It was one of those dreams that is so remarkably vivid, it feels as if it is trying to say something to you, to tell you something urgent. One of those dreams you wake from with your heart beating faster than normal, a sense that something important has shifted, deep in the ocean trenches of the mind.

The dream was something like this. I was sharing a meal with the rest of my family. We were seated together around a single table in a way that by then rarely happened any more. The meal was good, or as good as a dream meal could be. But then I looked up to see my grandfather in the doorway. He had an air of awkwardness, almost of embarrassment. I knew he wanted to join the feast. I gestured to him. He stepped out of the doorway towards the table, as if to sit down. But there was no chair, and I knew nobody else could see him. He stood there, outside the warm circle of light and conviviality, unable to enter. And he seemed confused, unsure why he had not been invited.

Then I woke up. I was sleeping in a shared room and I could hear the breathing of other retreatants. I cried, because it seemed so sad. Then I turned on my side and went back to sleep.

Later that morning in meditation, I was unsettled and uneasy. I had the deep-rooted feeling I should do something, but I was not sure what. It made no rational sense. He was dead. Gone. It was only my mind conjuring fictions. But fictions matter too. They deserve to be taken seriously.

For the rest of the day, I was dogged by a nagging sense of obligation. It was not troubling or upsetting; it was just the sense there was something to be done. So that evening, after the meditation ended, I continued to sit on in the shrine room, waiting for the other retreatants to leave. It was late when I opened my eyes to check I was alone. Candles flickered in front of the Buddha statue. I was tired, my eyes heavy. I looked at my watch. It was well past eleven. I got up, stretched my legs. I knelt before the shrine, took a stick of incense and lit it. I returned to my meditation cushions and sat in silence for a while. Then I spoke directly to my grandfather, reciting his virtues out loud.

He was not the most virtuous of men. I knew this. But he was also capable of kindness and generosity. And there was no harm, just then, in focusing on the good stuff. I addressed him in the second person as 'you'. I spoke of my childhood memories. I remembered out loud how one winter he had dug up a nugget of raw lead in the garden, how together we had melted it down in the fire in an eggcup. We had smashed the eggcup to get the lead out. He made me swear not to tell my grandmother. I kept the lead in my bedroom drawer for years, a dull silver lump made more fascinating by the knowledge that it was poisonous, that I shouldn't handle it too often. I kept it alongside the bird skulls and bones and plaster casts of animal footprints, and the other bits and pieces that I had accumulated in my explorations of the world.

By the time I finished speaking, it was almost midnight. I thanked my grandfather and wished him well. Then I told him it was time to go. You are dead, I said out loud. It is time to leave the table.

I felt better after this. I got up and blew out the candles. Then I left the shrine room. I did not dream of my grandfather again. He did not return to the table.

Ghosts are ever-present strangers in the world of the living. I do not believe in ghosts. I never have. The evidence for their existence is thin and vaporous. But ghosts exert a strange power, even over those who do not believe. They disturb your sleep. They come to say hello in dreams. They interrupt the feasts of the living. Often they turn up uninvited: they simply appear, and you have to deal with them. At other times, we invite them in, hungering for a connection with the dead.

Six months after Elee died, I was living in Yangon in Myanmar. I had gone to get away from the world we had shared, to rebuild my life in the company of strangers, to find out what life could be. I lived in a small ground-floor apartment and taught classes at a local postgraduate institute. When I had spare time,

I wrote furiously, or studied Burmese, or walked through the dusty streets until I was exhausted.

One day, I left work early and headed to the park. The grief had got too much for me and I needed to be alone. In the park, I went into a small pavilion, took off my shoes and lay down on a bench, watching the sparrows in the rafters bobbing in and out of their nests. I closed my eyes and listened to the sound of the nearby fountain. I was exhausted after nights sleepless with grief.

As I lay there, I realised I had not dreamed of Elee for a long time, for months. I had imagined I would dream of her all the time, that I would wake up sobbing at her absence. I wanted her to visit me in my dreams, to have this sense of enduring connection. I worried that I was not grieving properly. But Elee was never showy. She always disliked grand gestures, and had little patience with big statements. She wasn't the kind of person to march into my dreams uninvited.

The wood of the bench was warm, reassuring. I felt myself begin to drift off. As I did, I remember issuing something like an invitation: come visit me, I said. And then I slept.

The dream was light and brief. I dreamed of Elee, there in front of me. It was good to see her. I reached out and she hugged me lightly. The hug felt good. Then she released me, and she was gone.

I woke to the sound of the sparrows in the rafters, slipped on my shoes and left the park.

Globally, ghost belief is strong. It is everywhere from South-East and East Asia to Africa to the Americas to Europe. In the UK, more than 50 per cent of people believe in ghosts. In the US, the figure is 42 per cent.[2] And it is on the rise. 'The extraordinary fact about the history of ghosts,' Owen Davies writes in his book *The Haunted: A Social History of Ghosts*, 'is that it is not a story of decline.'[3] While belief in fairies, demons and the devil has fallen over the previous decades, when it comes to ghosts, this belief is intensifying. And even those who do not believe in ghosts often act as if they do. Research shows that if you tell students an exam room is haunted, they will be less inclined to cheat, even if they have explicitly said they do not believe you.[4]

Ghosts are strangers in the world of the living. They can be visitors, sometimes even guests. And we respond to their arrival accordingly. If we perceive them to be hostile, we bar our doors and keep them out. We drive them away when they come uninvited. Or, if the visitation is longed for, we welcome them in, make them at home, even feed them. In the Buddhist tradition, ghosts – called *petas* – are characterised by their hunger. They hunger as my grandfather's ghost hungered. They long to eat at the same tables they shared in the past, to join the feasts of the living. There is a text in the ancient Indian Pali language dedicated to *petas*, called the *Petavatthu*. The book is virtually an anthropology (or a phantasmology) of the ghost realm. In the *Petavatthu*, the Buddha's disciple Moggallana goes on a fact-finding mission to the world of hungry ghosts. Of all the Buddha's disciples, Moggallana is said to be the most skilled in the use of psychic powers. It is this that enables him to enter into the ghost realm, to speak with ghosts and to understand their world. Like an anthropologist of the afterlife, he reports back on what he has found. The *Petavatthu* tells us that ghosts can be found 'outside the walls and at the open spaces and at the crossroads; they are standing at the doorposts'.[5] One day, Moggallana is going with his alms bowl for food in the city of Savatthi when he runs into a crowd of hungry ghosts by the roadside. He recognises them by their thinness, their pronounced veins and their protruding ribs. He stops to interview them. 'Famished and fainting with hunger, Reverend Sir,' the ghosts say, 'we are smitten to the earth. We are stretched out and lie sprawling; we fall down head first . . .'[6]

The hunger of ghosts cuts across cultures. In the *Odyssey*, when Odysseus wants to converse with the ghosts of those close to him, he convenes an underworld focus group. He makes offerings of food and drink, and summons the ghosts to feast on honey, sweet wine, sprinklings of barley, a sacrificed cow and the blood of his best black sheep.[7] Hungry ghosts haunt more recent myths too. In the French TV series *Les Revenants*, known in English as *The Returned*, a small mountain village is torn apart by the death of a coach-load of schoolchildren. Then one day the children unexpectedly return. They take up residence in their previous homes. They seem just as they were before, except for their hunger. They are always poking around in the fridge, or snacking, or pushing down platefuls of food. They eat, and eat, and eat. They eat like beings who will never be satisfied.[8]

In the customs hall of Suvarnabhumi Airport in Bangkok, there is a concrete pillar where people leave offerings of snacks. They bring bracelets too, as well as rings and other jewellery, and gold leaf which they stick onto the column. If you look at the column closely, you can see two indentations, 'as if the column was jabbed in two spots and then plastered over'.[9] The offerings are gifts to the ghost of a Burmese woman who worked on the construction of the airport. Like many ghosts in South-East Asia, she suffered a horrific, violent death. When they were pouring concrete for the pillar, the Burmese woman fell into the mould and was suffocated. They had to wait, the story goes, for the concrete to set to get her body back. They tried to chip her out, but with limited success. The concrete was too hard. They removed all the parts of her body they could; the rest remained within the column.

The ghost of the Burmese woman is doubly a stranger. First, she is a foreigner; second, she is a ghost. Now it is said she comes back to haunt airport workers on the night shift. The column has become a place of offerings. These small gifts help ease her suffering and assuage her hunger. Sometimes airport workers go to the column to seek supernatural advice on winning lottery numbers. If the ghost divulges the winning numbers, they return with gifts of thanks.

According to Buddhist belief, the hunger of ghosts, although terrible, can eventually be eased and ghosts can be reborn as happier beings. Over the border in Laos, on the new moon of the ninth lunar month, people celebrate the festival of *boun khau padab din*, or 'rice packets decorating the earth'. For two weeks, hungry ghosts walk among the living, desperate and needy. Families make sticky rice and fruit, bundle them together in banana leaves and take the packets of sweet rice to the temple so the ghosts can feed off the vapour. As they feast on the fragrant steam, the ghosts take on a new substance and are reborn outside of the ghost realm.[10]

At other times in South-East Asia, like unruly guests, ghosts need to be dealt with more firmly. The seaside village of Cam Re in central Vietnam has a particular problems with ghosts. And no wonder. The entire village of horticulturalists, tangerine growers and small-time farmers is built on top of a wartime cemetery. There is the one-legged American soldier who hops through the forest and who is often spotted following an old Chinese scholar-ghost. There is the entire ghost platoon that, at night, marches past the pagoda. There is the skinny, perpetually hungry Vietcong ghost who sits with crossed legs on his own grave and terrifies the women coming back from the market. Then there are the two huge ghosts of American GIs who appear underneath an areca palm, where they chat to each other in the language of ghosts, making an unsettling noise like 'a spoon clinking in an empty can' or 'a few bullet shells rattling in an empty munitions box'. The ghosts are bashful, polite. They don't seem to want to cause trouble. But local villagers are uneasy with the presence of these strangers in their midst. Just in case, they burn incense sticks to propitiate them. They also burn votive paper money, in US dollars, so the ghosts can make purchases in the afterlife in their own currency.

Not far away, on the road between Cam Re and Da Nang, a group of Vietnamese soldiers was undertaking a military exercise when they encountered the ghost of a ragged American army officer. The ghost was tall, unarmed and had torn clothes. He was soaked in mud. The Vietnamese lieutenant decided to get rid of the ghost by urinating on the spot where it had appeared. The ghost disappeared as expected. But then the lieutenant fell sick: he had headaches, he stuttered and he was diagnosed as borderline psychotic. Eventually, the lieutenant went to see a ritual specialist, a local woman skilled in dealing with restless ghosts. They dug at the spot where the lieutenant had urinated and found the body of an American soldier. The remains were repatriated. The ritual specialist reprimanded the lieutenant for his hostility towards the ghost, reminding him instead of the ghost's hunger. 'Dead people don't fight,' she said. 'They are not really even angry. They simply want to be remembered. They want someone to know what they went through.'

The ritual specialist performed a ceremony to quieten the tall American. 'Aunt, thank you, thank you. Forgive me, forgive me,' the ghost said to her. And she replied, 'It's all fine now. Go and rest.'[11]

It is not clear why, in many places, belief in ghosts is on the rise. Perhaps we are more inclined to believe in them as a consequence of the hyper-mobile world in which we live; this world of many thresholds, where liminal spaces proliferate. It is as if movement conjures ghosts, as if their rootlessness and their hunger to connect mirror our own. Ghosts, like all strangers, haunt the margins and the boundaries between worlds. They are found by the doorways and at the crossing places. In the bland, anonymous spaces of airport terminals in Thailand, and in Myanmar too, where they interfere with the cockpit instruments, annoying the pilots, or flit across the tarmac, distracting the people on duty in the control towers.[12] Or they are found beside highways: phantom hitchhikers, spectral vintage cars, ambiguous figures standing by roadside crosses and flowers, memorials that mark out the places of traffic accidents. In the UK, the space between junctions sixteen and nineteen on the M6 motorway has been referred to as 'Britain's most haunted road'. Crashes are attributed to everything from Roman soldiers to ghost trucks.[13] In Myanmar, when buses driven by overtired drivers high on betel nut, skid off the badly surfaced road, the authorities blame the ghosts of Japanese soldiers and call in the monks.[14]

Back in 2010, the Burmese government was hard at work building a new capital city in Naypyidaw. It was the tail end of military rule. Four years before, the military government had decided to move the capital city from crumbling colonial-era Yangon in the south to a new city in the country's dry zone. The reasons for the move were complex. The multi-billion-pound project was undertaken on the advice of military strategists who feared a sea invasion and on the warnings of soothsayers who said only in this way could Myanmar regain its former glory as an abode of kings. But the regime also wanted to make a clean start somewhere new, a blank slate, free of the ghosts and shadows of the country's colonial past.[15]

It was in this year Captain Aung Khant of the Burmese army was given a strange task to complete. In the township of Tatkon – the name literally means 'high military ground' – there was a large graveyard that needed to be moved. The plan was to build a monastery and a local courthouse on the land. But the graveyard was a problem. It was easy enough to move the graves to a new site beyond the city limits. The bigger problem was the ghosts. There were many Japanese war dead buried in Tatkon. According to Burmese belief, those who die violent deaths 'create spiritual residues that funerals cannot completely release'.[16] Even after the graves have been moved, the ghosts may hang back and cause trouble. One thousand ghosts: without a proper send-off, they would amount to a supernatural army.

Six years after the graveyard was cleared, I went to Naypyidaw to meet the captain. I caught the bus up the perilous highway from Yangon, when the dry season was at its height. When my translator and I arrived at the restaurant, the captain, a relaxed, handsome man in his forties, was already there. We sat outside in the shade. Along the nearby drainage channel, the tamarind trees were blazing orange.

I had thought the captain would be cagey, unwilling to talk about the project. But he was at ease, eager to tell his story. 'There are some people who are close to ghosts,' he said. 'They are ordinary people, but they have a special ability. They can tell the spirits it's time to move. We are afraid of the ghosts. If they don't want to move, they become angry. They are dangerous to the people in the town. So we do it systematically – we use monks and other people. People like Whoopi Goldberg in the movie.'

It took me a moment to catch the reference. I double-checked with my translator. 'Whoopi Goldberg?' I asked. The translator nodded. 'Yes,' he said. 'Whoopi Goldberg.'

'Who are these people like Whoopi Goldberg?' I asked.

'They are *natsayas*,' the captain said. Spirit masters, skilled in talking with ghosts, gods and other spiritual entities.

With the help of a group of monks and a local *natsaya*, the captain supervised the removal of the ghosts. The ghosts were loaded onto Japanese trucks, under the supervision of the *natsaya*. A good truck can fit up to ten ghosts. Burmese ghosts are not light and insubstantial: they can be up to seven feet high, and they have huge ears, tusks and long tongues.[17] To those who can see them, they are terrifying. And they make for unruly passengers. The captain told me the ghosts fought to get into the front seat. Ghosts care about status too. As the ghosts got into the trucks, the wheels sank further into the soft ground.

The whole operation took three days, with each truck making twelve trips a day. I did the maths in my head: 108 journeys, an auspicious number in Buddhism. I asked Aung Khant if he had photographs of the ghost removal, but he just laughed. It was not clear whether this meant there were no pictures or he was unwilling to show me.

There were a few hiccups. Some ghosts got left behind and caused trouble. One ghost decided it was unwilling to be relocated. It hung around the compound of the Naypyidaw Development Committee spooking small children, pushing people out of bed, and generally being a nuisance. They called in a monk who mopped up the remaining ghost.

After that in Naypyidaw, all was well; the city was at peace.

After the conversation with Aung Khant, I asked my translator if I could meet the *natsaya* who had been involved in moving the ghosts. Apparently he was no longer around, but my translator said he could introduce me to a local spirit medium called U Nain La Shwe. The following day, the spirit medium came to my hotel. I went down to reception and found him sitting cross-legged on the hotel sofa, a stocky man in his sixties with silver hair, dressed in a white, pressed shirt and an expensive *longyi*. U Nain La Shwe told me that he sold his services with the slogan 'Believing is Seeing'. It came to him, he said, in a dream. As he talked, he occasionally took a small plastic bottle of cold remedy from his bag and put it up each nostril in turn, sniffing deeply. U Nain La

Shwe was a habitual meditator in the graveyards of Naypyidaw. He was on good terms with all the spirits, foremost among them Ma Phae Wa, known as the Coffin-Carrying Spirit, or the Yellow Ribbon Lady. Until the 1990s, it is said, Ma Phae Wa snacked on baby flesh, but then a monk from Kayin state persuaded her to switch her diet to dogs. Even so, parents were still uneasy about the Yellow Ribbon Lady. When they had young children, they sometimes posted signs on their door reading, 'Baby's flesh is bitter, dog's flesh is sweet.'[18] But Ma Phae Wa held no fear for the *natsaya* U Nain La Shwe. They got on well. They often crossed paths out in the graveyard. 'She is chairman of the board,' he told me. 'She is in charge of all the other graveyard spirits in Myanmar. She is very clean and beautiful.'

Before he left the hotel, the *natsaya* asked if I had experienced any trouble myself with ghosts and spirits. I said I hadn't. He told me that if I did, I should call him immediately and he would sort my problems out.

Like all troublesome guests – those strangers who hang around and outstay their welcome – ghosts need a firm hand. If they will not take their leave of their own accord, you need to send them on their way. To exorcise is literally 'to bind by oath'. In Tibetan Buddhist cultures, when demons and malign spirits are exorcised from the body, they are pinned down with the *phurba*, a demon dagger, so they can be better dealt with. The demon dagger plays such an important role in Tibetan Buddhist ritual that it has been personified as the deity Dorje Phurba, who is associated with removing malign influences. Similar rituals exist across the Buddhist world. In Sri Lanka, ghosts who do not depart are believed to disrupt the lives of the living. Capricious and unpredictable, they cause sickness and malaise. It takes a ritual specialist to bind them with the use of *mantra*, the recitation of sacred words with magical power, and then to expel them.[19]

These tales of ghosts and exorcisms can seem like a quaint relic of the past, but we know that the reverse is true. Exorcism is thriving more than ever in the modern world. As one contemporary Catholic scholar puts it, 'The exorcists, it seems, are here to stay.'[20] Exorcism in Christianity, once a relatively niche pursuit, is undergoing a huge renaissance. The Vatican has established a new training course for would-be exorcists, set up in 2018 in the face of what the Catholic Church calls 'an unprecedented rise in demonic activity'.[21] The Anglicans have an exorcism programme of their own, staffed by 'mature Christians who are priests, with a track record of being reliable, trustworthy, professional, and with a sound knowledge of Christian theology'.[22] According to the *Church Times*, the 'deliverance missionary team' take a holistic and multi-disciplinary approach to exorcism. When a Muslim family in Wrexham on the Welsh borders reported the appearance of a ghostly monk who was causing 'low-level poltergeist activity', the social services called in the Anglicans. Reverend Jason Bray of St Giles's Church, a trained exorcist who told the *Sunday Times* that he inhabits 'the hard edge of the spiritual world', determined that this was a low-level threat. It took no more than a few words of blessing and a recitation of the Lord's Prayer to still the ghost.[23] Reverend Bray declined to say how he dealt with more aggressive hauntings. In an aside that played into the deep-rooted obsessions of the British middle classes, he said that even low-level hauntings can have a deleterious effect on house prices.

The dead are gone; but the dead are here to stay. Strangers, they interrupt our lives and we have to manage them as best we can. We have much the same complex, tangled, difficult relationships with the dead as we have with each other in the world of the living: love, hate, jealousy, resentment, fear, hope. And the ways we manage these strangers are similar to the ways in which we manage the living: through invitation, through feeding and, in extreme circumstances, through driving them away and bolting our doors. No wonder Aristotle believed that the dead remain vulnerable to harm, regardless of whether they are still able to experience suffering or pleasure.[24] They remain a part of our imagination, the fabric of our shared, social worlds. And our obligations to them extend beyond their death. In caring for the dead, for their needs and their hunger, we care for all our relationships among the living. In offering snacks or gold leaf to a pillar where a Burmese woman may or may not have been entombed, we testify to the things we judge to be important – quirky, oddball social beings that we are.

What was I doing on that night years ago when I sat in the dark of a Buddhist meditation hall and spoke out loud to my grandfather, telling him it was time to leave the table? Was I grappling with my own sense of loss? Was I talking my unconscious mind into accepting the fact of death? Was I reaffirming to myself the importance of this relationship? Was I finding a way to refashion my life in the face of this new absence? Perhaps all of these things. I do not know.

But this, at least, is clear. Being dead doesn't let us off the hook. Whether or not we believe in ghosts and afterlives, even when we are gone we will continue to be enmeshed in the complex social webs of which we are a part. We will come to other people in imaginings, memories and dreams. We will turn up uninvited at mealtimes, strangers now in the land of the living. Parasites, we will continue to cause disruption and inconvenience. We will speak to those left behind when they are least expecting it. We will disturb them and comfort them in equal measure. We will bring them unease and hope.

And all this when we ourselves are perhaps absent, no longer there, beyond all experiencing.

Part Two

8

Pilgrims

In the weeks before Elee died, knowing that the end was close, she asked me what I would do after.

After, she said.

It was the first time we had talked about after. We had made arrangements. We had done the paperwork. We had outlined a plan for the funeral. We had, as people delicately say, 'put our affairs in order'. But we hadn't talked about what life would be like when I would still be there and Elee would be there no longer.

I said I didn't know. I had no idea what I would do. I had no idea how I would feel, how life would change. I had no plans beyond the next day, and the next, and the next. I was just doing as best I could, until Elee was gone.

'You should get away,' Elee said. 'Once everything has settled down.'

'Do you think?' It seemed strange to sit together and plan this.

'Yes, you should travel. Go elsewhere. Get some space.
China. Taiwan. Anywhere.'

'I don't know,' I said. 'I really don't know.'

Elee paused. Then she said, 'I think you'll go away.'

'You do?' I asked.

'Yes,' she said. 'You'll go away, because that's what you do.'

Elee knew me well. Over thirteen years, she had become accustomed to my restlessness. We travelled a lot in that time, both together and apart. Elee took long road trips alone in America, touring the natural history museums she loved. I spent time in China, and hung out with philosophers and small-town fortune-tellers. When together, we usually travelled closer to hand: to visit friends in the UK, a Christmas spent with strangers in southern Germany, summer breaks in the mountains of Bulgaria.

And this is how, less than six months after Elee's funeral, I found myself on a flight to Yangon. I quit my job. I left my home and cat in the care of two friends. I said goodbye to everybody I loved. I packed my bags. And armed with only a beginner's guide to the Burmese language, I left home. My departure was open-ended. I didn't know how long I would be away. I was committed to spending five months in Yangon in the first instance. After that, I had no plans. Five months was already unthinkably long. But something about the decision felt like a continuation of my shared life with Elee, rather than a complete break.

In the January after Elee's death, in my first week in the new job, I stood on the roof terrace of my new workplace on the top storey of a small tower block in Yangon, gazing out at the traffic on the concrete flyover, the black kites wheeling in the sky above me. Those first few weeks were giddying. The disorientation was less a kind of homesickness than a kind of seasickness. I was trying to find my feet, trying to regain my balance, trying not to plan for anything. I was seeing what life would become, there in the company of strangers.

Before I left, some friends asked whether I was wise to uproot myself. They asked me: wasn't I just running away? But my relocation to Yangon didn't feel like a flight. It wasn't an escape. It wasn't the desire to lose myself in the world, to bury my grief or to forget things. It was a desire to find a new way of being in the world, now all the reference points were different and strange. I went to Yangon because sometimes movement feels like the only option, because sometimes home is not where you want to be, because there is no better place to loosen the bonds of your past, to reimagine your life, than somewhere where you are living among strangers.

In Yangon, the grief nagged and pulled at me. Every night, on the bed in my grimly spartan ground-floor apartment, I curled into a ball and shuddered with tears. I sat at my new desk at work, looked out of the window at the circling birds and tried not to cry. I walked for miles in the heat through the Yangon suburbs, because I did not know what else to do. I wasn't escaping myself. I was reshaping myself. I was looking for new possibilities, trying to reimagine what life might now mean.

What Elee said was true: I have always been restless. I have always fluctuated between a hunger for home and a hunger for elsewhere. I have always found something profoundly freeing in the experience of being among strangers, far from home ground.

When it comes to the physics of human lives, it's easy to assume we are Aristotelian objects, that we stay put unless we are pushed or pulled. But if our ancestors were homemakers from the very first, they were also wayfarers, spreading out from Africa to cover the surface of the globe. Migration, as historian Michael Fisher writes, 'has always been central to human identity'.[1]

The advantages of home seem obvious. But why this hunger for elsewhere? What benefits does it confer on us to take the risk and set out for somewhere over the horizon, to live out a portion of our lives among non-kin, among strangers? No doubt both push and pull factors can stir us to movement. Since prehistory, people have moved because home is intolerable, because they have been forced out, because they are sick of their kin, because of climate change and natural disasters. And they have moved because they are curious for elsewhere, because they want to know what is over the horizon, because they want to access new resources or seek out new opportunities.

But movement is also its own reward. We like the thrill of it. If home makes us feel good, so too does being on the road. Research suggests travel leads to greater creativity, to cognitive flexibility.[2] It wakes us up, makes us feel more alive. As the poet Ken Smith once wrote, 'If I don't take long journeys and meet different strangers, I grow blunt and rusty like a knife left out in the rain.'[3] Restlessness and movement sharpen the blade of the mind.

Our obsession with movement, with roads and paths, is written into some of our oldest myths. Metaphors of paths and journeys are also common to all the major religious traditions. Buddhism and Hinduism talk about the *marga*, the path trodden by the faithful. The Bible too is preoccupied by paths. 'Shew me thy ways, O Lord,' it says in Psalm 25, 'teach me thy paths.' The metaphors are picked up again in the New Testament, where Jesus says, 'I am the way, the truth, and the life.'[4] Paths and roads – sometimes metaphorical, sometimes not – abound in the Quran too: 'We guided him to the way; then he is either thankful or ungrateful.'[5] The religious and philosophical traditions of China talk endlessly about the *dao*, the path or the way. 'A way is created,' says the ancient philosophical classic, the *Zhuangzi*, 'by somebody walking it.'[6]

The metaphor of the path may be universal, but its meanings vary. Sometimes the journey we are on is a kind of exile, an Odyssean homecoming. According to St Augustine, 'Things which are not in their intended position are restless. Once they are in their ordered position, they are at rest.'[7] For the exiled believer, in Augustine's view, the path to be taken is the path that leads homeward to rest in God. Elsewhere, in Buddhism and Hinduism, the path leads outward – to a different way of being: to awakening, enlightenment or liberation. And in some versions of Daoism, the path leads nowhere in particular: what matters is not that you get to your destination, but that you engage in a 'free and easy wandering' that is its own reward. What is important is not where you get to, but that you can keep on meandering, without ever getting bogged down.[8]

Bruce Chatwin claims that all these religious metaphors of paths are a compensation dreamed up by settled peoples who are nostalgic for a lost hunter-gatherer past. 'All the transcendental religions,' he writes, 'are stratagems for peoples whose lives were wrecked by settlement.'[9]

I do not know whether Chatwin is right or not; but somewhere in my childhood, I came to see my own restlessness as a vice in need of correction. Sitting in the classroom at school, I squirmed to stay in my seat. It wasn't that I was a sporty kid. It was just that I liked the freedom to move, to plot my own paths through the world. In the interminable church services of my youth, I was sometimes afflicted by a boredom so terrible, so all-enveloping, I felt like running out, screaming for my life. And the very worst thing was I knew I never would; I knew I would continue to sit with every outward sign of calm. When I started to practise Buddhism seriously, I learned to see restlessness as a hindrance to meditation, a regrettable lapse in the air of unruffled serenity that a Buddhist should, ideally, exude. When I sat in meditation, I was unstill, torrents of agitation surging through me. It took two years of daily meditation to get the knack of stillness. Through the strange, simple magic of focusing my attention on the breath, my desire for rootedness and my restlessness began to rebalance, and I began to relish this tranquillity, this silence. But years of meditation didn't drive out the restlessness entirely, nor did I want them to. There was something about this restlessness that seemed worth keeping hold of, something worth cherishing; and after a few more years, I began to wonder if what I had been told about the undesirability of restlessness was wrong. The better I got at finding channels for my restlessness, the more clearly I saw that the desire to wander is not a failing, but instead a fascination with the world, an expression of philoxenia – the hunger for strangers and for strangeness.

Standing there on the roof in Yangon, the buses surging across the flyover, the knot of grief in my chest, I knew that here were new possibilities, new ideas, new encounters, new thoughts, new futures. I wasn't on some grand homecoming. Nor was I escaping home. Instead, I was sharpening the blade of my mind. Immersed in strangeness, surrounded by strangers, suddenly strange to myself, I was allowing myself to become other than I had been. Exhausted, utterly incapable of rebuilding my life by my own resources, I was allowing myself to be refashioned by this vast, inexhaustible world.

Before quitting my job and leaving for Yangon, I went to see the head of department in the university where I worked. She was a professor of religious history who had written on pilgrims and travellers in sixteenth- and seventeenth-century Europe. I sat in her office and we chatted about her pot plants for a while. Then she asked me what she could do for me. I said I wanted to quit.

She asked if I was sure and said she would do what she could to support me if I stayed. But I told her I needed to be on the move, to find ways of remaking my life.

'What you are talking about,' she said, 'is a *peregrinatio*.'

The Latin *peregrinus* means 'stranger', 'sojourner' or 'outsider'. The *peregrinatio* is a self-imposed exile. It is a wandering, a movement outward without a fixed goal, a pilgrimage of sorts. The word was used by classical authors, including Cicero, to indicate 'the state of being abroad' or 'the condition of being a stranger'.[10] It was picked up by St Augustine in his *City of God* to reflect on alienation and homecoming; and then it was used by

later Christian thinkers to indicate a journey outwards, without a
fixed destination, a journey among strangers, the object of which
was, as the scholar Stephanie Hayes-Healy writes, 'a complete
physical and spiritual shift of the most basic elements of . . .
existence'.[11]

The idea made sense. A *peregrinatio*: that was what I needed,
more than anything else. I handed in my notice.

Traditions of pilgrimage go back at least to the Neolithic era.
After the Natufian shaman was buried in the cave at Hilazon
Tachtit, along with a leopard pelvis, an eagle wing and shells of
many tortoises, after the funeral feast was done, the site was not
abandoned. Instead, it became a ritual centre to which people
returned again and again.[12] Archaeological traces of pilgrimage
are found also in the Arabian Peninsula, where ritual sites for
'gathering, sacrifice and feast' date back to 5550 BCE.[13] The archaeologist Joy McCorriston says such sites 'provided inter-cultural
spaces to integrate peoples of different cultural backgrounds'.[14]
They were places where strangers far from home gathered
together, to eat, share their lives and offer sacrifices.

But even in the ancient world, people travelled for reasons
other than trade, economic need and pilgrimage. When writing
about people in the distant past, we almost always imagine them
to be more high-minded, less frivolous and vacuous than we
know ourselves to be. This is almost certainly an error. As far
back as 1244 BCE, there is evidence that people in the ancient
world were driven to move not just by need, or by lofty religious
principles, but also by the desire to have fun, by simple curiosity
and by the thrill of movement for its own sake. It was in this

year that two brothers caused boisterous trouble in the city of Memphis, the ancient capital of Inebu-hedj, in northern Egypt. They left an inscription scratched into a monument: 'Hadnakhte, scribe of the treasury, came to make an excursion and amuse himself on the west of Memphis together with his brother, Panakhti, scribe of the Vizier.'[15] Theirs was not an official mission, or a pilgrimage. Instead it was a journey born out of a desire to move, to experience new places and new people, to take pleasure in this newness.

In ancient Greece, people moved for many reasons. They travelled to visit sporting events, to watch plays, to take in culture, to visit shrines, to seek out cures for illness, to see friends or just to go exploring.[16] The world of ancient China was no less mobile. People travelled for trade and for religion, but also because they wanted to find out how things were elsewhere.

The possibilities for this kind of wandering were extended by the growth of infrastructure: from the road-building of Qin Shihuang in China, to the developments in Greek shipbuilding that opened up the sea routes that criss-crossed the Mediterranean, to the Roman roads of Europe. Well before the turn of the common era, the world was already a network of roads and paths along which travellers, tourists and strangers moved, either in pursuit of some goal or simply because movement felt good, because they wanted to know what was around the next corner, because sometimes there are better things than staying at home.

Human beings are creatures of high inertia. Once in motion, they tend to stay in motion. Once they settle down, they tend to stay put. But while cities and towns, pilgrimage centres and trade routes in the ancient world offered a free-for-all of multiple encounters, beyond these hubs the world turned more slowly on its axis. This is true even today. For all the restlessness of the age in which we live, it is easy to overstate our appetite for movement.[17] A recent study from Oxford University, published in the journal *Nature*, shows a genetic fault line between Devon and Cornwall, one that almost exactly mirrors the current county boundary. The same research shows that most people from east, south and central England belong to a single genetic group, sharing a large dollop of Anglo-Saxon DNA. Even more surprisingly, genetic clusters in south-east England map remarkably well onto what we know about the boundaries of sixth-century kingdoms.[18]

In a slow-turning world, strangers are a novelty. When I was a child in rural Norfolk in the 1980s, the arrival of a stranger in town was always a noteworthy event. When my uncle came visiting from Colombia, he put on his jogging shorts and went trotting through town at dawn. His behaviour provoked consternation and alarm. Who is this strange, suntanned man, people asked, who canters through the streets at daybreak, his bare legs showing?

Movement has always created suspicion among settled populations, where the presence of strangers can still be worthy of comment, or a cause for alarm. According to the 1824 Vagrancy Act – still on the statute books, and used to prosecute rough sleepers and the homeless[19] – 'every person wandering abroad, or placing himself or herself in any public place, street, highway, court, or passage, to beg or gather alms, or causing or procuring or encouraging any child or children so to do; shall be deemed an idle and disorderly person . . .' Vagrants, wanderers and the terminally restless turn up in our lives and worlds, and for those who would rather everything remained predictable and the same, these unanchored strangers present a problem.

We might be quick to call out xenophobia, but this fear of wandering strangers in our midst is not wholly unreasonable. When I was in my early twenties, I found myself in Barcelona. I had been travelling in Europe, playing classical guitar on the street to fund my trip. When I hit Spain, my earnings dried up: Spain was awash with guitarists far better than me. I booked into a cheap hostel and planned my next move. I was aiming to get to Morocco, where I had a temporary job starting in a couple of weeks, but in the meantime I was trying to make my budget last.

I didn't feel at home among my fellow travellers in the hostel. They were too brash, too loud. I was the weird, hesitant English kid with the guitar. In the evenings, I hung out in the Plaça Reial with the Pakistani drug dealers, chatting about Lahore and Karachi and Rawalpindi, about the deserts and the mountains of their homeland.

On my last evening in Barcelona, I went out for food with two Norwegian travellers from the hostel. They were tall and confident and smiled easily. We went down to the harbourside and they suggested an expensive place I could barely afford. I was too awkward and shy to protest. We drank a beer, ate some food. The waiter treated us with an edge of disdain.

When he brought the bill, the Norwegians looked at me and grinned. 'Now we run,' they said. They pushed back their chairs, stood up and ran out of the restaurant.

My decision was instantaneous. I grabbed my bag and bolted after them, out into the street, down into the backstreets. When we knew we were no longer being followed, we stopped and caught our breath.

'That was fun,' one of the Norwegians said.

But it was not fun. I was angry and ashamed. And I was afraid. Not just afraid of being caught, but afraid of how easily I slipped into this petty theft. On the train out of Barcelona the next day, I asked myself what had come over me. Was it momentary panic? Was it my desire to be liked? I was certain of one thing: I would not have done this at home. So what was it about being there in Barcelona, far from home, that made me run? What was it that made me steal?

The cognitive flexibility movement gives us can be a mixed blessing. On the plus side, researchers have found that those who travel are more likely to default to trust when they encounter strangers. Those who travel are also better at themselves creating trust and making connections.[20] Travel can fuel our creativity, making us looser, more flexible, more aware of opportunities and possibilities.[21] But loosening up and creativity also have a dark side. From the point of view of settled populations, the prospect of armies of unknown creatives descending upon their lives and worlds has always been a cause for alarm. Creativity may offer fresh possibilities, but it also potentially brings new risks.[22] Research undertaken at Columbia University suggests the experience of being on the move can throw our moral compass into disarray. In one task, participants were asked to solve anagrams and to mark them solved to earn a reward. The twist was that one anagram was insoluble. In this study, those who had spent time studying abroad for more than six months were more liable to cheat. The strange thing about this research is it suggests even *recollecting* travel experiences leads us to be less honest. The researchers told one group of people to recall a travel experience and another group to recall an experience of home, then set them the same task with the anagrams. They found the first group cheated more than the second. The researchers concluded, 'Although foreign experiences can elevate people to new heights of creativity, they can also pull people down into the depths of immorality. The person who has broad foreign experiences may be a more creative thinker, but not necessarily a more moral one.'[23]

Cheating in an anagram task may not, as the researchers suggest, be quite the same as sinking into the depths of depravity; and other factors as well may lead to those far from home committing such petty misdemeanours – here there are complex questions of privilege and entitlement, politics and culture.[24] But the sheer unknowability of untethered strangers – the inability to tell what they are going to do next, the fear that they may be up to no good – has meant that, from earliest times, settled populations have sought out ways of managing the risks of transient populations. Inns, hotels and other institutions set up to provide hospitality to strangers are not just about catering to the needs of temporary visitors. They are also ways of better containing and minimising the dangers, whether real or simply perceived, that are posed by people on the move.

These institutions are as old as civilisation itself. The Code of Hammurabi, dating from 1754 BCE, sets out laws regarding public inns that catered to the needs of travellers. In the Greek world, *katagogia* – taverns, inns or hostelries – served not only travellers and pilgrims but also the interests of the city-state, providing an infrastructure that supported trade while keeping troublesome strangers corralled. Xenophon writes, 'When funds were sufficient, it would be a fine plan to build more hostels for ship owners near the harbours, and convenient places of exchange for merchants, also hostels to accommodate visitors. Again, if houses and shops were put up both in the Piraeus and in the city for retail traders, they would be an ornament to the state, and at the same time the source of a considerable revenue.'[25] One such hostelry, built at the pilgrimage centre of Epidaurus, had seventy rooms, and could accommodate hundreds of guests.[26] By the time the Roman Empire was at its height, those magnificently straight Roman roads were punctuated by lodging places that charged a small fee for their service: the more high-end *hospitiae*; and the rough-and-ready *stabulae*, where you could also stable your animals for the night. Both were notorious for bedbugs, fleas, parasites, violence, disputes and myriad other troubles. Many upper-class Romans preferred to rely on their friends and allies. If you were well-off and had connections spreading throughout the empire, you could lodge in style without needing to resort to public inns.

In the Europe of the Middle Ages, these duties of hospitality towards strangers were taken over by religious orders. In his monastic rule, St Benedict makes hospitality a religious duty: 'All guests who arrive should be received as if they were Christ, for he will say, "I was a stranger and you took me in."' Guests should be greeted, invited to pray, given food and accepted freely, without any expectation of return, regardless of their social standing or wealth. 'Special care and attention should be shown in the reception of the poor and of pilgrims,' Benedict writes, 'because in such people Christ is more truly welcomed.' And yet, guests in Benedictine monasteries were also quarantined and carefully managed. They were not permitted to wander round, to interfere with the life of the monastery or to chat to the monks. 'The house of God should be looked after by sensible people in a sensible way,' Benedict says. 'No one should associate with guests or converse with them unless he is told to do so. But if a brother meets or sees a visitor, he should greet him with humility . . . and ask for a blessing as he passes, explaining that he is not permitted to converse with a guest.' As for visiting monks, they should be invited to join in with the life of the monastery, but only if they are 'happy to accept the customs of the place' as they find them. Excessively demanding, awkward or insubordinate monks 'should be asked politely to leave, so that the others are not corrupted' by their bad behaviour.[27]

Free lodging appears again in the Islamic world, where lodging places were established to support long-distance trade and travel. Rural caravanserais and urban *hans* provided lodging without charge for up to three days, and the building of caravanserais was seen as a religious duty alongside the building of mosques. In the tenth century in Central Asia, the governor of Samarkand was ordered to 'establish inns in your lands so that whenever a Muslim passes by, you will put him up for a day and a night and take care of his animals; if he is sick, provide him with hospitality for two days and two nights; and if he has used up all of his provisions and is unable to continue, supply him with whatever he needs to reach his home town'.[28]

Meanwhile in China, by the end of the Western Zhou dynasty (1045–771 BCE), there were government post houses where messengers travelling on government business could rest their horses and themselves. In the Chinese bureaucratic manual the *Rites of Zhou*, dating from the third century BCE, it says, 'On all the wild roads of the country, every ten *li* [a *li* is 300 paces] there was a hut, and the hut provided food and drink; every thirty *li* there were lodgings, and the inns had roadside rooms, and these rooms were staffed; every fifty *li* there was a market, and the market had watchtowers, and the watchtowers were large.'[29] By the Tang dynasty (618–907), hotels, trade and travel were flourishing. Some hotels were huge and accommodated hundreds of guests. And by the fourteenth century, when the Muslim traveller Ibn Battuta was in China, he found a system that both catered well to travellers' needs and also made sure that these religious outsiders could be managed. When a Muslim enters any town, Ibn Battuta said, he is given the choice of staying with a local Muslim merchant or staying in an inn. If he chooses the latter, then 'his property is deposited under the charge of the keeper of the hostelry [and] the keeper buys for him whatever he desires and presents him with an account'.[30]

All these inns and taverns, hotels and hostels, guest houses and pensions were not just places of welcome, but also places of containment. They were places that aimed to set apart dangerous outsiders, to monitor, manage and control them. In the Indian treatise on statecraft the *Arthashastra*, which dates to as early as the second century BCE, the wise ruler is counselled to pay attention to the services provided to tourists and travellers. It recommends the appointment of a 'Superintendent of Liquor' to build and supervise taverns 'that have many rooms, contain separate beds and seats, advertise drinking, have perfumes, garlands and water, and are comfortable in all seasons'.[31] And it advises that these taverns be populated with spies to track 'normal and unusual expenditures', and with 'charming female slaves' to find out the dispositions and the secrets of drunken (male) guests.

While visitors to inns, hotels or taverns may have to put up with bureaucracy, surveillance, bedbugs and other hardships, there is nevertheless something freeing about being hosted not by individuals and families but by institutions. You are released from the obligations and demands you might encounter as a guest in somebody's household. You don't have to worry about stepping over the threshold with your right foot first. You can enjoy the perfumes, garlands and water without the house guest's ever-present fear of offending their host.

Sometimes, when I was doing anthropological fieldwork in Indonesia, staying in the homes of my patient, long-suffering hosts, I fantasised about the sheer freedom of being in a hotel. Imagine, I thought, how delicious it would be to sit around, read books and drink beer or coffee, with nobody commenting on my behaviour, disapproving of my indolence or giving their opinion about my conduct. In a hotel, your time is your own. You don't have to perform any role. You can relax. As long as you don't smoke in your room, or make noise after eleven o'clock, or throw the TV out of the window, the hotel will provide you with shelter, food, whatever it is that you need. There is a freedom, David Graeber says, that comes from 'the possibility of dealing with other human beings in ways that do not demand either party has to engage in all those complex and exhausting forms of interpretive labour' that come about through unmediated social relationships.[32]

The German language makes a distinction between 'hospitality as friendly and inclusive sociability (*Gastfreundschaft*), and hospitality as a service-like interaction (*Gastlichkeit*)'.[33] *Gastfreundschaft* can be fun, but it can also be exhausting: it opens up all kinds of interpersonal complexities and troubles. With *Gastlichkeit*, life is easier. What you get up to in the privacy of your hotel room is, within reason, nobody else's business. Bureaucracies and institutions remove us from the warp and weft of the interpersonal. And then, freed from the obligations that weigh heavy on household guests, you can, as Graeber writes, 'simply place your money on the counter and not have to worry about what the cashier thinks of how you're dressed . . . Surely this is part of the appeal.'[34]

The infrastructure and bureaucracy that manage transitory guests have a long history; but it was not until the nineteenth century that, in an explosion of restlessness, the modern tourism industry was born. The genius behind its birth was an itinerant preacher called Thomas Cook.

On 5 July 1841, a crammed train pulled out of Leicester station. On board were a full band and 500 high-minded teetotallers, all of them in a party mood. In a flurry of speed and soot, smoke and sparks, the train shuddered its way towards the nearby town of Loughborough. The band played rousing tunes. The bridges over the railway lines were crowded with well-wishers cheering the travellers on their way. When the train reached its destination, another band was there on the platform, adding to the chaos: a cacophony of drums, bugles, trumpets and trombones. Crowds pressed together to greet the brave travellers, all of whom had paid one shilling for a return ticket. The welcoming committee waved flags reading, 'Do not drink wine nor strong drink.' The passengers spilled into the station and headed to the marketplace to sing hymns and listen to speeches on the virtue of temperance. After the speeches, the travellers shared a picnic lunch and played children's games: tag and blind-man's-buff. There was dancing, there were further speeches from clergymen with names like Reverend Boot and Reverend Babbington, and there was more high-minded partying. Then the travellers were herded back to the station, where they boarded the train home, pulling into Leicester at 10.30 in the evening. Cook, the organiser of the tour, wrote that 'all went off in the best style'.[35] It was modern history's first ever package tour, and it was to revolutionise global travel.

Cook's statue still stands outside Leicester station. He wears a waistcoat, overcoat and bow tie. On his face is a serious expression. In one hand he holds a watch and in the other an umbrella. A suitcase rests by his feet. He looks like a man who is confident of his place in the world. But Cook's own journey from impoverished childhood to tour operator was a long one. As a child, he worked as a gardener's assistant. His boss was a drunkard, which gave him a lifelong distaste for alcohol. After a religious conversion at the age of seventeen, Cook became a committed

Baptist and got involved in the growing temperance movement. In 1833, he took the Temperance Pledge: 'We agree to abstain from all liquors of an intoxicating quality whether ale, porter, wine or ardent spirits, except as medicine.'

But abstention did not tame Cook's ardour. He was one of life's fidgeters, a habitual walker unable to stay in one place, a man who was always twiddling his thumbs or pacing around: the embodiment of restlessness. When he walked, he thrust his hands deep into his pockets and moved in long strides. He hated excess and extravagance. He liked rousing marching bands that could stir the heart to pious thoughts, without stirring up bodily lusts. He was industrious and impassioned. He spent several years as a wandering preacher, travelling from town to town to spread the Gospel, usually going on foot, only occasionally allowing himself the indulgence of a journey by carriage or on horseback. In one year, he travelled over 2,500 miles, most of it on foot.

It was while on one of these journeys that he had the idea for his first package tour. What, he thought, if 'the newly-developed powers of railways and locomotion could be made subservient to the promotion of Temperance'?[36] He got in touch with the Midland Railway Company. They said they could provide a train. Thomas Cook was in business.

Cook's preaching career gave him skills in oratory and crowd control. He was known for his ability to put down hecklers. And he passionately believed in the value of opening up travel to those for whom it had hitherto been impossible, to provide respite from lives of drudgery. Until this point, travel had been a luxury for the middle and upper classes with their grand tour itineraries. Cook wanted to make use of these new connections, these new

roads, to provide new possibilities for ordinary people. It was a
mission that he set about with an almost mystical, apocalyptic
fervour. In his *Handbook to Scotland*, he wrote, 'The prejudices
which ignorance has engendered are broken by the roar of a train,
and the whistle of the engine awakens thousands from the slumber
of ages.'[37]

After his first successful tour, Cook expanded his enterprise.
The package became more complete, covering accommodation as
well as travel and food. He diversified the destinations on offer:
Liverpool, Scotland, Wales, the Lake District. Soon Cook became
more ambitious, adding Antwerp, Brussels, Strasbourg and Paris.
In 1865, he ran a tour for over 1,500 people to Switzerland.
Remarkably, nobody died. He took people on trips to Rome and
Naples. He arranged journeys across the Atlantic to the United
States, and was seasick all the way. He took advantage of his
American tours to preach the Gospel in the towns and cities of the
New World. In 1868, he visited the Holy Land, a lifelong
ambition, with a trip to Egypt and Palestine. And then in 1872, he
led a world tour, travelling from Liverpool to the USA, and from
there to Japan, China, India and Aden, before heading back
through the Suez Canal to Egypt and home. The planning was
meticulous; again, nobody died.

Cook retired from running tours in 1872. He returned to
Leicester. And there he remained, striding and fidgeting, until his
death fourteen years later.

Thomas Cook democratised restlessness. The idea was simple
and revolutionary: the right to travel belongs to everyone. Cook
wanted to give people who were fixed in place by poverty and

waged labour the right to explore the restless urge for elsewhere. For those whose lives were reduced by industrialisation to endless repetition, Cook's package tours brought back a sense of quest and newness. And in doing so, they multiplied the opportunities for meeting with strangeness and with strangers. Because Thomas Cook was not only selling holidays. Nor was he just providing moments of relief in lives of drudgery. He was dreaming of the awakening of humanity from the slumber of ages. He was creating a new generation of pilgrims, a new society. Like Mr Valiant-for-Truth in Bunyan's *Pilgrim's Progress*, a book he knew well, he was on fire with the idea of life as a pilgrimage. The package tour was the *peregrinatio* democratised. It was a vision for remaking lives, and for remaking the world.[38]

Cook would have been horrified by what the package tour later became. There is not much temperance to be found in Ibiza or in Bulgaria's Sunny Beach. But it is not clear those first revellers on the train to Loughborough really were inspired by a love of temperance, despite what Cook himself may have believed. For many of them, perhaps it was more about adventure, about difference, about the possibility of chance encounters, about the opportunity to meet new people with whom to talk and to flirt, about the smoke and steam and sparks, the blare of trumpets, the bugles and trombones. It was about our human longing to move, and in movement to be refashioned. It was about a deep-rooted, almost metaphysical desire, a hunger, as Levinas writes, to go forth 'from a world that is familiar to us . . . toward a yonder'.[38] And for all the harms of the global travel boom, there is something revolutionary in this desire. There is something joyously hopeful in the way we seek to always open new journeys, new quests, new lines of flight.

Standing on the rooftop in Yangon, I was no different from those pilgrims at Hilazon Tachtit in the ancient Near East, or from those wastrel brothers Hadnakhte and Panakhti, scratching graffiti onto the walls of Memphis more than 3,000 years ago, or from one of the many holidaymakers stumbling off the flight to Sunny Beach. I was doing what many of us do, given half the chance. I was taking hold of the restlessness that is an ineradicable part of who we are. I was following my hunger to be uprooted from the same old realities. I was setting out on a *peregrinatio*, a pilgrimage of sorts. I was immersing myself in strangeness, spending time in the company of strangers. And I was nurturing the hope that in these encounters I might become other than I was and I might be remade.

9

Who Goes There?

At Strymonas station, in northern Greece, the stray dog now knows me. When I get off the minibus that has brought me from the Bulgarian border, he pads over to say hello. I make a fuss of him and he wags his tail. 'Hello, friend,' I say. The dog's tail wags harder.

I am on my way back from Sofia to Thessaloniki, my temporary home. The train journey already feels like it has taken most of the day. If I'd wanted to get there quicker, I could have caught the direct bus: it takes only half as long. But I prefer the train. I like the slowness of it. I like the time the journey gives me to read and think. And I like the station dog.

By now, I've made this journey several times. I'm getting used to it. It is by far my favourite way of travelling between the two cities; but it is not the most straightforward. First you must take the train to one side of the border. Then you hang around for one of the minibuses that shuttle back and forth over the road crossing. At the border, the guards check everyone's passports.

Then the buses continue to the station on the other side, where once again you hang around until, at last, another train takes you on to your destination.

Once there was a direct train: you can still see the tracks from the road border as you sit waiting on the minibus. The official reason the service was suspended is that the small stretch of line between Strymonas and Kulata on the Bulgarian side is under renovation. But there is no work taking place. The real reason for the closure of the border is political. In the wake of the migrant crisis that, between 2015 and 2016, saw over a million refugees arriving in Greece by sea and overland, the Bulgarian authorities sought to harden their southern border.[1] In June 2016, they turned back a Greek train suspected of carrying migrants. Soon after, all direct services were suspended.[2] Since then, the journey by train has taken an extra three hours, sometimes four.

On the station platform at Strymonas in Greece, the dog and I finish saying our hellos, and he wanders off to talk to somebody else. The sun is starting to set. I look round at my fellow travellers. Everybody else on the platform is a tourist like me. Most Greeks and Bulgarians, pressed for time, prefer to catch the direct bus, or else to drive. It is only writers and travellers who have the appetite to spend extra hours hanging around in deserted border villages, chatting to the stray dogs. With me on the platform are a French woman on holiday, an Irish train enthusiast, a quiet Bosnian man, a young Swedish man with a guitar and a band of Croatian musicians. We exchange stories about our journeys, make connections. As dusk rolls in, the Croatians take out their instruments and play music: 'Wish You Were Here', 'Blackbird', 'Norwegian

Wood'. The stationmaster comes to sit with the band, dangling his legs over the side of the platform, pulling on his cigar. He phones a friend and holds up the phone, so his friend can hear the music too.

Eventually, the train to Thessaloniki arrives. It has come from Alexandroupoli, capital of the Greek province of Evros, bordering Turkey. When we climb on board, I am surprised to find the train crowded. Our fellow passengers are asylum seekers and refugees, and they are almost all men. They smile in greeting as we few ragged tourists get on the train. But there is an air of awkwardness: the awkwardness that comes from knowing you exist in different worlds, from wanting to connect but not having any idea how. It is the young Swedish man with his guitar who breaks the ice. He stands in the aisle and serenades the carriage with sweet tunes. His voice is mournful and high-pitched. We all applaud. Then the men on the train start to talk. They tell us where they have come from and where they are going. They say they are from Afghanistan, the Middle East, Pakistan; and they are on their way to Athens, after two months in the internment camp at Fylakio, near the Turkish border.

As Dina Nayeri writes in her book *The Ungrateful Refugee*: 'Asylum *seekers* is so mild a phrase – we weren't politely seeking, we were ravenous for it, this creature need for the safety for our bodies. Even as we learned English and swam and erased workbooks, we thought of nothing else. How do we survive the memory of so much wanting?'[3]

This creature need – this movement of human populations in search of safety from harm – has always been with us. For all of recorded history, people afflicted by war, by environmental degradation and by natural disasters have set out on the road, risking long and arduous journeys in the company of strangers, in the hope that they may meet with kindness, with safety, with the asylum for which they hunger. The word 'asylum' has its roots in the Greek notion of *asulia*, which literally means 'inviolable', or 'not plundering'. In its original sense, it referred to the practice of taking refuge at a sacred site, rendering you safe from abduction, exploitation or violation. For the ancient Greeks, *asulia* was the responsibility to offer 'refuge for all, irrespective of a person's political affiliation, socioeconomic status, ethnicity, or any other qualifying condition'.[4] Even a barbarian could seek *asulia*. Many Greek temples had accommodation for those who sought sanctuary, while the asylum seekers petitioned to become settled residents. Long-term safety wasn't guaranteed for these ancient asylum seekers; but for those who were without protection, uprooted from their kin and their webs of allegiance, exposed to the possibility of exploitation, it was a start.

According to the historian Livy, the same tradition of sacred asylum existed in Rome from its foundation. He writes that when Romulus first established the city, 'so that this large city was not empty' he set up a place of asylum on the Capitoline Hill. And many people fled from neighbouring states to take refuge in Rome. 'They came without distinction,' Livy writes, 'slaves and freemen alike, eager for a fresh start. This was the first move toward beginning the increase of Rome's might.'[5]

The asylum seekers on the train tell us how, two months before, they crossed into Greece where the River Evros forms a natural border with Turkey. They were taken to the camp and there they were registered by the Greek authorities. The registration process should have taken seven days, but the men had been in detention for two months, waiting for their onward papers. The conditions in Fylakio were grim: overcrowding, limited infrastructure, verbal and physical abuse from the police, lack of adequate health care.[6] After two months, having finally issued them with their papers and not knowing what else to do with them, the authorities in the camp gave them tickets to Athens. In Athens, at least they would be someone else's problem.

After two months in these conditions, the released men are demob happy, glad to be out. Even if they are heading into the unknown, it is better than Fylakio. One man – an Afghan, still in his late teens – is making his second trip to Europe. Three years before, he fled to Norway and sought asylum. He lived there for a year or two, and he learned the language. He wanted to stay. But his request for asylum was turned down and he was deported to Afghanistan. Once back in Afghanistan, he immediately left on his second journey. Some places are so intolerable, you have to leave twice.

When we arrive at Thessaloniki station, I pick up my bags to leave and say goodbye to my travelling companions. As I am about to exit the station, I hear somebody calling out to me. It is one of the men from the train: I have left a bag of snacks by mistake. He hands it back to me, wishes me a good onward journey and climbs on to the night train bound for Athens with his fellow refugees. Only after I leave the station do I think I should have given him the snacks, that his need is so much greater than mine.

*

In the days after, I think often about these men, the danger and difficulty of their journeys. I wonder about the hopes they had for safe passage, the destinations they dreamed of reaching. How easily we tourists slid across the border, holding up our passports and our identity cards, our travels born out of no other need than a pilgrim restlessness. For our other travelling companions, it was different. Their journeys were urgent and desperate, born out of a hunger for safety, out of the hope they might find freedom from plunder or violation. And for them – travelling with the wrong passports, or with no passports at all – every border was an ordeal, an unimaginable barrier, an existential risk.

The Albanian writer Gazmend Kapllani gives a name to this cruel triage at the threshold between nations, this sorting of strangers into the welcome and unwelcome: he calls it 'border syndrome'. Born in 1967, in the central Albanian town of Lushnje, Kapllani was in his early twenties when the Stalinist regime in Albania collapsed. In 1991, he joined the protests against Enver Hoxha and his government. Hearing he was wanted by the secret police, Kapllani went into hiding. Soon after, he fled over the border to Greece.

Border syndrome, Kapllani says in his book *A Short Border Handbook*, is a complex phenomenon made up of the longing to cross the border and the trembling of fear as one does so. It is opportunity and threat, the key and the cudgel. In Kapllani's fictionalised account of his flight, the narrator takes a truck to the border between Albania and Greece. He walks the final stretch, part of a 'caravan of human beings moving forward with one single demand: to break through that terrifying taboo otherwise known as the border. Escape as an end in itself. Escape as illness.'

At the border, the guards interrogate the refugees, but then they let them pass. 'We broke into a run,' Kapllani writes, 'scared that the soldiers might shoot us in the back with their Kalashnikovs. We got through the barbed wire, which was still intact, meaning that we were the first to cross at this point. We started bashing at it with a stick to see if it was electrified and then we opened a hole in it with some sticks that the drivers had brought from their truck until it was big enough for us to get through, one at a time.'[7]

Borders are places of fear and hope. But how these are mixed in your cup depends on the luck of who you are. The luck of where you were born, your country, your class, your colour, your ethnicity, the passport you carry. The luck of having a passport at all.

The Iranian-Swedish poet Athena Farrokhzad writes: 'If you do not tremble when you cross a border / it is not the border you have crossed.'[8]

A preoccupation with borders and thresholds has always been with us. It predates even the beginning of human settlement. The hunter-gatherer societies in which our ancestors lived were not borderless. On the evidence drawn from more recent hunter-gatherer groups, it is likely that in early human societies there were 'complex strategies for regulating membership, territory, and resources that intermingled notions of exclusivity and reciprocity'.[9] And yet in a fluid, mobile world, the boundaries between different communities are often changeable, porous and open to negotiation; it is only with the coming of agriculture that these boundaries become more tangible. Crops stay put, so to look after them you have to stay put as well. You have to build fences to keep out wild animals, to fend off the encroachment of strangers parasitic on your hard work. Settlement forces us to harden our thresholds.

As early settlements turned into cities, fences became walls. In fertile river valleys from the Middle East, through the Indus Valley culture of India, all the way to China, urban centres appeared, surrounded by ramparts to keep out marauding strangers, and to better monitor and control those inside.[10] In Mesopotamia, the walls of Uruk were seven metres high and several metres thick.[11] *The Epic of Gilgamesh* sings their praises: 'Climb Uruk's wall and walk back and forth! / Survey its foundations, examine the brickwork! / Were its bricks not fired in an oven? / Did the Seven Sages not lay its foundations?'[12]

If city walls were the most tangible boundaries of these early civilisations, the territorial ambitions of ancient city-states often extended far beyond. These cities depended for their survival on the resources that lay in the lands beyond the city limits. But the status of these areas was often unclear. The Egyptians erected stone pillars at the outer limits of territories they claimed, but these were less borders in the contemporary sense and more checkpoints which could help regulate the flow of trade and manage taxation. A similar system existed in Central America, among both Olmec and Mayan cultures.[13] The Chinese emperor Qin Shihuang, who founded the short-lived Qin dynasty in 221 BCE, built a wall at the fringes of his empire, beyond which lay the feared Xiongnu nomads. This was the precursor of what is now called the Great Wall, a series of fortifications stretching across swathes of north-east China, built piecemeal over the centuries.[14] Three hundred years after Qin Shihuang, the Romans built Hadrian's Wall, which still snakes over the barren hills of northern England. It is easy to see these boundary markers of political control as something akin to modern borders, lines on the map that clearly demarcate and divide up territory. But both in China and on the chilly hills of northern England, the walls served a range of different functions. They offered tangible signs of the outermost limits of political and military power. They were zones of cultural contact around which marketplaces and settlements grew up. They were places where goods could be taxed. And they acted as roads along which troops could pass, to manage the porosity of these frontier zones.[15]

Today, the map of the world is tessellated into myriad nation-states, each one distinct and sovereign, bounded by a tidy border; and we take for granted the existence of linear borders, of nations and of the passports that ideally allow us safe passage from one to another. And yet this way of imagining the world is remarkably recent. As late as the nineteenth century, when the idea of the nation-state had not fully taken hold in the imagin-ation, a 'foreigner' was not necessarily somebody from outside the nation's borders. Instead, a foreigner could be anybody designated as an outsider.[16] People were as likely to regard those in neighbouring provinces as foreigners as they were people in neighbouring countries.[17] According to local lore in my native Norfolk, well into the 1970s, the train station at Downham Market divided destinations into two camps: 'King's Lynn', fourteen miles away, and 'foreign'.[18]

The historian Benedict Anderson famously referred to

nation-states as 'imagined communities'. They are communities of those who are not kin, but who are called upon to act as if they are. Nation-states, Anderson writes, are cemented together by an idea of 'deep, horizontal comradeship', by thickets of myths and obligations so compelling that millions are prepared 'not so much to kill, as willingly to die' for them. In this way, the idea of the nation not only marks out territories on the map, but also divides humanity up into tidy categories. When we meet someone new, one of the first things we ask is: where are you from? And by this, usually, we mean to ask what their nation is. Because when you know the answer to this question, then you can begin to place them in the order of things.

Myths of national belonging are a powerful way of forging connections between strangers who might never meet. Anderson writes, 'The members of even the smallest nation will never know most of their fellow-members, meet them, or even hear of them, yet in the minds of each lives the image of their communion.'[19] In this way, national myths divide all strangers into two camps: those who are in some fundamental way like us and those who are unlike us. The tendency has a long history, one that stretches back until well before the birth of national myths. The Greeks distinguished between Greek-speaking *xenoi* – the foreigners with whom one could have relationships of *xenia*, or guest friendship – and the babbling barbarians, with whom you couldn't do much at all.[20] Meanwhile, over in China, there was a long-standing distinction between the 'cooked', or civilised, Chinese and the 'raw', or allegedly uncivilised, barbarians who lay beyond the Chinese cultural world.[21] The sorting of strangers into those who resemble us in some fundamental way and those who do not acts as a powerful social glue. The sense that we are different from those people over there is one of the most powerful ways we have of binding together a community. As the Greek poet Cavafy once wrote, 'What will now become of us, without the barbarians / those people were a sort of solution.'[22]

Nevertheless, life is never as tidy as myth; and the lines on the map that divide nations one from another are often at odds with the mess of allegiances, affiliations and desires that make up the fabric of our lives. For many of us, our connections are both fine-grained and multifarious. They sprawl untidily across borders and thresholds, messing with the clean lines of national myth-making. We might feel ourselves to be part of multiple communities, united by gender, race, religion, shared history or a common vision of the world. It is no surprise that nation-states are often suspicious of these sprawling allegiances over which they have little control. Nationalism is an ideology 'that assumes the nation commands the primary allegiance of its members'.[23] It asks that you nail your colours to the mast and renders other allegiances suspect. And if you want to find the cracks in these myths of national belonging, the places where they break down – revealing their madness and sometimes their cruelty – then you need look no further than those communities who live on the nation's borders. Because in communities such as these, people often find their richly textured allegiances disrupted by boundary walls and barbed-wire fences, by the machineries of surveillance and the hostility of border guards.

After the dissolution of the Soviet Union, the administrative boundaries between former Soviet states became international borders. In the years that followed, these international borders increasingly hardened and communities found themselves divided. The anthropologist Elina Troscenko carried out fieldwork on the border between the former Soviet states of Uzbekistan and Kyrgyzstan, a place where villages that were once just down the road from each other came to exist in entirely different worlds. One Uzbek women interviewed by the anthropologist spoke of her married daughter, who lived in the next-door village in Kyrgyzstan. In the past, she said, 'I could just walk for fifteen minutes down the road and I was at my daughter's house.' But now the trip took four hours, two taxis, queues at the border post and bribes offered to the guards. She did not see her daughter very often any more.[24] When borders harden, cross-border communities find themselves broken apart in the name of national security; and those who seek to maintain connections across the clear lines drawn on the map become an object of suspicion, sometimes of outright paranoia. In her book *Border*, Kapka Kassabova tells the story of a shepherd in Turkey during the Cold War, watering his horse in the river that divided the country from Bulgaria. On the other bank, he saw a Bulgarian shepherd. The Turkish shepherd, Kassabova writes, 'shouted *Merhaba!* Hello! The man on the other side waved back.'[25] That was all: a simple, human exchange. But a nearby Turkish army patrol overheard the greeting. They arrested the shepherd and he was sentenced to fourteen years in jail for espionage. The horse – knowing its owner would not return – died of a broken heart.

As the border guards come onto the bus at the Bulgarian–Greek border, we fumble for our passports. I know that my British passport will not cause me any problems. But not all passports are equal: were I travelling on a Ghanaian passport, or a Venezuelan passport, or an Iraqi passport, I would not be so lucky.

I have travelled this route enough times to know the pattern. Those whose faces or passports don't fit are taken off the bus and into the border office, where they are interrogated about their intended movements. Because there is no document that more powerfully divides the world into those strangers who are welcome and those who are unwelcome than the passport you carry.

As long as there has been bureaucracy, travellers negotiating a passage through strange lands have relied on documents, letters of safe passage and tokens of trust. Documents to ensure the safety of travellers are mentioned in the biblical Book of Nehemiah 2:7: 'If it pleases the king, let letters be given to me for the governors of the region beyond the River, that they must permit me to pass through till I come to Judah.' In India, in the *Arthashastra*, the ruler is instructed to appoint a superintendent of passes. 'Only someone who possesses a sealed pass,' the book cautions, 'should be authorized to enter or to exit the countryside.'[26] Han dynasty China issued permits and passports in the form of wooden strips.[27] In the medieval Islamic world, tax authorities kept their eye on the movement of people by granting permission to travel only to those who had receipts for taxes paid.[28] But the idea of the modern passport as an internationally recognised document only emerged in the early twentieth century, to address the need of stateless refugees fleeing the Russian civil war.[29] The passport was originally a document for those of no nation, a guarantee of safe passage for those seeking asylum. Only later in the twentieth century did it become a sign of national belonging, cementing the identity of the person who carried it: their identity and their fate.

Back in the early 1990s, it seemed that border syndrome might be a temporary condition, a sickness for which we would eventually find a cure. The Berlin Wall had fallen. Totalitarian regimes were collapsing. The Soviet Union was breaking apart. History seemed to be on the turn. Some even believed – as Francis Fukuyama famously argued – that we were at the end of history, and this great cycle of human struggle had reached its terminus in Western liberal democracy.[30] We were arriving at a place where borders and walls would matter less and less, where border syndrome would be consigned to the past.

But this hope has turned out to be a fantasy. The last three decades have seen a rapid increase in wall-building, hardening existing borders not just in Europe but across the globe. The increased border security between Bulgaria and Greece is not the exception but instead the rule. In his book *Divided: Why We're Living in an Age of Walls*, Tim Marshall writes: 'Despite globalization and advances in technology, we seem to be feeling more divided than ever.'[31] And where there are borders, there are people who are excluded and marginalised. The hardening of borders multiplies suffering. According to Daniel Trilling, who has written extensively on migration: 'Border defences often produce or exacerbate the very problems they purport to solve, by forcing irregular migrants to take more dangerous routes.'[32]

I knew that many of the journeys made by the men I met on the train to Thessaloniki had involved sometimes unimaginable dangers. Many migrants have died of exposure, drowned or been

shot by border guards when crossing the Evros from Turkey.[33]
The sea passage into Greece is no safer, with people crowded
onto rickety boats where they risk death from drowning in the
Aegean. The risks of these journeys are not accidental. They are
the result of deliberate policy decisions. The reason people cross
by unseaworthy boats, paying tens of thousands of pounds to
people smugglers, or the reason they struggle across the River
Evros is that they have no means of just catching a flight, or
making the journey by legitimate means. Under EU law, airlines
can be fined hundreds of thousands of euros for transporting
passengers without valid travel documents.[34] And so these un-
wanted strangers – driven by warfare, by economic need – resort
to other methods, vastly more dangerous and more expensive.

One summer day in Thessaloniki, wanting a break from writing,
I went with friends down to the local beach in the suburb of
Kalamaria. The beach was not a glamorous place. The sea floor
was stone and seaweed, the water murky. There was a kiosk that
sold grilled meat, beer and Greek coffee. A stray dog dozed in the
shade of the crumbling concrete, hanging out with the two ducks
it seemed to have befriended. Local pensioners sunned themselves.
One local man – in his sixties with a large handlebar moustache
– came to the beach every day, carrying a five-litre bottle of water
into which he put sprays of fresh, colourful flowers. He set up the
flowers on a plastic table outside the kiosk, pulled up a chair and
looked out to sea. A few days before, he had come over and
wordlessly given us handfuls of hand-painted shells.

We came to the beach a lot. We liked the down-at-heel vibe,
the absence of glamour, the sense of people unhurriedly going

about their lives. We knew the woman in the kiosk. She was impatient with our bad Greek. When we ordered food or drink, she sighed and rolled her eyes. When we misunderstood the kiosk queueing system, she snapped at us.

On this particular day, we stripped down to our swimsuits and idled in the shallows. And there we got chatting with four fellow swimmers. They were a journalist from Thessaloniki, a woman from Holland who was making a documentary about unaccompanied minors seeking asylum, and two boys from Afghanistan. The boys were fifteen years old and had been on the road for six months. They'd left their families, travelling overland via Iran and Turkey. I tried to imagine what it must be like, how fifteen-year-old me would have survived such a journey. The film-maker had spent a few days with them, interviewing them for her documentary. The Afghan boys had been several weeks in Thessaloniki, but Greece was only a staging post; their time in Greece was coming to an end. That evening, they planned to move onwards, to the border with North Macedonia. They dreamed of going to France, they said, or to Germany.

We bobbed around in the sea together, me, my friends, the journalist and the boys from Afghanistan. We talked about their journey, about the Pashto language, about how good the water felt. 'So nice,' the boys said. 'So nice,' we agreed.

Eventually, we got out of the water. The boys stayed in a while longer. When they got out, they smiled and gave us thumbs-up gestures.

In the line at the kiosk, I talked to the film-maker. 'They are so young,' she sighed. 'They have such a long way to travel. There are so many dangers ahead.'

*

For those far from home caught up in the inhumane machineries of borders, nations and passports, often the best hope lies in the kindness of strangers. I arranged to meet with Eleni, a friend of a friend, in a bar in Valaoritou, a grungy hipster district in downtown Thessaloniki. Eleni worked for an NGO that ran projects with refugees, but it was her personal story that I was interested in.

It was a hot night at the end of summer when we met. The city had been half-deserted for weeks, the businesses closed up as families headed down to the coast to cool off. But as summer crawled to an end, life was returning to the city. Shops were rolling up their shutters. The streets were beginning to fill with people again. Eleni arrived at the bar straight from the office. We ordered ourselves drinks and she started to talk.

Back in 2015, Greece was reeling from the government debt crisis that hit the country hard in the aftermath of the financial crash of 2007 and 2008. The punishing austerity measures adopted in response to the debt crisis drove the country into recession. Taxes were hiked up, businesses closed, people lost their homes and their livelihoods. Then the boats started arriving – on Lesvos, on Chios, on Samos – carrying refugees from Afghanistan, from Iraq and from the war in Syria. At the time, Eleni was living on the mainland, in the village of Profitis, with her husband and their two-year-old child. They were in a two-storey house in which each floor was independent of the other. They inhabited the first floor; the ground floor was empty. Eleni's husband had trained as an electrician, but was now running his own bar. Times were not easy, but they were weathering the crisis better than many.

Then the authorities set up a refugee camp nearby to house migrants relocated from the closed-down Idomeni refugee camp on the Macedonian border. A Syrian Kurdish couple were among the first to move in. Their names were Viktor and Aisha, and they had two children. They had lived through several years of war in Syria, but when bombs started to fall close to their home they fled for Turkey. After two years in Turkey, they realised that, as Kurds, they would never feel welcome among their new neighbours. The prejudice and discrimination ground them down. So they decided to try to make it to Europe. They crossed the Mediterranean from the coast of Turkey while their daughter was still only one year old. Then they made their way to the mainland and to Idomeni. When, in 2016, the Greek authorities forcibly closed the camp, Viktor and Aisha were relocated to Profitis. But there their luck changed. While in the camp, they befriended a local police officer who said he would find the family a place to stay. He spoke with Eleni and her husband, who confirmed the ground floor of their house was free. In August 2016, Viktor and Aisha moved in.

Eleni and her husband paid the Syrian family's rent and electricity and water bills. 'Hosting people means you effectively double your costs and expenses,' Eleni said. 'It is not just about being nice. This is also a practical matter. But it was an extra cost we were willing to pay.'

Aisha, who spoke fluent English, Kurdish and Arabic, found work as a translator. Viktor stayed home to care for the kids. He found it hard, Eleni said, to be out of work. But he gave free haircuts to the young people in the village, so he could feel useful. He made food for Eleni and her family. They could smell his cooking wafting up from below. He cooked stews of chicken and vegetables, home-made Arabic bread, spicy lentil soup. When Eleni's husband finished shutting up the bar in the early hours of the morning, Viktor would be waiting for him at the door and would invite him in for dinner.

Life was hard for Viktor and Aisha; their status was uncertain, caught in the nightmare bureaucracy of the asylum system. But they were luckier than many. In April 2017, they were granted permission to relocate to France, to have their asylum application processed there. They moved to Angers in the Loire Valley, where they started to study French. Aisha, who had helped out in the emergency room in a hospital in Syria, treating those suffering from traumatic injuries due to the war, retrained as a nurse. The children took to the French language more quickly than their parents. Viktor got a job cutting hair again, setting up his own barber's salon. Their right to remain was granted.

Shortly before I met with Eleni, she had taken her family to see Viktor and Aisha in France. It was the first time they had met since their departure from Greece. It was wonderful, Eleni said, to see their former guests' lives were going well for them. 'I feel good to have them in my life,' she said. 'They made such a huge journey. I am happy for them now.'

Eleni was not alone in her welcoming of strangers into her home. Between 2015 and 2016, there was an extraordinary explosion of philoxenia in Greece, an astonishing generosity extended towards the bedraggled strangers turning up on the coast: a chef who travelled to the border with North Macedonia four times a week to spend eight-hour shifts cooking lentil soup for refugees;

a taxi driver who spent days distributing food to asylum seekers at the port of Piraeus in Athens; countless people who opened up their homes and their lives.[35] One reason Greek friends gave for why people extended this welcome to those turning up on their shores was Greece's long cultural tradition of valuing philoxenia. But they also cited history as a reason. Many Greeks, particularly in Thessaloniki, were still marked by their family's own refugee experience a century before, during the great and traumatic population exchanges of 1923 after the crumbling of the Ottoman Empire.

But for Eleni, this response wasn't just about Greek culture or history: it was also something more fundamentally human. 'When Aisha and Viktor first came,' Eleni said, 'their morale was quite low. They kept feeling they had to thank us. But I told them, "If I was in your position, I would really hope that someone would help me." Because you never know where your life will end up; and solidarity has something to do with that. What you do for others is not charity. It is like doing it for yourself. It is not exactly selfish, but it is about seeing yourself in another person. And thinking about the kind of world you want to live in. I'm not a particularly charitable person; but on a purely human basis, it feels nice because I feel connected. It is really about connecting. And you don't know where this connection takes you.'

For those fortunate enough to have never suffered from border syndrome, it is easy to see the machineries of nations, borders and passports as orderly and just. It is easy to imagine there is something natural in these mechanisms we have created to deal with the bewilderment of living in a world of strangers. It is only those who stand on the threshold, without the right papers, seeking *asulia* or freedom from violation, who can see how monstrous the system truly is. Injustices on this scale take a lot of unpicking. But one step towards seeing the horror our myths have created is a recognition of the vast contingency of life: the fact, as Eleni said, that 'you never know where your life will end up'.

Because, who knows? Having created these systems, there is no guarantee that one day we won't be the ones who are clambering onto leaking boats, or struggling across the river, or standing by the border post with the wrong documents in our hand. And this is where solidarity begins: when we start to see through the distorting lenses of our collective myths; when we recognise that a relaxing of our vigilance and a friendly *Merhaba!* yelled across the river border may do more for the nation's well-being and security than unfurling yet another row of razor wire.

10

Crowds

I got off the plane in Chengdu and waited in line at immigration for the border officials to stamp my passport. As the queue shuffled forward towards the immigration desk, I wondered how I could ever feel at home in a city of fourteen million people.

It was mid-September 2015 and I was in China to take up a one-year post at Sichuan University, in the College of Literature and Journalism. I looked forward to meeting my colleagues. I had sent them my flight details, which told them when I was arriving. I thought about Elee back home. It was early afternoon in China, so morning in the UK. She'd be getting up, making tea: I missed her already. I was looking forward to seeing her again. Christmas, I told myself, was not far away.

The previous few years had been difficult. Elee's cancer diagnosis came in late 2012, just as she was about to start writing up her PhD. She was studying how museums can help young children make sense of the natural world. She worked in the Oxford University Museum of Natural History, where she gave cameras to four- and five-year-olds. Then she sent them hurtling around to take snapshots of cheetahs, rocks, great auks, dinosaur skeletons, monkeys and spider crabs. Just as Elee was beginning to write up her research, she found a lump in her left breast. A doctor friend said it would be fine, but that she should go and get it checked. When she did, Elee was referred to the breast clinic.

I caught a taxi with her to the clinic. After we had checked in, a nurse led us down the corridor to the line of chairs and asked us to wait. Opposite us was a door with a sign reading 'Quiet Room'. We saw a nurse going in carrying two mugs of tea and a plate of biscuits. She closed the door discreetly behind her. 'You really don't want to find yourself in the Quiet Room,' Elee said.

When Elee's name was called, I asked if she wanted me to go with her. 'No,' she said. 'No, it's OK.'

I waited in the corridor, trying to read my book. The nurse took Elee for an ultrasound. They photographed her breast lump and her armpit. Then they gave her a mammogram. She winced in pain. She could see the bloodless, yellow shape of the lump beneath her skin. They examined both breasts, then her armpits. Elee put her gown back on and joined me in the corridor.

'I need a biopsy,' she said. 'I won't be long.'

When the call came for the biopsy, I stayed in the corridor with our things. They took two biopsies: a fine-needle biopsy and a core biopsy, scraping for cells to examine, then stamping out a piece of the lump. When they were done, the nurse taped up the wound and Elee came back into the corridor, crying from the pain. She sat down and lay her head in my lap.

'Is it bad?' I asked.

She hesitated. 'Yes. I think it's bad.'

A nurse came down the corridor. 'Eleanor?' she said. 'And . . . ?'

'Will,' I said.

The nurse smiled kindly. 'Will,' she said. She turned to Elee. 'Please,' she said. And she indicated the Quiet Room. 'Would you like some tea?'

We glanced at each other. Then we got to our feet and followed.

The tumour was two centimetres across. There were cancer cells elsewhere too in Elee's lymph nodes. It was treatable, the nurse told us. I remember thinking that treatable was not the same as curable. We could come in next week, when they had more results back. Then we could talk further. We caught a taxi home and sat out the rest of the week in numb discomfort.

The treatment began just after Christmas: chemotherapy, surgery, radiotherapy. It was a hard few months, but by the summer it was done. The oncologist said everything had gone well and Elee's chances were good. We took a train down to Aix-en-Provence for a break, where we drank coffee and wine, ate bread and cheese. We felt the tension of the previous few months drain away, the sense of future come creeping back. Elee resumed her PhD. We talked about the coming years, what we wanted to do, how to manage the uncertainty of not knowing if the illness would return.

The year after, Elee's PhD was finished. She continued to go into hospital for six-monthly check-ups and the results came back clear. We bought a small terraced house in Leicester. Elee took a job at the Institute of Education in London. And then one day, I received the email offering me the post teaching at Sichuan University. Elee told me she thought I should take it. It would mean a year away from home, but she would come and visit at Christmas. I would be back home for a few weeks at Easter. In the summer, we would travel together. I suggested the high mountain passes of west Sichuan; Elee favoured Japan. It felt good to have a future again.

It was late morning by the time I passed through immigration. I had that stretched-out feeling you get after long-haul flights, as if half of you has been left behind somewhere along the way. When I came out into the arrivals lounge, I saw a group of young women holding flowers, craning their necks eagerly. 'He's arrived!' one of them shouted in Chinese. I beamed at them. But they weren't there for me. They looked straight past me and then broke loose to mob a slick young man in a suit who had passed through immigration after me. A minor celebrity, perhaps.

The excitable group disappeared. Soon, I was alone, and I realised nobody had come to meet me. I didn't have an address, or any instructions where to go. I hung around for a while, hoping someone might turn up to rescue me. With some currency from my last trip to China, I bought a bowl of noodles. I tried to check my email for messages from the university, but my phone did not work and I couldn't get online. I made the noodles last an hour, just in case my colleagues were late. When it was obvious that nobody was coming, I decided to head to the campus and hope for the best.

I caught a cab into town. As we sped down the highway everything looked unmanageably large. I gazed out of the window at the high-rise condominiums looming through the smog, the giant digital display screens. I was overawed by the sheer scale of it all. I didn't know how I could ever belong somewhere so huge, how I would ever find my tribe.

The cab drove me to the university campus. 'Where to?' asked the driver. I had no idea. But I had a map of the university and on it was a building marked Foreign Teachers' Hotel, so I asked the driver to take me there. At the front desk of the Foreign Teachers' Hotel, they were not expecting me, but they let me go online. When I logged in, I found a cheery welcome email from my new colleagues, sent to my email address only an hour or so before. The email contained a phone number. I asked the receptionist to call the number using the hotel phone. Ten minutes later, somebody came to meet me. By the time a couple of hours had passed, I had already met with my new colleagues and was unpacking my things in my new on-campus apartment on the twelfth floor.

I started to settle into life in Chengdu. My students tolerated my patchy Chinese with a mixture of good humour and encouragement. My colleagues were welcoming. They guided me through the endless mazes of Chinese bureaucracy with good grace. After several weeks, I moved off campus into my own place. The new apartment was on the seventh floor of a down-at-heel block where I was the only foreigner. The complex had been built in the 1980s, but looked much older. It had a shambolic, decaying charm. There was no lift. There was a leafy, chaotic courtyard at the bottom of the stairs where the owner of the shop that served the apartment block did synchronised exercises with her friends. My neighbours on one side were a family with a young child and on the other side an elderly couple who piled their household waste outside their door, until I got sick of it and took it down to the trash cans for them.

In the first few months, I worked hard on my Chinese. I enjoyed teaching and got on well with my students. Then one evening, I wandered into a local bookstore and bar and started chatting with the owner. We drank too much wine together, and I suggested setting up a philosophy salon, a public event where we could discuss philosophy in English and Chinese. He agreed immediately. It would be fun, he said. So I negotiated my fee: a glass of red wine, on the house. It seemed a fair trade. The bookstore put up posters and sent out advertisements on WeChat. I set about planning the first session. I expected the salon would be small and intimate, but on the first night seventy people turned up to talk about Confucius and Aristotle, Epicurus and Zhuangzi. Through the salon, I built new connections, made new friends.

It was around this time that I bought myself a second-hand bicycle from the campus store. The bike was heavy and battered, but very cheap. Chengdu had a rampant bike-theft problem and there seemed no point in buying an expensive bike only to see it disappear. I kept the bike in the communal apartment bike store. When I went to pay my dues after the first month, the bike store official pulled out his ledger and asked my name. He traced his finger down the list of names in Chinese, muttering to himself, 'I can't find it . . . I can't find it . . .'

I leaned over and pointed to the two characters that read *lao wai*: foreigner. 'I think that's me,' I said.

'Ah, yes,' he said, embarrassed. 'Of course it is.'

It was only then that I looked down at my bike and saw he had put a sticker on the frame as well, to better identify it. '*Lao wai*,' it said.

Lao wai literally means 'old outsider'. The 'old' suggests these outsiders are nothing new, but are instead strangers of long acquaintance. It is a term that goes back to the Kangxi Emperor, who ruled the Qing dynasty between 1661 and 1722. China scholars debate how to translate it effectively. Denis Mair, the translator and poet, suggests 'foreigner in our midst', denoting strangeness but also familiarity. The historian David Moser, not entirely seriously, suggests that an adequate translation might be 'overseas amigo'.[1]

I knew foreigners who hated the term. But I always liked it. I liked the tone of it: sometimes dismissive, sometimes disdainful, sometimes good-humoured, sometimes teasing, sometimes affectionate. It reminded me I was a stranger, but it encouraged me to feel at home in my strangeness. It reminded me that even as an outsider, I had a place there in Chengdu, that I was a problem of long acquaintance, the kind of problem people were practised in dealing with. When I rode around town, I would sometimes glance down at that sticker and, knowing that I sort of belonged, I felt more at home.

Still, the vastness of Chengdu was bewildering. I tried not to think about the city as a whole, the size of it. It was too large, too sprawling to be held in the mind. I focused instead on finding my own pathways through this new world. I made connections, cut new passages through the bewildering hugeness of it all, drew my own map of the city.

Across the globe, more of us now live in urban centres than in rural areas.[2] And the percentages are only going to rise. Megacities – which the UN defines as cities with ten million inhabitants or more – are proliferating: Tokyo, Delhi, Shanghai, São Paulo, Mexico City, Cairo. In northern China, there are plans to integrate the urban agglomerations of Beijing, Tianjin and Hebei province into a single megatropolis called Jingjinji with a population of over one hundred million. And as populations flood into the cities, the countryside empties of life.

We were not made for this world of millions of strangers, piled on top of each other. We are creatures with brains evolved to keep tabs on 150 others, more or less; and yet we are crowded into megacities and tower blocks, surrounded by tens of thousands of others who are, and will always be, strangers. But if we are not made for dealing with living in such large agglomerations, it is remarkable how well we manage. Despite all the rumours to the contrary, we are a pretty peaceable species. The next time you feel despair for humanity, go and sit in a busy city street. Grab yourself a drink so you can people-watch. And look at the people going past, all strangers to each other. Almost everywhere, you will see that human beings are remarkably good at making room for one another. People step aside to let each other pass. Strangers catch each other's eye and smile. Somebody buys something from a street vendor and, having exchanged money for goods, the two of them spend a few moments chatting about the weather. How many people can you see walking past in an hour or two? A thousand? Five thousand? In one single day, you might see more people than your hunter-gatherer ancestors saw in their entire lifetime.[3] Yet most of the interactions in a busy street take place agreeably, without any significant problems. We are now so used to living like this that we take it all for granted: so many human beings, strangers to each other, and everybody, most of the time, getting by. It is a testament to our remarkable flexibility, our adaptability and our amiability.

Cities, however, make the problem of how to deal with strangers even more urgent. For most of human history, the people with whom we were most intimate were the people who we kept physically close. They were the people whom we saw day by day, with whom we shared the everyday business of living. But in an increasingly urbanised and mobile world, these networks of kinship and alliance are more widely distributed. Our intimates may share the same apartment, or live in the same street; but for many of us they are instead in a different town, a different country, even a whole continent away. Nevertheless, we maintain our connections across these vast distances thanks to the technologies that stretch the threads of our belonging until they extend in invisible filaments across the whole globe. Banished to Thessaloniki, Cicero was alone and despairing; his fragile, crumbling sense of himself depended on the letters he, his friends and his family members sent back and forth. But these days, we sustain our sense of connection by means of social media, by text, by instant message. The technologies that are often decried as drivers of loneliness and isolation are equally ways of keeping connected to those we care about. Take any public bus or subway in almost any major city in the world, and you will be surrounded by a mass of strangers, all with their own allegiances, all belonging to different tribes. That tired worker who glances down at his screen? He has just received a message from his family on the other side of the world, thanking him for the money he has sent home, saying they are looking forward to seeing him on his next annual visit. That woman next to you? She is calling Kenya, talking to her relatives on the phone in Swahili. That student looking down at her phone, the screen filled with intricate Chinese characters? She is scrolling through WeChat, keeping in touch with friends in Henan, or in Ottawa, or in Tokyo. There is something sweetly ingenious about the way we continually connect and reconnect in the twenty-first century, maintaining our links through instant chat, through video calls, through the sharing of photographs, through the exchange of messages.

Thus the strange paradox to city living: the people with whom we are most intimate are furthest away; and the people in closest proximity to us – those we crowd up against, jostling for room – are complete strangers. But it is easy to underestimate the continued role close networks of kinship and friendship still play in urban environments: urbanisation does not automatically break the kinship networks that characterise more traditional communities. Cities are not just big melting pots where individuals run up against each other in Brownian motion, each of them carrying around their own personal histories. If the city as a whole is made up of countless strangers, in one quarter or another there may be complex webs of friendship, kinship and other social ties. Whole families, whole communities even, move to the city *en masse*. Incomers migrate to quarters where they will be near their kin.

In my neighbourhood in Chengdu, I could never work out who was exactly related to whom. The families who lived there were connected in complex ways, forming a tight-knit social fabric; and working it all out was made more complicated by the liberal use of kinship terms in Chinese.[4] In Chinese, it is normal to refer to an older man as 'uncle' and to an older woman as 'auntie', or for those closer in age, to use terms such as 'younger brother' and 'older sister'.[5] As a result of this proliferation of kinship terms, I could never be sure who in my block was actual kin and who was not, but in the end perhaps this doesn't matter that much. Kinship is never just about biology, or about affiliation. It is about closeness, about what is shared, about the way we connect and reconnect, and between us forge enduring bonds.[6]

'Cities are miracles,' the art historian Christopher Dell writes, 'cities are hell.'[7] When we imagine city life, we often find ourselves oscillating between utopia and dystopia. But for much of human history, the balance sheet has been pretty unfavourable. The risks of urban living, since the foundation of the very first cities, have been great. And one of the things that always threatens to turn a city from a miracle into a living hell is the risk of disease. Cities have always been exposed to diseases of crowding. The political scientist and anthropologist James C. Scott argues that most of the greatest killers in human history – cholera, smallpox, mumps, measles, influenza, chickenpox, even possibly malaria – 'arose only as a result of the beginnings of urbanism'.[8] When you pile up countless strangers together in one small, cramped space, you have the perfect environment for pathogens to multiply. In the present-day, Covid-19 spreads fastest when people gather together in large numbers: from Singaporean workers' dormitories to Protestant churches in South Korea. In the earliest of all cities, Uruk, the walls laid by the Seven Sages could not keep out sickness. Ancient texts are a testament to the prevalence of infectious diseases, including diphtheria, tuberculosis and cholera.[9] There is even evidence that the people of the ancient Near East understood the use of quarantine as a tool for stopping the spread of infectious disease.[10] In ancient China, oracle bones – the scapulae of cattle used for divination – record mass epidemics as early as 1500 BCE.[11] Ancient Egyptian medical papyri display a forensic attention to the variety of diseases, their symptoms and their possible causes, testifying both to the problems of transmissible illness in ancient Egypt and to growing medical knowledge that sought to treat or cure the afflictions of urban living.[12] The Old Testament is more broad-brush. It doesn't care so much about diagnosis, treatment or cure of the successive tides of plague that sweep through the books of the Old Testament. Instead, it is obsessed by the idea these are sufferings sent by a vengeful God. Later on, in the fifth century BCE, during the Peloponnesian War, plague ravaged Athens, killing tens of thousands, up to a third of the population, leading to a breakdown in public order. Thucydides wrote: 'The plague was the beginning of increased lawlessness in the city . . . Immediate pleasure, and any means profitable to that end, became the new honour and the new value. No fear of god or human law was any constraint.'[13] Thucydides himself was infected, and was lucky enough to survive; but even for survivors, he wrote, such events 'can enslave the spirit', being the kinds of things that 'happen suddenly, unforeseen, and quite beyond any reasonable prediction'.[14] In the early

Renaissance, in Boccaccio's *Decameron*, seven women and three men flee to a countryside villa to tell stories as plague ravages the city of Florence. When the plague arrived, Boccaccio says, 'In the face of its onrush, all the wisdom and ingenuity of man were unavailing.'[15]

Each individual plague, says Thucydides, is unforeseen and beyond reasonable prediction. But for all of human history, when it comes to urban living, the persistence of plagues and tides of sickness has not been the exception but the rule. And the risks have not been eradicated, even after the coming of modern sanitation, and the development of deeper knowledge of the causes and transmission of disease. Up to the nineteenth century, life expectancy in urban Liverpool was less than half that in rural Devon. And right up to the start of the twentieth century, as P. D. Smith writes in *City: A Guidebook for the Urban Age*, 'more people died in cities than were born in them, a situation referred to as the "urban graveyard effect"'.[16] Nevertheless, throughout history, cities have acted as a draw. For millennia, people have flooded into urban centres to take the place of those who have died, Dick Whittingtons looking to make their fortune where the streets are paved with gold.[17]

It can be hard to understand why anybody would ever have chosen to risk overcrowding, bad sanitation, noise, noxious smells and the chaos of city life, when they could be living the good life elsewhere. One answer is that many people throughout history have been compelled to live like this: they have been trapped in cities by poverty, bonded labour, forced resettlement or economic need. They have been city dwellers because they have had no other choice, because they have had nowhere else to go.[18]

This is part of the answer; but it is not the whole answer. The other reason is that cities are not just hells, they are also miracles. There is something in these great agglomerations of human life that gives us a buzz, that attracts us, that wakes us up to new possibilities. There is something about us that likes a crowd.

As a species, we are not just social but *ultra*social.[19] We have a hunger for grouping together. We are, as the biologist Frans de Waal points out, 'obligatorily gregarious'.[20] We love a good huddle. Our ultrasocial natures cause us to reach out beyond our immediate kin to connect with strangers. Neuroscientist Matthew Lieberman argues: 'This is what our brains were wired for: connecting with and interacting with others.'[21] Connection is what we are about.

This ultrasociality predates both urbanisation and agriculture. As we have seen, it is demonstrated by Neolithic feasting sites in the Near East, where mourners and pilgrims cooked up shared feasts with strangers, and even earlier by the bones around Neanderthal hearth fires that are testament to shared feasts. Our hunter-gatherer ancestors and their close cousins, although they lived day to day in small kin groups, would also get together in much larger numbers to share food, to undertake rituals, to make friends, to find mates.[22] Sedentism and urbanisation were not the origins of our love of crowds, but they were fuel to the fire. And from the very first cities, this delight in being together in large numbers, in being numerous, gave us a love of urban environments that somehow managed to outweigh the downsides. The ancient Sumerians were so enamoured with cities, they dreamed that Eridu, oldest of all Sumerian cities, was the creation of the god

Marduk. Eridu, they claimed, predated the great flood that overwhelmed humanity. It came before even humankind itself.[23]
It was the original, perfect, primal city, and the template for all
cities to come. Because, they reasoned, what could be more
perfect, more complete, more befitting of the gods than a city?

Other than my few weekly classes in the university, I had time on
my hands in Chengdu. So I took my bike out and explored the
city. I hunched on low plastic chairs at cheap street stalls
and slurped noodles. On weekends, I went to the parks where
grandmothers practised ballroom dancing, families ate picnics,
pensioners wrote calligraphy on the flagstones with large brushes
soaked in water and, among the bamboo, people practised
taijiquan and *qigong*. Or I visited temples and hung out in the
incense-fragranced dark, where people drank tea, chatted, bustled
round in groups and performed divinations with *jiao bei* moon
blocks, asking questions of the gods: should I leave him? Should
I marry her? Will my business do well this year?[24] In the evenings,
I went out to night markets to eat street food, losing myself in
the hubbub. And the heat and noise – the burning of the chillies,
the fizzing, numbing tingle of Sichuan pepper – helped me feel a
little less alone.[25] The *renao* hot noisiness that characterises all
Chinese social gatherings is played out a thousand times larger in
temples and in parks, on streets and in markets. This collective
fun, lived out in the company of strangers, is one of the things
that, for many people in China, make life worth living. City
dwellers leave their houses to stroll the streets, in search of this
'commotion, hustle and bustle, collective liveliness, excitement,
the activity of crowds, heat and noise'.[26] Because the whole point

of being in the city – at a dumpling stall, in a night market or in a temple – is that it is *renao*.[27]

Being together in large numbers can give rise to a collective joy, a festivity that, as Barbara Ehrenreich writes, 'generates inclusiveness'.[28] This festivity is its own kind of philoxenia: a love of strangeness and strangers. And in the busy chaos that results, Ehrenreich writes, strangers are the 'very source of this joy'.[29] In Chengdu at lunchtimes, I would order a plate of dumplings at the crowded street stall (the sign said they were 'award-winning') and nudge into a shared table. My fellow dumpling eaters budged up and grinned. Sometimes they smiled, said hello, asked where I was from. On occasion, we connected via WeChat, scanning each other's phones. But the point was rarely building long-term friendships. The point was the sheer delight being there together, enjoying the buzz of conversation, the fragrance and the steam.

In China, this delight in crowds has a long history. One of the most famous of all Chinese paintings is the long scroll 'Along the River during the Qingming Festival'. The first version of this scene was painted by Zhang Zeduan in the early twelfth century. It is more than five metres long and only twenty-five centimetres high. Zhang was a painter who – according to the colophon attached to the scroll – 'especially liked boats and carts, markets and bridges, moats and paths'.[30] The painting is a masterpiece, one much copied throughout Chinese history. Zhang's original is in the palace museum in Beijing; a Qing-dynasty reinvention of the scene, dating from 1737, is in the palace museum in Taipei. Both versions of the painting are miracles of minute detail. The scenes are like early Chinese versions of the *Where's Wally?*

books, but without the character in the striped top and bobble hat. On a crowded bridge, traders hawk their wares. The crew of a boat on the river, realising at the last minute it will not clear the bridge, rapidly lower the mast. The crowds on the bridge look on eagerly, pointing, gesticulating and helping out. Weary scholar-officials slump in tea shops. Two women ride together on donkeys, chatting. Traders carry goods into town by ox-drawn cart, by camel or on their own backs. A knife seller hawks his wares. As you follow the scroll to the right, the population thins: there are trees, streams, bucolic huts, mountains disappearing in the mist. It is as if the painting is telling us that these people are gathered together not because there is insufficient room in the world, but instead because sometimes it is worth gathering together simply for the excitement and the pleasure this brings. A similar enthusiasm for hot and noisy gatherings is there in literature too. In the Ming-dynasty novel the *Jin Ping Mei*, dating from around 1610, a small huddle of onlookers gazes down from an upper-floor window onto a bustling city street: 'dense crowds gathered in the lantern market, extremely hot and noisy. Hanging facing the street were tens of lantern-stands, and there were merchants lined up on all sides. Men and women came to enjoy the lanterns – red as flowers, green as willows – whilst carts and horses thundered past.'[31]

'What is the city but the people?' asks Shakespeare in *Coriolanus*. The rich interaction of city life is not just something many of us both crave and relish, it is also a spur to invention. 'Our move to the city,' P. D. Smith writes, 'produced an unprecedented flowering of culture, commerce and technology.'[32] There is something anarchic in the sheer fecundity of cities, something that resists orderliness and predictability. Cities have always pulled in two directions: on the one hand, they have tended towards centralised control, towards hierarchy and the repetition of the same old order; but on the other hand, they have tended centrifugally towards fragmentation, to the break-up of this centralised control, as the myriad encounters that make up the life of a city spiral off in new and unexpected directions.

The tension between the centripetal impulse towards order and the centrifugal forces of human interactions that fizz and pop like firecrackers is a large part of why cities have always been places of invention and reinvention. Ancient Athens was the cradle of Greek philosophy; Hellenistic philosophy flourished in Rome; multicultural Tang-dynasty Chang'an saw a flowering of poetry, storytelling and art;[33] medieval Baghdad was a centre for invention in everything from medicine to cuisine to science; Renaissance Florence gave birth to new philosophies, new approaches to art; and in the New York of the 1920s and 1930, the ferment of creative invention known as the Harlem Renaissance was to transform American culture and lead the way for the Civil Rights movement.

If cities are places of invention, one reason why people move to cities is to reinvent themselves. In his book on solitude, Michael Harris asks, 'Didn't some of us move to the city in the first place to become anonymous, to be uncounted, to go solo amidst a disorganised crowd – and thus, to find *ourselves*, lest we be informed too much by the findings of others?'[34] But although we might move to the city as an act of solitary reinvention, this is only one side of the story. Few move to the city simply to become hermits. There are, after all, better places to escape from the society of others. While we might move to become strangers from who we once were, we are also looking to reconnect, to be counted among new communities. And as we reconnect amid the city's disorganised crowds, we seek out new ways of finding ourselves, new ways of inventing ourselves, informed by the new connections that we make with strangers, by what we can find together.

This was why I went to Chengdu; it was why Elee took her job in London. After the years of being fixed in place by illness and fear, we wanted to open up the doors and windows. We wanted futures we could neither plan for nor anticipate. We wanted the kinds of unanticipated possibilities that can only come from taking risks, from journeying in strange places among strangers. 'The thing I would hate most,' Elee said as she recovered from her cancer treatment, 'is playing it safe, making our lives smaller. What happens if in ten years' time, we've not done the things that matter to us, because we're afraid of the cancer returning? What happens if we make our lives small, unnecessarily?'

As I settled into life in Chengdu, we talked often. We sent messages back and forth. I called home, caught Elee up with my news, and she told me hers. 'You sound well,' Elee said. 'You sound happy.' And I was. But I still found Chengdu disorientating. It was too big, too bewildering, impossible to hold in the mind all at once. I tried not to think about the big picture, but to focus on the small details instead: my new apartment, the routes and paths I took as I made my way through the city, teaching at the university, the philosophy salon. If I focused on these things, I said to myself, eventually I would find my tribe and Chengdu would become home.

The turning point came one weekend several months in, when I was visiting the Wenshu temple with a friend. It was a weekend afternoon and, as we had nothing else to do, we decided to visit the temple tea shop, where we ordered tea and sunflower seeds. Gusts of sparrows chirped in the bamboo. We cracked the seeds between our teeth and chatted. The sun glimmered weakly through the smog. It was then that I heard somebody calling my name: a philosopher from the salon who had decided he too wanted to spend his Saturday afternoon idling in the temple precincts. He came and joined us at the table, and we talked for an hour or so, as the sunflower husks piled up between us.

When it was time to leave, I realised what this encounter meant: that if in this city of fourteen million I could run into friends, Chengdu was a place, another place, where I now belonged.

11

Trouble with the Neighbours

As we crowd together into cities, we find the boundaries of our lives rubbing up against others who are neither kin nor complete strangers. Instead, these people occupy that strange, in-between state of neighbours. They are people with whom, in the absence of a shared past or even a shared future, we nevertheless share our corner of the world: so close that we may see them every day, so distant that we may know nothing at all about them.

Back when I was living in Myanmar in my ground-floor apartment, I used to worry about my neighbour. Every day, I stood at the sink washing dishes and looked out of the window to see her busying herself in the alleyway between our apartments. She hung up clothes on the bamboo drying racks she had built. She swept and cleaned. Sometimes she stared back at me through the window and I smiled. She never returned the smile. Instead, she turned away, her shoulders hunched, and retreated into the dark of her apartment.

My neighbour had taken control of all the space between our apartments. According to the terms of the lease, it belonged to us both equally, but she took it for her own. Along with the drying racks, she had built makeshift shelves and cupboards that blocked my back door. I couldn't get out into the alleyway even if I wanted to. She spent hours out there, and when I saw her, I tried to win her over. We were neighbours after all. But it was no good. She didn't like me.

Early mornings, she swept the back alley clean and left the sweepings outside my kitchen window. She dragged over things she had no more use for and piled them up against the outside wall of my apartment: old bits of furniture, sheets of glass, broken plastic toys. When I had the energy and the inclination, I picked up her rubbish and put it in the public rubbish bins only a few metres away. Sometimes, when I passed her apartment, I raised my hand to greet her, or asked her if she had eaten – a common form of greeting in Burmese.[1] She never replied.

The apartment was in a crumbling block in Bahan, a township that was developing fast. Set back from a busy intersection, the area in which I lived had so far been overlooked by developers; it was shabby and uncared for. On Google Maps, the satellite images showed the rusted roofing of the apartment blocks, anomalous among the new developments. It was so neglected that nobody had even bothered to name the streets. What passed for my address was more a set of instructions for finding the place. 'Apartment six, block eight, on the third street behind the hotel,' I told taxi drivers.

There were around 200 apartments in each of the three blocks. With most apartments housing a family, this made a population of well over 2,000. My apartment was at the end of the middle block, on top of the hill. My windows faced onto the street. Satellite dishes clustered on the walls. In the hot season, air conditioning units dripped water. Trees and plants grew out of the broken concrete. A fractured pipe on the upper floors meant that water cascaded continually down the wall outside the bathroom. Ropes hung down from the upper apartments, with bulldog clips attached to the ends. In the morning, the newspaper delivery man clipped copies of the *Light of Myanmar* and the *Mirror* to the ends of the ropes, and the residents reeled in the daily news.

It was a good place to live. The neighbourhood was always busy. The unnamed streets were lined with general stores, snack shops and dressmakers. At the lower end of the street a market opened morning and evening, selling fruit, vegetables, fish, meat and snacks. I woke every morning to patriotic songs blasted out on the school loudspeakers. Sometimes I would go to sit at the tea stall where the local men hunched over cups of tea made to order: *cho saint* (sweet and creamy), *cho paw* (light on sweetness) and *poun mhan* ('as it comes'). It was never quiet. Sellers of lottery tickets and *shwe yin aye* – Myanmar's punishingly sweet dessert made of sago, milk, sticky rice, white bread, ice and vast quantities of sugar – wheeled carts up and down the streets, calling through bullhorns. Only during the hot part of the day did the noise abate. The shops closed up. The stray dogs and cats lounged in the shade. People waited for the evening cool. Then it all started up again.

Over the months, it came to feel like home. I got to know the fried rice vendor who set up his cart every night in the market. He made the best fried rice I had ever tasted, a dollar a portion. Slowly, I made friends. The tea stall knew my order – a cup of *poun mhan* – without asking what I wanted. The woman who sold fried things at breakfast time picked out the best spring rolls. When I walked down the street, people said hello or waved. In the evenings, as I cooked in the kitchen, the local kids clustered round the window and asked me questions in Burmese: Where was I from? What was my name? How long was I there? What was I doing there? What was I cooking? What were my favourite Burmese foods? Why did I have a beard? Was I a Muslim?

At Thadingyut, the November full moon festival, the fried rice seller's son put on a bra and red dress. He danced in the street with a life-sized papier-mâché puppet. People threw banknotes and cheered. I showed the pictures of the puppet to my Burmese friends, but they just shook their heads. They were urban, modern Yangonites. They didn't know what any of it signified, and neither did I.

At religious festivals, the Buddhist monastery installed loudspeakers to broadcast chanting in Pali and sermons in Burmese. The sermons went on for ever. The pious local dogs joined in, barking their approval. On Independence Day, our neighbours set up a pole several storeys high, smeared with black engine oil. At the top of the pole was a plastic bag containing a small quantity of money. In teams, the young men from our district, dressed only in *longyis*, shinned up the pole to snatch the money. That evening, on the stage set up outside my window, a series of cross-dressing, gender-fluid performers sang, mimed and made lewd gestures to the popular songs that crackled through low-quality loudspeakers.

The apartment might have been crumbling, the windows ill-fitting, the bathroom blackened with mould and home to a small, ill-tempered frog; but increasingly Yangon felt like home. It was only in the mornings when I stood at the sink and caught the neighbour staring at me that I felt uneasy, aware I didn't fully belong.

Your neighbour is the person who – both literally and etymologically – 'dwells near'.[2] This 'nearness' is relative and depends to a large extent on culture. Several years ago, a friend from Finland told me a Finnish joke about a man who went to the forest so he could be alone. Tired of being bothered by others, he wanted to get away from it all. Deep in the wilderness, he built a hut by a stream. He cut the wood and built a snug little home. He hunted for deer and rabbits. He fished. When it got cold, he stoked up the fire in his hut and smoke curled from the chimney. He was happy in the forest. What more could a man want other than total solitude? But one day, as he was gazing at the surface of the stream, he saw some wood chips come floating by. The man was outraged. Somebody was impinging on his isolation. He took up his axe and walked upstream for two days. Eventually he saw the offender. There was another hut by the stream, much like his own, with smoke curling lazily from the chimney. And outside the hut, a man was sitting fishing. They were so alike they could have been brothers. The hermit crept up on the interloper, swung his axe and cut his head off. Then he walked two days downstream and returned to his cabin, happy to be alone once again.

'Ha-ha!' my Finnish friend said when he got to the end of the joke. If it was a joke, rather than a reminiscence of happier times. 'Ha-ha! This is Finland!'[3]

The idea of neighbourliness has a moral dimension. You might find that your relationships with your neighbours involve alienation, distance and the hostility that leads us to cut off each other's heads. But ideally, and for most of us at least, neighbourliness involves an ethic of mutual support and aid. Particularly when infrastructure is poor and people are pressed together into crowds, neighbourliness can become the fabric that holds communities together. It is, as one seventeenth-century writer in Lincolnshire wrote, a matter of the 'mutuall comforts of neighbourhood and intercourse one with another'.[4] In working-class communities in post-war Britain, Richard Hoggart writes, neighbourliness was 'part of the received, the orthodox, wisdom that you had to help each other, that this was almost essential to survival'. In a world where people 'could hardly ever afford to pay for services from elsewhere', neighbourliness mattered: it meant you could get your plumbing fixed, that there would be somebody to call upon in an emergency.[5] Neighbourliness is about attending to the web of interconnection by means of which we all get by. There is reciprocity here. One seventeenth-century poem reads: 'Lending to neighbour, in time of need / Wins love of thy neighbours, and credit doth breed.'[6] To be a good neighbour in an uncertain world is to gain credit, and who knows when this credit might need to be redeemed?

In Yangon, when the frequent power cuts and water outages in the ageing apartment blocks became too troublesome, I too came to rely on these neighbourly ties. Other than the old lady out the back, I got on with my neighbours well. So when the water pump broke down, I found myself standing in my *longyi* squinting at the pump with the man who lived in the apartment across the corridor in that friendly, easy camaraderie of mutual aid. Often these were problems without solutions – the pump didn't respond to any of our efforts to repair it. ('This is Myanmar,' my neighbour concluded philosophically. 'When there is power, there is no water. When there is water, there is no power.') But sometimes the knowledge that there is mutual support should you need it is more important than the problem itself.

From a young age, I had the virtues of neighbourly mutual aid instilled into me through the troubling commandment that you should love your neighbours. This injunction goes back all the way to Leviticus – 'Thou shalt love thy neighbour as thyself' – and is repeated in the New Testament so often as to become a slogan. As a child, part of the duty of neighbourly love involved visiting old ladies in our street. There was the woman across the road whose armchairs smelled of dust and piss, and who gave us sweets from an old tin. She was lonely and unhappy, and we found her company stultifying. We visited out of obligation and for the sweets. We stayed because we couldn't get away. And when we left, we were resentful for the time spent with her, and guilty for our resentment. Then there was the widow further down the street who took a liking to me. She was more interesting, and more frightening. She had thick net curtains that kept out the light. When I was eleven or twelve, she held me hostage with tea, biscuits and strange tales. She told me about a mysterious orb of light that one day came hurtling down her chimney. It danced around her living room, she said, then it shot back up the chimney and was gone. I can still see her hands, pale and fluttering in the darkness, her voice high and thin, as she talked about how the glowing ball danced in the air. And there was Betty, whom we liked. She was kind, and she had a colour TV. We went round to her house every week to watch David Attenborough's *Life on Earth*. Mum and Betty drank brandy, and I lay on my front, my head propped in my hands, enthralled by the axolotls and the sea slugs.

From the first, it was clear to me that the greatest difficulty posed by the commandment to love your neighbours lay in the fact that our neighbours are rarely chosen. They are the people who just happen to be next door, who just happen to be in the neighbourhood. Not only are our neighbours unchosen, there is no guarantee that their interests are the same as our own. No wonder, then, that trouble with the neighbours is an old, old story.

The Code of Hammurabi sets out laws for how to deal with your neighbours, covering everything from accidentally flooding your neighbour's fields to gossiping about their matrimonial affairs.[7] Records of official correspondence show that in ancient Greece officers of the law spent large parts of their professional lives tangled up in disputes between neighbours, particularly those relating to boundaries.[8] Boundary disputes are a recurrent concern throughout history. 'Love your Neighbour, yet pull not down your Hedge,' the poet George Herbert wrote in his *Outlandish Proverbs* of 1640.[9] In the same year, Reverend Ezekiel Rogers wrote to John Winthrop, governor of Massachusetts Bay

Colony, saying, 'A good fence helpeth to keep peace between neighbors, but let us take heed that we make not a high stone wall, to keepe us from meeting.' It is a proverb that goes back to the medieval Latin *Bonum est erigere dumos cum vicinis*, it is good to erect fences with the neighbours; and it is one that has equivalents elsewhere – in Japanese, in Hindi, in Norwegian and in German.[10] In Russia in the nineteenth century, boundary agreements between neighbours were sometimes guaranteed by the taking of oaths upon the lives of landowners' children – oaths taken in the presence of the children themselves.[11] And according to contemporary English law, if you are affronted by the branches of your neighbour's trees hanging over your garden, you have the right to cut them off, as long as the offending tree doesn't have a protection order; but you don't have the right to dispose of the branches at will, as they still belong to your neighbour, and you are required to politely return them.

Boundary disputes are not the only problems you might have with the neighbours. In ancient Greece, other complaints were common too: that they were not pulling their weight when it came to collective duties and obligations; and insinuations of moral and sexual depravity.[12] In the Tanimbar islands of Indonesia, my host, Ibu Lin, was a relentless observer and fierce critic of her neighbours, telling me who was trustworthy and who was not, who was liable to *main nakal* or 'play at evil', causing harm through witchcraft and black magic, and who was engaged in illicit sex. Among the last group, her complaint was usually that somebody was indulging in forbidden sexual acts 'under the banana palms' – a location I took to be more metaphorical than actual, given the lack of privacy a banana palm affords.

This moral surveillance is the flip side of the care that often characterises neighbourly communities. Aristotle lamented how, when engaged in joint ventures that serve the public good, it is easy to find ourselves finely attuned to our neighbour's faults and seemingly blind to our own.[13] And this human tendency to censoriousness is only intensified by the close, fierce bonds of community, the division between those who belong and those who don't, between the neighbours who are *like us* and the neighbours who are different, unsettling and troubling.

'Every neighbour is ultimately creepy,' writes Slavoj Žižek.[14] In Yangon, the more I tried to connect with my neighbour in the back alley, the more I failed. And eventually it dawned on me: as far as she was concerned, it was me who was the creepy neighbour. I was living in her back yard, but I was cut loose from the social fabric. I was there on her doorstep, going about some obscure business she knew was no business of hers. I wasn't obviously a Buddhist. I didn't have any ties with the place or the community. When I wore a *longyi*, I was creepy because I was trying to fit in. When I wore trousers, I was creepy because I didn't fit in. If I spoke to her in Burmese, I was creepy because I was trying to bridge the gap between us. If I didn't speak to her, I was creepy because I was keeping myself to myself.

At first I thought she might soften towards me, that all it needed was time. But it was no use. My presence at the sink every day spooked her. By being there, I made her world worse. And it was hard to see this as solely an irrational hatred. Yangon was changing fast. Foreigners were flooding in, with their fancy MacBooks, their strange habits, their coffee-slurping ways. As investment capital poured into the country in the wake of the reforms that started in 2011, the streets of the old colonial-era city were undergoing a creeping gentrification. Downtown buildings were being turned into swanky bars and clubs. In some areas frequented by foreigners, you were now never more than twenty metres from a flat white. Property prices were rising fast. In my neighbourhood, there was a new cafe – Singapore style – which served international food, fancy coffees, cocktails, gluten-free options. I used to go and hang out there with friends. I knew the owner and the staff. It was a welcome reprieve from the heat and the chaos. But all of this was a world where my neighbour had no foothold. No wonder she found me creepy: I was here on her back doorstep, the most obvious representative of this brave new world.[15]

Recently, an urban development project in the Netherlands designated Yangon a 'city of the future'.[16] It is not hard to see why. Yangon has a thriving artistic culture: writing, visual arts, photography, film, art galleries, feminist performance art collectives and an audacious punk activist scene. As capital flows inwards, it is becoming increasingly cosmopolitan. Yangon is, and always has been, a multicultural and multi-religious city. Alongside the famous pagodas, the downtown area in Yangon is crowded with other places of worship that testify to this diversity – mosques, churches of all kinds, a synagogue, numerous Chinese temples, places of Hindu worship. Yangon was the original 'plural society', a term coined by the colonial administrator James Furnivall in 1948 to refer to the mixture of communities and religions within the city.[17] Military rule put a lid on this richness of culture; but it did not eradicate it. And when I was there, Yangon was stretching its limbs again. Alongside the resurgent local culture, there were foreigners everywhere. Many of them lived downtown, where investors took old colonial apartments, refurbished them and let them out at a premium to long-term foreign residents. It was a lucrative game. With enough capital, you could fancy up an apartment, put in the things foreigners like and charge much more than a local tenant would pay. As Yangon was being gentrified, in the process local tenants were being priced out.

It is easy to see where the foreign hipsters live in Yangon. All you have to do is stand outside an apartment block at night and look up at the windows. You can tell where they are by the colour of the light streaming out onto the street. Burmese people like their light bulbs cool and tinged with blue. Many of the newly arrived foreigners prefer their lights warm and yellow-hued. Downtown, the light streaming from Yangon's colonial-era apartments was slowly turning from blue to yellow. And I was part of this. After I arrived in Yangon, I spent days scouring the supermarkets for yellow-tinged light bulbs. When I found them, I changed the cool lights in the apartment for warm ones, shifting the apartment along the colour spectrum. My neighbour was right to mistrust me. In Bahan, I was the vanguard of an uncertain future. I was another foot soldier in a rag-tag invading army, colonising the high-rises with our strange habits, our incompetent Burmese and our yellow light bulbs.

In Yangon, as in many cities across the world, there is a tension between cosmopolitanism and localism, between the transient strangers who make the city their home and those whose belonging is anchored by deeper, more long-standing ties of family and community. The fluctuating, cosmopolitan pluralism that characterises life in many contemporary cities is nothing new. To flourish, cities have always depended both on passing strangers and on those anchored more firmly in place. In her book on strangers in medieval cities, Miri Rubin writes that, in the Middle Ages: 'Living in towns and cities meant living with strangers.'[18] Some of these strangers were temporary migrants – merchants, students, those on church or government business, travellers, thrill-seekers, refugees fleeing war and poverty; others were members of settled communities – like German merchants in London or Tuscan bankers in Provence – who nevertheless maintained their difference and their strangeness.

The idea of cosmopolitanism as a way of managing living alongside difference goes back, like so many other things, to the plural society that was ancient Athens. It was the invention of the philosopher Diogenes of Sinope. Diogenes lived unconventionally, deliberate in his attempts to flout social mores. In Athens, he made his home in a large, abandoned wine jar. Has was notorious for his odd behaviour, in particular a fondness for public masturbation. When challenged, he'd roll his eyes and say, 'If only one could put an end to hunger by rubbing one's stomach.'[19] But Diogenes's disreputable behaviour had a philosophical intent. He wanted to break free from the shackles of a culture he found self-deceiving and dishonest. He argued that the best life could be found not through our affiliations to kin, or to a tribe, or to a city-state, but instead through seeing ourselves as citizens (*polites*) of the entire *kosmos*. Diogenes was the first *kosmopolites*, the first cosmopolitan.

Because of his unconventional lifestyle, Diogenes's enemies referred to him as 'the dog'. Diogenes embraced the insult. A dog does not have affiliation to a flag or to a nation. As long as it has food, shelter, water and companionship, it can be happy anywhere. Diogenes and his followers came to be known as the dog-like philosophers: the *Kynikos*, or Cynics. You could tell Cynic philosophers by their backpack, robe and stout stick. The early Cynics were the original counter-cultural dropouts. They were footloose, travelling from place to place, shrugging off the demands of polite society, preferring to curl up in a warm spot in the sun and snooze, like the dogs they were.

But for those who are less footloose, more fixed in place, the forces of cosmopolitanism need to be resisted. One Saturday afternoon in Yangon, I found a red plastic bowl on the kitchen work surface. Somebody had slid back the mosquito screen, put down the bowl and slid the screen closed. Inside the bowl was a brown, greasy porridge. It smelled faintly of fried beans. When I poked at it with a fork, I found underneath the porridge a black, fibrous sludge. The sludge smelled of oil and badness. I emptied the contents into the toilet and flushed. Only later, when I looked into the toilet bowl, did I see the gleaming metal screw and rusted nail.

Burmese friends knew what it was. Black magic, they said. It was the hairy sludge that was the main giveaway. In Burmese, the sludge was called *apin*. The word literally means something that stops something up, something that blocks or wedges. It is used to refer to any foreign body that, insinuated into the body of its victim, causes harm. In his book *Burmese Supernaturalism*, the anthropologist Melford Spiro writes that *apin* is 'usually human hair, but sometimes leather, raw beef, or animal sinew'.[20] When ingested, according to Burmese belief, *apin* multiplies. It fills up the victim's stomach, leading to excruciating pains. In extreme cases, it leads to death.

Fear of *apin* makes people mistrustful of taking food from strangers. Even in the cities, parents tell their children living away from home for the first time that they shouldn't accept food from strangers, out of fear of black magic. 'Did you eat the porridge?' my Burmese friends asked. I told them I threw it away. They said I did the right thing. I spoke to my Burmese teacher. She told me I was lucky. Once she had eaten a *pau'si* – a steamed bun – prepared by an expert in black magic. The Burmese equivalent of Chinese *baozi*, these buns are usually filled with meat, sweet molasses or bean paste. But when my teacher bit into the bun, it was full of *apin*. She ended up with a mouthful of black, fibrous hair. She threw the bun away.

Later that day, she fell ill. Her belly distended. She became delirious, broke out in a fever, had strange hallucinations. Her husband and one of his relatives took her to see a monk. As they led her across the threshold of the monastery, her body recoiled in disgust. They had to carry her into the monastery by force. The monk exorcised her. She vomited up a whole bellyful of black fibres. And then she recovered.

A week after it appeared so unexpectedly, I saw the same red bowl in my neighbour's back yard, propped up by the door. It was there all day. It looked as if it had been left there as a sign or a warning. Then, by dusk, it was gone.

I wondered in the weeks that followed whether it really was my neighbour who had left the porridge or somebody else. I could not be certain; but I couldn't think who else would want to cast a spell on me. And if it was her, it was hard to blame her. If Yangon was becoming a city of the future, what place did my neighbour have in this future? And, from her point of view, what was I if not *apin* – a foreign contaminant in the community where I had made my home?

Cosmopolitanism, in its contemporary form, may seem to many like an appealing idea: an urbane ethic for the modern age. In his book on cosmopolitanism, Kwame Anthony Appiah writes, 'One distinctively cosmopolitan commitment is to *pluralism*. Cosmopolitans think that there are many values worth living by and that you cannot live by all of them.'[21] This recognition seems like a good start when it comes to getting on with the neighbours. But such pluralism of values becomes problematic when, as I did, you plonk yourself down in the midst of a community whose values are anything but plural.

In Yangon, I tried to fit in with the community. When there were festival days, I went out and joined the revellers. One day, our street was closed off for a *naikban ẓay* or 'nirvana market'. Members of the local community – both small businesses and individual households – set up numbered tables laden with free gifts: food, snacks, small presents. At the end of the street, members of the public queued up for lottery numbers, written on pieces of card at random. Then when the street was open, the crowds ran to find the table that corresponded to their number to collect their free gift. It was a ritual that, despite its Buddhist origins, was observed by Christians, Buddhists and Muslims alike.[22] I loved days like this, the buzz of it, the sense of community. I did my best to get involved. On Independence Day, as my neighbours were celebrating their liberation from British colonial rule, I made chocolate chip cookies to give out. I thought it was the least I could do. My neighbours, fearful perhaps that the cookies contained not only chocolate chips but also *apin*, took the cookies only reluctantly. But while I tried to fit in, my neighbours knew I also had commitments elsewhere, a foot in another camp. They knew that, cosmopolitan that I was, I never *fully* belonged.

The partialness of this belonging has always been a problem with cosmopolitanism, at least from the point of view of more settled communities. The fear – not entirely unjustified – is that citizens of the cosmos cannot have the same commitment to the local. At worst, cosmopolitanism translates into a disdain for localism. This was true of Diogenes; and it was true of the ancient Cynics who tried to undercut the problems of living with strangers by finding a common ground in nature, ducking out of the game of culture altogether. Diogenes and his fellow cosmopolitans held all states, all cities, all cultures in contempt. If they could be equally happy everywhere, it was because they were also equally disengaged everywhere. This image of the cynical (in both senses), disengaged cosmopolitan still haunts today's political discourse. In her Conservative Party Conference speech of 2016, the then prime minister of the UK, Theresa May, conjured the spectre of untethered cosmopolitans, with a glassy disdain for everyone and everything, a privileged metropolitan elite, aloof from all affiliations, who despised everyone equally. 'If you believe you are a citizen of the world,' she said, 'you are a citizen of nowhere.'[23]

But a different kind of cosmopolitanism is possible, one that, as Kwame Anthony Appiah writes, is rooted in 'a simple recognition that our lives are interrelated in ways that transcend boundaries'.[24] A cosmopolitanism built on the desire not to disconnect but to connect. Because from the very beginning, the problem with cosmopolitanism was not that the cosmopolitans were dogs, but that they were not dog-like enough. Dogs, after all, love to connect. They work the room. They go round wagging their tails, asking, Will you be my friend? What about you? And *you*? If dogs are natural cosmopolitans, their cosmopolitanism isn't built upon universal disdain, but instead upon multiple loves, multiple engagements and multiple affiliations. Any reasonable cosmopolitanism recognises that we *need* others, that even Diogenes with his stout stick and his backpack and his robe was enmeshed in webs of mutual dependence. The choice we face, social animals that we are, is not between dependence and independence. It is not even between cosmopolitanism and localism. It is between different ways of allowing our mutual dependence to play out.

When I saw my neighbour in Yangon, I was often reminded of my first year of living in Birmingham, back in the UK. I was new to the city and desperately short of cash. I rented a cheap flat in Balsall Heath. It had no heating, and when it snowed in winter, it was colder inside than out. Most of my neighbours were Pakistani Muslims from Kashmir. The languages of commerce were south Asian – Urdu and Mirpuri – with a smattering of English. I managed to get by with English mixed with the fragments of Urdu left over from my time in Pakistan.

Balsall Heath immediately felt like home. It brought back memories of Pakistan. There were cheap restaurants where you could get roti and curry for next to nothing. The supermarket at the end of my street sold piles of inexpensive fruit, vegetables and spices. I liked my neighbours. They waved at me when I passed, calling out, '*As-salam alaykum.*' I waved back and replied, '*Wa alaykum as-salam.*' Although I was new to the community, it felt like a place of mutual aid, a place where people looked out for each other.

The boundaries in Balsall Heath were fluid. Kids spilled out into the streets, people sat out on the doorsteps and called out to passers-by. I liked the blurring of the public and private, the way my neighbours hammered on the door to say hello, or ask if I could help them out with filling in official forms in English, so they could claim the benefits they were entitled to. There were fences, but none were high enough, or solid enough, to prevent friendly chat. The wall that separated my tiny front garden from that of my neighbours only came up to my knees. Out the back, the Yemeni kids who lived in the house behind clambered onto crates to peer over into my back yard, or looked through the gaps in the fence and called out hello. Cats came and went, slipping between worlds. Cooking smells and noise seeped through the walls, the way they would in a Manggarai village. People yelled to have their ball thrown back into the street. Unruly buddleia blurred the human-made boundaries in a fuzz of purple flowers, a feast for bees.

Balsall Heath seemed to me a kind of paradise. But sometimes

I saw the lonely old woman who lived on her own in a small house down the road. She was white British and I guessed she had been born and bred there, that she had spent her whole life in the area. Perhaps her ancestors had lived there too. But over the decades, the world had changed around her. As she walked down to the supermarket, I could see her shoulders hunched with misery, as if she felt she did not belong. Sometimes she cursed people, angry at them being there at all, angry about the world that had changed around her.

It would be easy to dismiss her as a xenophobe, to say she just needed to get over it. But sometimes I wondered what it must be like to see businesses closing and then reopening so they were strange and new. To find yourself surrounded by new neighbours, who came from a world you didn't understand and, because of not understanding, that you didn't like. To go to the corner shop and fail to make yourself understood. To have yourself become a stranger as the world changed around you. A different culture. Different food. A different language. The shops full of different things.

'The reality is,' writes Jon Bloomfield in his book on the changing face of multicultural Birmingham, 'that successive waves of migration have changed the character of all the major European cities for ever. Living with difference is one of the greatest challenges for European politics in the twenty-first century.'[25] How do you build bridges between neighbours in places that are a hubbub of religions, ideologies, lifestyles, cultures and foods? In this kind of environment, what is the glue that can hold communities together?

One answer to this question was provided in the early Middle Ages by the philosopher and etymologist Isidore of Seville. 'A city,' he wrote, '*civitas*, is a multitude of people united by a bond of fellowship . . . it decides upon and holds the lives of many people.'[26] What constitutes a city, the city's fabric, is this warp and weft of human connection. To allow these connections to flourish, the right conditions need to be in place. Bloomfield gives an outline of some of the conditions that can help: a willingness to look at economic inequality and the role it plays in community division; building human-scale infrastructure; supporting education; the provision of public space where people can 'meet, socialise and relax'; a commitment to civic and human rights; and an equal access to justice.[27] These are the things that support the flourishing of our philoxenia and that work against the fear and suspicion of our in-built xenophobia.

But when these things are lacking, the social fabric frays. I knew in Yangon that my trouble with the next-door neighbour wasn't personal. It wasn't that she disliked me individually. It was that for her I represented a real harm, a genuine injustice. Her city was changing about her. Her community was changing. And she was marginalised, excluded from these changes. Yangon's rush to development involved multiple injustices, and it hit the economically disadvantaged most of all.[28] It would have been easier for the old lady in Yangon to tolerate me, her neighbour, if she was secure in the knowledge that her home and her community were safe. But in the face of the blind cruelty of rapidly developing Yangon, the awesome, terrifying powers of investors and property developers, in the end, she resorted to the only tool for resistance she had.

*

Eventually, my contract in Yangon was up and it was time to leave. I said goodbye to my Burmese friends. I ate fried rice for a final time at the market. I visited the tea stall, where I sat watching the monsoon rains and drinking a last cup of *poun mhan*. Then I packed my bags and called a cab to take me to the airport.

As I was leaving, I thought of my neighbour. Whether or not she was responsible for the porridge, it must have been a relief for her to see me go. And if it was her doing, perhaps she consoled herself with the thought the magic had worked, at least for the time being: the *apin* expelled from the body of her community; the sickness in remission; the lights from the apartment – for a while at least – turning back from yellow to blue.

12

Loneliness

Sometimes I wonder why I do it to myself. Why do I leave the company of the people I know and love, and seek out new ways of living among strangers? Why do I put myself in the path of loneliness? Now, when I read my diaries from Pakistan – a shy, vulnerable eighteen-year-old, travelling alone 5,000 miles from home – I see how achingly lonely I was. This was long before email, before social media, before the internet. What communication I had with home came from letters I picked up poste restante from small-town post offices. If the letters arrived at all, the postmarks were weeks, sometimes months old. Occasionally I sent a telegram, paid by the word: *In Dera Ghazi Khan. Stop. All well. Stop. Missing you. Stop.* In a cheap hotel in the small town of Thatta, feverish and delirious after days of sickness, I wrote in a spidery hand in my diary: 'I want somebody to bring me a cold lemon squash.' In Rawalpindi, I had a dream that I was back home and when I woke in the morning I jotted down: 'The distance is so big, I cannot think about it clearly.' Up in the damp, misty hill resort of Nathia Gali, I dreamed my hotel room, with its blue expanse of carpet, was my grandmother's house.

This loneliness recurs whenever I am far from home. In Indonesia, working as an anthropologist, I felt the tug of home even though I didn't want to be there. And in Chengdu, I stood at the window of my apartment every night and I looked at the pulse of neon lights in the city, learning their patterns and how they repeated, and I throbbed and ached with loneliness. I missed Elee. I missed my friends. I missed more or less everything.

To console myself, I translated classical Chinese poets. One of my favourites was Yu Xuanji, the ninth-century courtesan whose poems dripped with loss and loneliness and hunger. I felt a kind of solidarity with her loneliness, reaching across time and space.

> Drinking in farewell, a thousand cups
> will not wash away my sadness;
>
> I leave, my guts knotted a hundred times,
> no way of untangling them.
>
> The orchids gone,
> I return to the spring garden,
>
> willows on either shore,
> I stumble to board the boat:

meeting, parting, already grieving,
the clouds are all unanchored.

Our affection must study
the endless flowing waters.

In the seasons of flowers,
knowing it's hard for us to meet,

not yet ready for weariness,
I get drunk in the jade tower.[1]

I stood at the window, up in my jade tower, drinking beer, my head against the glass. In the sky, the clouds were all unanchored. My guts knotted and unknotted. And I dreamed of home.

There is freedom in this chosen loneliness. Despite the sting of it, I have always relished the experience of being alone.[2] In my Buddhist days, I courted loneliness on solitary retreats in cold, draughty bothies up on Hadrian's Wall, or in cabins, huts and caravans in remote corners of England and Wales. I spent weeks out in the wilds, looking for the 'humming silence' of which Rebecca Solnit writes – that space in which solitude seeps into your physical being, so even language becomes puzzling and strange, the place where words metamorphose into 'strange rocks you may or may not turn over'.[3] I imagined myself part of a long tradition of hermits and sages and misanthropes, seeking to commune with God, or with nature, or with their higher ideals. I meditated for hours a day. I picked nettles and boiled them up with lentils to eat.[4] I wore strange headwear. I gazed out at the rain, convinced enlightenment was just around the corner. After several years of making sporadic forays into the hills in search of spiritual truth, I tired of all the nettles and of the endless quest for enlightenment; but my love of solitude has continued, long outlasting my Buddhist aspirations. There is still something I relish in this kind of aloneness.

I have sought out loneliness in cities too. Years ago, I visited Prague for a philosophy conference. I arrived a day early, and had twenty-four hours to myself with nothing at all to do to fill the time. On the first morning I was there, it was misty. I left the hostel where I was staying and went to sit alone on a bench near the river. It was the kind of weather where you wouldn't be surprised to see Kafka himself looming through the fog. And all at once, I felt my body pulse with the sheer bodily thrill of solitude, with the knowledge that nobody here knew me. It was a physical bliss, something transporting and alive; and it was so overwhelming, it took my breath away.

But this sort of loneliness, this chosen solitude, is a privilege. I knew when I was out in the wilds that I was not truly alone, that I had people I could depend on, that if the nettles and the rain and the meditation got too much, I could flee my retreat and be welcomed back into the company of others. I knew in Prague that the following day I would be hanging out with a ragged bunch of philosophers, chatting and drinking wine.

But when loneliness is unchosen, when there is no other option, it can be ruinous. Today, loneliness proliferates, part-icularly in our vast, sprawling cities. Part of the reason is the mobility of the world we live in. When our intimates are no longer close by, when the fabric of kin and neighbourliness is torn and tattered, then we find ourselves without the support we need. A government survey in the UK in 2020 found that under Covid-19 restrictions, 5 per cent of the population felt lonely 'always' or 'often', and when asked about their well-being over 30 per cent said they had experienced loneliness in the previous seven days.[5]

According to *New Scientist*, a staggering range of disease risks coalesce around loneliness, including heart attack, cancer and neurodegenerative diseases.[6] Loneliness disturbs our sleep. It puts us at greater risk of chronic illness. It correlates with higher blood pressure, cardiovascular problems, depression, an increased risk of Alzheimer's disease and cognitive decline in old age, and a weakened immune system.[7] It is often claimed the impact of loneliness on mortality is the same as smoking fifteen cigarettes a day.[8] Loneliness, all the signs suggest, is dangerous to our mental and physical health, and to our well-being both individually and collectively.[9]

In her cultural history of loneliness, Fay Bound Alberti writes that loneliness lives as much in the body as in the mind. Loneliness 'does not happen in a vacuum but is deeply connected with all aspects of our mental, physical, and psychological health. Loneliness is a whole-body affliction.'[10] It is felt in the physical thrill that runs through us as we sit on a bench in Prague, in the ache that accompanies an unwished-for solitude, in the hungering to touch and be touched, in the sense of awkwardness when we long to connect – with a longing so fierce it feels it might burn – but don't know how, or do not dare.

What makes loneliness so devastating is our creature need to touch and be touched. We are tactile beings. Like our primate ancestors, at some basic level we want nothing more than to sit around in groups and engage in mutual grooming. We want to hold and caress, to reach out and poke each other, to tickle and hug and cradle.[11] Metaphors of touch pervade the language of social life – *get in touch*, we say; or, *it's good to be in touch*; and this obsession with touch is more than mere metaphor. Touch, even between strangers, builds relationships. It makes us feel less alone. It strengthens trust. It helps alleviate both psychological and physical pain.[12] Touch diminishes stress and boosts immunity.[13] Among children, it is essential not just to social and emotional development, but also to physical development.[14]

Even before the arrival of Covid-19, it was widely reported that in many parts of the world we were living in the middle of a crisis of touch.[15] In our mobile, online, fragmented society, people can go for days without touching or being touched. 'When disconnected, socially or emotionally, from others, people can get ill,' Alberti writes. 'Deprived of touch, of meaningful human engagement, people can die.'[16] The Dutch film-maker Lieza Röben invented a term for this deprivation: *huidhonger*, or 'skin-hunger'.[17] And this need for touch, this skin-hunger, is multiplied manyfold when we know that touch can mean contagion, even death. Covid-19 physical-distancing measures have compounded loneliness. Locked down in our individual lives, the risks of opening up our homes are vividly real. Invite somebody in and you invite in the potential for disaster. On the street and in shops, we skirt round crowds. On public transport, we shuffle up the carriage to where there are fewer people, because our lives might very well depend on it. The vast grief of it all – the physical distancing, the isolation – is hard to contemplate. During long periods of isolating alone, many suffer months without touching another human being. In hospitals, the dying spend their final hours without holding or being held by those they love. And with the easing of restrictions, when friends meet in the street, they knock elbows or tap toes, suppressing the urge to hold out their arms and step into an embrace.

We are social animals, made for connection more than aloneness. The primatologist Frans de Waal argues: 'We are not born as loners. Our bodies and minds are not designed for life in the absence of others.'[18] This goes against much of what the philosophers tell us about human life. In his book on the philosophy of loneliness, Lars Svendsen writes: 'In a certain sense, we are born, live and die alone. We all have a self that relates to itself and is conscious of its separation from others.'[19] Meanwhile, the existential philosopher Patricia Joy Huntington imagines loneliness as our 'true home', and says that the purpose of this 'wild venture of life' is to journey back to this aloneness.[20] Bertrand Russell, whom Svendsen quotes in his book, writes in his autobiography about the 'strange loneliness of every separate soul'.[21] Russell claims that our connection with others comes out of the discovery in them of the same loneliness that afflicts ourselves. If the philosophers are to be believed, loneliness is not something that comes and goes, something we might experience under certain conditions. Instead, it is a metaphysical burden, something rooted in who and what we are.

But anthropology and human history tell us that we are

social animals; and like other social primates, at the deepest levels of our being we are made for connection. In modern hunter-gatherer societies, like the societies in which our ancestors lived, people are rarely alone. Our ancestors spent their days huddling and snuggling, joking and teasing, telling stories and exchanging gossip, arguing and falling out, flirting and jockeying for power. And in these societies, people have a lot of time on their hands: the amount of leisure time in hunter-gatherer societies is far more than in agricultural communities, and far more than in the contemporary world.[22] This means there is a lot of time for all the social interaction: in these societies, even non-leisure-time activities like gathering food or hunting or tending to living spaces are inherently social. People living in societies such as this, as Jared Diamond writes, might have many problems, but loneliness will not be one of them.[23] Or if loneliness is a problem, it will be necessarily fleeting: not a psychological fault line or an unhealable rift, but the temporary experience of bodily separation from the rest of your crowd.

Loneliness researchers John and Stephanie Cacioppo see loneliness as the fear and anxiety that come from finding yourself on the social perimeter.[24] Fish get twitchy when they are on the outer fringes of the shoal. Birds try to avoid being on the outside of the flock. To be on the perimeter is to be exposed to danger, to risk. In this sense, loneliness is adaptive.[25] Those among our distant ancestors who enjoyed solitary, Wordsworthian wanderings were the ones who got eaten before they had a chance to pass on their genes. Meanwhile our ancestors who felt that familiar stab of anxiety at finding themselves alone hurried back to the warm huddle of their kin, and it was their genes that prevailed.

Sustained loneliness is not what we are made for; it is not an inherent part of the existential burden we carry. Instead, it is a bodily response to finding ourselves on the outside, one that told our ancestors it was time to reconnect, and plunge back into the circle of belonging where our best security and protection is to be found.

The historian Jill Lepore writes: 'Before modern times, very few human beings lived alone. Slowly, beginning not much more than a century ago, that changed.'[26] Loneliness has a history; and that history runs in parallel with the history of a loss of touch, with our bodily separation from each other. We no longer live in hunter-gatherer bands. We no longer hang out with our kin and our friends every minute of our lives. More than at any other time in history, we find ourselves bodily apart. Urbanisation, and the great reordering of social relationships that follows from our crowding into cities, has accelerated this separation. 'You can be lonely anywhere,' Olivia Laing writes, 'but there is a particular flavour to the loneliness that comes from living in a city, surrounded by millions of people.' It has the sting of cruelty about it, this knowledge that you are living alongside countless others, but there is nobody to touch or to hold, nobody with whom to talk, to share confidences, to joke around and to gossip. The loneliness of the city, says Laing, is 'an absence or paucity of connection, closeness, kinship: an inability, for one reason or another, to find as much intimacy as is desired'.[27]

One reason for urban loneliness is crowdedness: it is simply overwhelming to be surrounded by so many others. There may indeed be something in us that loves a crowd; but there is also evidence that crowdedness can itself lead to social withdrawal and to loneliness. When there are too many people out there, we don't have the machinery to deal with all those transitory connections, so we fall back onto our own resources, and we find ourselves lonelier than we were before.[28] How can we make sense of this many lives? We might know that there are people out there who are kind and good, people with whom we could connect, even become friends, but how to make a start?

Another reason for urban loneliness is the problem of trust. Living among strangers, it is hard to know how and when we should extend trust. Loneliness, the feeling of being on the periphery, gives us a heightened threat response. When we are lonely, it is then that we most tend to default to mistrust; and when we are inclined to mistrust others, it is then that we are at our loneliest.[29] We are less likely to connect, more risk-averse.[30] The cycle of mistrust and loneliness, once it kicks into action, is hard to stop. Research shows that when loneliness degrades our ability to trust, the consequent mistrust is directed not just outwards, towards strangers, but also towards those who are closest to us.[31] As loneliness becomes malignant, it shifts from being a symptom of the breakdown of our social relationships to playing its own part as a contributing cause.

Much of what is written on contemporary loneliness focuses on the landscapes of the cities where now more than half of us live. But cities do not have the monopoly on loneliness; and as people migrate from rural areas into cities and towns, they leave behind gaps and voids where loneliness can multiply. Communities are hollowed out. Houses stand empty and crumble away, or are bought up as holiday homes, occupied for only part of the year. Those who are left behind are often the very old or the very young, the curmudgeonly, the sick or the ones who love the land so much that they cannot bear to leave. In rural China, when adults move from rural villages to the city to find work, they often leave behind children in the care of grandparents and members of the extended family. This puts the left-behind children at significant risk of loneliness.[32] The elderly too, as their children migrate into the cities, experience increased loneliness and isolation.[33] And this pattern of increasing rural loneliness is replicated everywhere from the Americas to Europe, and from Asia to Africa.

Some places have attempted to turn the tide by reversing the flow, importing strangers from elsewhere. In the Sicilian town of Sambuca, the houses stand empty. The municipal authorities have put them up for sale starting at one euro each. Sambuca is famous for its Moorish architecture; the houses come complete with courtyard, palm gardens and citrus trees. All you have to do if you want to sign up for an idyllic new life in the shadow of Mount Etna is be willing to invest 15,000 euros over three years to restore your new home to its former glory. There are similar schemes elsewhere in the world, from Spain to Japan, seeking to revive rural communities by bringing in strangers who might, in future, become locals.

It is mid-September and I am in Vidin province in north-west Bulgaria. The provincial capital of Vidin is weirdly, eerily beautiful. It has spectacular views of the Danube, a fortress the foundations of which were first laid in the tenth century, a mosque surrounded by quiet gardens, the ruins of an abandoned synagogue and some impressive Bulgarian Revival architecture. But despite all this, Vidin is almost deserted. The whole town is blanketed with an air of somnolence. Even though it is the weekend, the streets are empty. Half the shops have their shutters pulled down. The restaurants and cafes have one or two customers at most. There are signs of life, here and there. Vidin has a functioning symphony orchestra. The local drama group is staging a performance of *Cabaret*. The pedestrian boulevards are being resurfaced. But nobody pretends Vidin is flourishing.

Over the previous decades, the province – one of the most impoverished regions in all Europe – has seen a catastrophic demographic collapse. The population has almost halved in the last three or four decades, from 166,680 in 1985 to an estimated 84,865 in 2018. The decline in Vidin itself has been less catastrophic, but over the same period the town has still lost almost a third of its residents.

I am in Vidin because I have been invited to a party out in Negovanovtsi village, several miles from town. There is apparently an erratic local bus service, but information is hard to come by. At the bus station in Vidin, they tell me that there are no buses and suggest I go to the bus stop for local services. I make my way there and stick my head round the door of a rusting minibus to ask the sleepy pensioners dozing on the wood and metal-tubing seats. The old people look surprised by my broken Bulgarian. They confer for a while, then tell me I should go to the bus station. I give up and flag down a taxi instead.

When the taxi drops me in the village square, the party is just getting started. A nine-piece brass band is playing fat, cheerful tunes. The logo on the bass drum reads '*Dunavski Ritmi*', or 'Danube Rhythms'. Outside the *chitalishte* – the 'reading room' that serves as community hall, library and education centre – the villagers have hung textiles and intricate lacework. A table, covered with red, traditional tablecloths, groans with local food: *banitsa* pastries both sweet and savoury, polenta cake, fig tart, stuffed peppers, soup, chocolate layer cake, bread. In the square, in the shade of pine, horse chestnut and birch trees, people are dancing the *horo*, the circle dance. Some of the dancers are old people. But there are young people too, dressed in Bulgarian traditional dress: embroidered smocks, woollen hats, shoes pointed at the end.

The party marks the end of the project called *Rezidentsiya Baba*: Baba Residence or 'Granny Residence'. The project, run by a Bulgarian organisation called Ideas Factory, sends urban young people on short residencies to live and work alongside elderly villagers. The website says the residency 'combines design thinking, ethnographic fieldwork skills and . . . the simple wisdom of a rural lifestyle – with a granny – for a period of 3 to 5 weeks'.[34] The purpose of the project is to build cross-generational solidarity and to develop new projects and initiatives to revive these rural communities. The young people are hosted by the elderly residents. They live together and work together. The young people learn local crafts and traditional skills. And together the participants devise creative projects that contribute to the longer-term welfare of the villages, to their economic and social development.[35]

In the years since it was first started, the project has worked in villages all over Bulgaria. It has led to releases of professionally recorded CDs sung by choirs of elderly residents. It has contributed to the revival of regional libraries, replaced church bells, renovated and reopened bakeries, opened up eco-trails, held public photography exhibitions of village life and given rise to computer games based on traditional Bulgarian weaving patterns. Working together, residents and locals have recorded countless stories, folk songs and recipes that might have otherwise been lost. All of this has added to renewed bonds and a strengthened sense of community. One grandmother who hosted a resident in her home said, 'You live the same life, in the same house and in the same village, but you are already a changed person: your life is fuller, your days and evenings are more pleasant. The bread you eat becomes more enjoyable.'[36]

Bread tastes better when it is shared, for the elderly residents and their visitors alike. When the young people return to the city, they do so with extensive knowledge of herbs and mushrooms, and dexterous skills in stuffing vine leaves; and after the scheme is over, they continue to work on the projects they have started, maintaining their connections with their friends in the villages, going back repeatedly to catch up, to drink tea and *rakiya*, and to keep these new friendships alive.[37]

In Sofia, I caught up with the folklorist Sarah Craycraft, one of the small number of non-Bulgarians who had been on a residency. She spent a month in the village of Sinagovtsi, close to Negovanovtsi, where she shared the house of a local grand-mother, Baba Ceca. Over the weeks of the residency, Sarah and Baba Ceca became good friends, and after the residency ended they kept up their connection. When the snows started to fall and winter began, Sarah headed back to the village to see her former host.

Baba Ceca spoke no English. Sarah spoke good Bulgarian, but the local dialect in the villages outside Vidin was hard to understand – a melange of Bulgarian, Serbian and Romanian; and Baba Ceca talked fast, at hyper-speed. Nevertheless, the two of them got by.

'I said to her, "Baba Ceca, you know I can't understand you that well, right?"' Sarah told me. 'And she replied, "It's no problem," and just kept talking!'

Sometimes interaction itself is gift enough; sometimes the act of speaking and of listening – when you are huddled together in a kitchen, hungering to connect – is more important than what is said.

The Baba Residence project is successful not just because it brings new life to depopulated villages, but also because it harnesses the creativity of these local communities, finding new ways of putting the traditional knowledge of the elderly people to work: their stories and songs, their language and wisdom, their recipes and crafts.

A society in which intergenerational links are broken gives rise to a particularly painful kind of loneliness. There can be nothing more isolating than the knowledge that you have nothing to pass on, the thought that your culture, the things that are closest to your heart, will die with you. Belonging lies not just in having people around us, but in the feeling of being part of a lineage or tradition. Research with elderly villagers just over the border in nearby Serbia brings home quite how isolating it is to find yourself the last in line in your community. 'When evening comes, I close the door because I'm afraid, because I'm alone,' one woman told the researchers. And another woman said, 'Back then we took care of four generations of old people. We were poor, we didn't have anything. But we managed. I buried great-grandmothers. Two of them. I buried my mother-in-law, then I buried my father-in-law, then . . . But we will die alone here.'[38]

There is an increasing recognition that one cause of loneliness in the elderly is this opening up of an intergenerational gulf.[39] And this is a problem not only for the elderly, but for younger people too. A sense of tradition, and of being part of a lineage, can anchor us within the world.

In passing on stories and songs, traditional village wisdom, recipes, proverbs and craft techniques, the elderly people in the Bulgarian villages where the Baba Residence project works find new ways of giving; because loneliness is not only the lack of what we can receive – care, recognition, appreciation; it is also the lack of the opportunity to give.[40]

The anthropologist Michelle Anne Parsons, who researched loneliness in post-Soviet Russia, argues that loneliness arises when we fall out of the cycle of gift-exchange that characterises shared living. Parsons carried out her fieldwork in Russia in the 1990s, after the fall of the Soviet Union. When the Soviet Union collapsed, rapid social and economic reforms led to many older men losing work or being forced into early retirement.[41] The loss of employment, the loss of social roles and the loss of a sense of purpose led in turn to spiralling levels of alcoholism and rapidly increasing mortality. Many of those Parsons spoke with talked about how, in the new world they were facing, they found themselves unneeded. They were, they said, *nikomu ne nuzhny*, needed by nobody. They were *ne vostrebovany*, not sought after.

Of all our needs, the need to be needed is among the greatest. One of the major sources of the loneliness and isolation suffered by the unsought-after, writes Parsons, is 'a constricted ability to give and experience mutual recognition'. When you have nothing to give, as one of the anthropologist's interviewees put it, 'Each person is alone. Each one has no one and that's it . . . Who needs us? Who is needed now? Now no one needs anyone else. The world has become terrible.'[42]

Social animals that we are, we build and rebuild our social relationships through the exchange of gifts and counter-gifts. Generosity spreads through social networks and, as it goes, it binds us together.[43] But to be a part of this open-ended cycle of gift and counter-gift, you need, as a minimum, to have the opportunity to give. You need the human dignity that comes from what you can offer others. Because when there is no way of giving, you fall off the edge of the social map, and loneliness is the result.

By the time the dancing in Negovanovtsi comes to an end, the village square is crowded. The band take a break. They drink local wine, mixed with the luminous yellow cordial that is sold as 'lemonade for wine'. There are speeches; the village mayor has to have his say. My Bulgarian is not good enough to follow what is being said, but nobody seems very interested. They are there for the food, for the chat, for the dancing, for the fun of putting on your best clothes and hanging out with friends, neighbours and strangers. After the speeches, there are games: the residents from the city compete to stuff vine leaves, showing off their new-found technique, while the grandmothers and grandfathers crowd round and comment on their prowess. Then the band strikes up again and everyone starts to eat. A sturdy-looking woman in traditional dress grabs my plate and puts a huge slab of something sweet and dense on it. She grins. I thank her and she pushes me towards the table. Clearly my plate is not yet full enough. I add a few more things – some Bulgarian *negarche* or chocolate cake, some stewed beans, a slice of savoury *kačamak* made from corn-meal, a small piece of *banitsa*, a hunk of bread. I sit on the steps of the *chitalishte* and look across the square. People are talking, connecting, having fun.

I am only a fleeting visitor to Negovanovtsi, but I feel at ease and at home. I know that the problems faced by these communities are huge. But nevertheless, as I sit on the steps of the *chitalishte*, my plate groaning with home-made delicacies, and watch the people dancing under the birch and horse chestnut trees, it seems the opposite of a village in decline. The square is filled with the hubbub of celebration. The old people and their young guests hug and touch and smile. There is laughter and noise and fun. One old lady sits on a chair on her own, holding a stick. But she doesn't look lonely. She stares at the crowd and she beams in happiness. This is how loneliness is overcome. Through opening up channels for generosity. Through the mutual giving of gifts. Through the way that pleasures are multiplied when they are shared. Through the sheer animal warmth we cook up together, as we meet – both strangers and friends – beneath the trees, with the brass band playing cheerful tunes and the table groaning with home-cooked food.

I chew on a hunk of bread and watch the party unfold. And there in Negovanovtsi, where today at least all the doors are open and anything seems possible, the bread does indeed taste better.

EPILOGUE

Keeping Open the Door

Four years ago, I left Elee's side for a final time, and arrived home from the hospice to find a hungry cat rubbing at my ankles and a tub of kedgeree on the work surface.

The cancer had come back more quickly than either of us had expected. Over the previous Christmas, Elee had visited me in Chengdu. We had spent three weeks together, hanging out, exploring the city, travelling to nearby towns, visiting museums. It had been good to reconnect, to introduce Elee to my friends, to slip back into the ease of each other's company. But in those few weeks, we already knew something was wrong. Elee was tired. She was pale and drawn, and when she climbed the stairs to my seventh-floor apartment, she was out of breath. Her voice was hoarse: the doctor had diagnosed laryngitis. She had little appetite. For much of the time, she was silent and anxious. We talked about going to a hospital in Chengdu to get her checked out. But there didn't seem any point. Once she was home, if she was still ill, she could go and talk to somebody there. If the news was bad, we decided, it would be really bad, so a week or two wouldn't make any difference.

When we said goodbye at the airport, I watched her wheel her case out of sight through emigration and I felt a choking unease.

Late that January, Elee collapsed with a pain in her side. She took a taxi to hospital. They kept her in for tests, then more tests. When the results of her scan came back, it showed shadows in her liver: a network of finely threaded darkness. Elee sent me an email. 'I'm sorry,' she wrote. 'I love you so much. I wish we could just go on and on for ever.'

I called home. We spoke for a short while. Elee's voice was distant and small.

'I'll book a flight,' I said. 'I'll be back as soon as I can.'

Early the next week, I was home, and we were sitting together in the oncologist's office.

'How long do I have?' Elee asked.

'It is hard to say,' he said. 'Everybody is different. But probably two years, maybe three.'

We both started to cry. Two years seemed like no time at all.

But it was time enough to go on living. 'I know I am dying,' Helen Dunmore wrote in a late poem. 'But why not keep flowering / As long as I can / From my cut stem?'[1] So we tried to keep on flowering, even though the stem was cut. In the weeks that followed, Elee quit her job to free her up to work on a book about her research.[2] She wanted a legacy, something to give the world before she left. We made plans for trips away. We planned a holiday in Copenhagen later in the summer: Elee had always wanted to visit Denmark. We invited guests and visitors over, and as usual I cooked up food for everyone. Now, more than ever, we needed to not harden our thresholds with the world. We hung out, walked in the rambling meadows on the urban fringes of town, spotting kingfishers and dragonflies and foxes slipping through the reeds. In the evenings, we watched TV or read books.

Towards the summer, Elee's health got rapidly worse. The cancer spread quickly, from her liver to her bones. By now, Elee was in a wheelchair. But when she was invited to give a public talk at the university, she accepted. It was six weeks before her death when she stood in front of the crowded auditorium, to talk about her research. Her voice was fragile, but she had always loved an audience, and in front of the crowd, she came alive. She told jokes, showed photographs of dinosaurs and stuffed polecats and whale skeletons. After the talk, she took cards from strangers and assiduously followed up afterwards, thanking them for coming.

By the summer, we knew it wasn't going to be three years; it wasn't even going to be two. We gave up on Copenhagen and settled for a weekend in Oxford instead. We booked a room just out of town. For most of that weekend, Elee slept. It was the weekend of the Brexit result. I read books, looked anxiously at the news, went for short walks, brought back things to eat. We tried to make it feel like a holiday, not a farewell. We went to the Museum of Natural History, where Elee had done her research. In the evening, we watched an indifferent and forgettable film. Afterwards, we went to a Japanese restaurant to eat. Elee no longer had much taste for food and it was hard to manhandle the wheelchair up the steps. But we drank beer and ate *gyoza*, and it was good. On the train home the following day, I watched Elee sleep, exhausted, in her wheelchair. I knew it would be our last trip.

Then, on the first day of August, Elee was gone; and the day after, I sat alone in the house we had shared, fussing the cat, not knowing what to do with myself.

A week after Elee's death, a friend from London put a message on Facebook. He had to move out of his apartment, he said, and he was looking for a place to live. He was not quite a stranger, but we didn't know each other well. I sat at the table, thinking about the emptiness of my home, how it had always been peopled. It would have been easy to keep the doors closed, to go into retreat, to hug my loss close. But something instinctive told me that here was an opportunity, a lifeline. I fired off a message. 'Move in,' I said. 'There is a spare room.'

My friend arrived exactly one week after Elee's funeral, with a van full of stuff. And it was good, in the weeks that followed, when the world seemed utterly broken, to have somebody else around, to feel the walls of the house expanding outwards again. My friend cooked up Chinese feasts. We invited people over to eat. As the autumn turned to winter, we ate and drank and sat by the gas fire.

The doorbell rang often. The house became clamorous, hot and noisy. Another friend brought over stacks of Motown records. We opened bottles of wine, put on the records and danced.

And in this way, I started to restitch the torn fabric of my world.

Author's Note

I finished the first draft of this book the summer before the Covid-19 pandemic hit. By the time I was working through the first batch of edits, everything had changed and half the world was under lockdown. It was a strange time to be working on a book about the virtues of opening our homes to strangers.

Now, several months on, it is the height of the summer and I am in Bulgaria, sitting at my desk in my apartment in Sofia. The quarantine restrictions of the previous few months have eased. The door is open to the balcony. Outside, the sun is shining and in the square a string trio plays Astor Piazzolla's 'Libertango'. It almost feels like an ordinary day – except no days are ordinary any more. It is a long time since I have had visitors; it's been months since the apartment was full of the noise of friends or strangers sharing food and conversation.

If I go out onto the balcony, I can watch the musicians play. People sit on benches listening to the music, keeping more or less to the recommended two metres apart. Strangers pass by, walking their dogs or heading to the supermarket. Trams rattle down the tram tracks, emptier than they were before the pandemic. Like everybody else, I'm still trying to make sense of the past few months, the isolation, the fear and the grief of it. Every day, I check the news, see what has changed. The world still holds its breath. And if the future is perhaps no more uncertain than it has ever been, this uncertainty is more palpable than before.

But pandemics come and go, as they always have done. And if, out of necessity, our doors remain barred, this is precisely when we most need to resist the temptation of making our lives small, and to remind ourselves of the futures strangers can bring. Because if we can only hold on to this creature need we have for each other, then – when the storm has passed – we will be ready to throw open the doors, to reconnect, to embrace and to go on building a shared world worth living in.

Acknowledgements

This book is dedicated to Elee Kirk, with whom I first discussed the idea more than a decade and a half ago. I am grateful for the many years during which I shared her friendship, her kindness, her humour and her irrepressible philoxenia. After Elee's death, many people – family, friends and strangers – stepped up to help mend the rift in my world. I want to thank everyone who shared their table with me, or came over, or invited me out, or gave me the opportunity to be a guest or a host, thereby keeping that spirit of philoxenia alive.

In Myanmar, I'm grateful to Sayama Thuthu, who guided me through the complexities of the Burmese language and who was a wealth of information on traditional Burmese systems of belief. Many of the ideas of this book were shaped while I was teaching at the Parami Institute in Yangon, and my students were brilliant, sceptical and enthusiastic partners in the quest to explore more deeply what it means to connect with strangers. In particular, my thanks go to my small research group, Than Toe Aung,

May Thant Cynn, Lawoon Yan and Khin Chit Win, for their insights into Burmese life, and for making me feel among friends when I was far from home. Over in Indonesia, I learned a lot from Grace Susetyo and her enthusiasm for the nuances of Indonesia's *ramai* cultures. I am grateful too for the generosity of the Rafeeqi family, in particular Yusra Rafeeqi and Samrah Sehar, who took time to answer my questions about their brilliant 'Dine with a Muslim Family' campaign.

In Thessaloniki, Tracy Lucas and Rory O'Keefe were the best ouzo partners, and our mutual friend Eleni S. generously shared her experiences of hosting strangers. I'm grateful also to Refugee Trauma Initiative for their insights into the refugee experience in Greece and beyond. In Bulgaria, Yanina Tanvea and the crew at Ideas Factory were both welcoming and enthusiastic. I am in awe of their brilliant, necessary work. Also in Bulgaria, I want to thank Hasan Yakub Hasan, for his wonderful storytelling, his even better *tarhana*, and for sparing me the cudgel.

I am grateful to the many scholars and researchers who helped me out while I was researching this book. In particular, my gratitude goes to Bénédicte Brac de la Perrière and Jane Ferguson, who were invaluable on Burmese ghosts; Caroline Humphrey and Gregory Delaplace, who filled me in on the *yos* in Mongolia; and Sarah Craycraft for her knowledge of Bulgarian folklore. Poet Ana Marija Grbić gave me the lowdown on the tradition of *sikteruša* coffee in Serbia. My former student Rubina Bala answered my questions about Albanian hospitality. And poet and travel writer Dr Tom Phillips provided rich insights into the concept of *besa* and the nuances of life in highland Albania.

In the early stages of this book's genesis, my brilliant agent, Emma Finn, pushed me again and again to clarify my ideas. The book would not exist at all without her support, her endless encouragement and her determined tenacity. At Granta my editor, Anne Meadows, helped me see the possibilities lurking in the roughly hewn stone of the first draft. It is a lucky writer who has an editor who is at one time so astute, so exacting and so relentlessly enthusiastic. I'm grateful to Lesley Levene for her meticulous copy-editing of the text, which saved me from myself more than once. And my nieces Liberty and India Abbott were excellent research assistants, and in the final stages of the book were tenacious in tracking down the last stray references.

I am grateful also to the Society of Authors, who provided an Authors' Foundation grant to help fund the research towards this book.

Much of this book was written while on the road, travelling among strangers. These journeys would not have been anything like as richly fulfilling, or as much fun, without the company and insightfulness of my collaborator and friend, Hannah Stevens.

Finally, the ideas in this book owe a debt to innumerable conversations with strangers whom I have met along the way. To everyone who has been willing to open up the door – literally or figuratively – and say, 'Hello, stranger', thank you!

Credits

Credits

Notes

Introduction

1 Naja Marie Aidt, *When Death Takes Something from You Give It Back* (Quercus Books, 2017), p. 88.

2 Quoted in Gaston Bachelard, *The Poetics of Space* (Beacon Press, 1969), p. 52.

3 Emmanuel Levinas, *Time and the Other* (Duquesne University Press, 1987), p. 77.

4 Donald N. Levine (ed.), *Georg Simmel: On Individuality and Social Forms* (University of Chicago Press, 1971), pp. 143–5.

5 Robin Dunbar, *How Many Friends Does One Person Need? Dunbar's Number and Other Evolutionary Quirks* (Faber and Faber, 2010), p. 37.

6 Ibid., p. 39.

7 See Hannah Ritchie and Max Roser's useful article 'Urbanization' on the Oxford University Our World in Data website: https://ourworldindata.org/urbanization.

8 See, for example, Malcolm Gladwell, *Talking to Strangers* (Little, Brown and Company, 2019).

9   The root here is in Proto-Indo-European, the ancestor of
     Sanskrit, Latin and Greek – a language that is believed to have
     been spoken up to 6,500 years ago, in the area of steppe that
     spreads east from the northern coast of the Black Sea.
10   K. D. M. Snell, 'The rise of living alone and loneliness in history',
     Social History, 42:1 (2017), pp. 2–28.
11   Fay Bound Alberti, *A Biography of Loneliness: The History of an
     Emotion* (Oxford University Press, 2019), p. 31.
12   Marina Keegan, *The Opposite of Loneliness* (Simon and Schuster,
     2014), p. 1.
13   This is true not just for *Homo sapiens*, but for all social primates:
     see John Capitanio, Stephanie Cacioppo and Steven Cole,
     'Loneliness in monkeys: neuroimmune mechanisms', *Current
     Opinion in Behavioral Sciences*, 28 (2019), pp. 51–7.

1   Welcome Home

1   Cicero, *Selected Letters*, translated by P. G. Walsh (Oxford
     World's Classics, 2008), p. 64.
2   Ibid., p. 68.
3   Plutarch, *The Age of Caesar: Five Roman Lives*, translated by
     Pamela Mensch (W. W. Norton, 2017), p. 104.
4   Some later scholars have questioned the plausibility of the
     charges. In his book *The Patrician Tribune: Publius Clodius Pulcher*
     (University of North Carolina Press, 1999), W. Jeffrey Tatum
     examines the arguments and concludes that, however unlikely the
     story sounds, the weight of evidence tips the balance in favour of
     Clodius's guilt.

5 This was originally a religious penalty, the forfeiting of home and property for violations of sacred law: see Gordon P. Kelly, *A History of Exile in the Roman Republic* (Cambridge University Press, 2006), p. 28.

6 See Anthony Everitt, *Cicero: The Life and Times of Rome's Greatest Politician* (Random House, 2001), p. 143.

7 This story is well told by Kathryn Tempest in *Cicero: Politics and Persuasion in Ancient Rome* (Continuum Books, 2001), pp. 122–4.

8 Cicero, *Selected Letters*, p. 76.

9 Cicero, *Back from Exile: Six Speeches upon His Return*, translated by D. R. Shackleton Bailey (American Philological Association Classical Resources, 1991), p. 84. See also Jack Lennon, 'Pollution and ritual impurity in Cicero's *De domo sua*', *Classical Quarterly*, 60:2 (2010), pp. 427–45.

10 See Jerry D. Moore, *The Prehistory of Home* (University of California Press, 2012), p. 18.

11 Martha C. Nussbaum, *Political Emotions: Why Love Matters for Justice* (Harvard University Press, 2013), p. 154.

12 John S. Allen, *Home: How Habitat Made Us Human* (Basic Books, 2015), p. 1.

13 Verlyn Klinkenborg, 'The definition of home', *Smithsonian Magazine Online* (May 2012): https://www.smithsonianmag.com/science-nature/the-definition-of-home-60692392/.

14 Wendy Dongier (trans.), *The Rig Veda* (Penguin Books, 1981), p. 100.

15 J. P. Mallory and D. Q. Adams, *The Oxford Introduction to Proto-Indo-European and the Proto-Indo-European World* (Oxford University Press, 2006), p. 222.

16   Cicero, *The Nature of the Gods*, translated by Horace
     C. P. McGregor (Penguin Books, 1972), p. 161.

17   According to J. A. J. Gowlett, the human discovery of fire had
     several stages: see 'The discovery of fire by humans: a long and
     convoluted process', *Philosophical Transactions of the Royal Society
     B: Biological Sciences*, 371 (2016), pp. 1–12.

18   Laura Spinney, 'Cosy up with the Neanderthals, the first humans
     to make a house a home', *New Scientist* (6 February 2019).

19   In *Sapiens: A Brief History of Humankind* (Vintage, 2011), Yuval
     Noah Harari sides with the theory that Neanderthals were wiped
     out by *Homo sapiens*, speculating that perhaps they 'were too
     familiar to ignore, but too different to tolerate' (p. 20). But it may
     be that what did for the Neanderthals was more bad luck than
     genocide: see Ian Sample, 'Bad luck may have caused
     Neanderthals' extinction – study', *Guardian* (27 November 2019),
     reporting on the paper by K. Vaesen et al., 'Inbreeding, Allee
     effects and stochasticity might be sufficient to account for
     Neanderthal extinction', *PLoS ONE*, 14:11 (2019).

20   This is consistent with more recent studies of hunting and
     gathering communities where access to territory by outsiders is
     managed socially, rather than defensively, by means of 'kinship,
     friendships or partnerships', and through the exchange of goods:
     see Steven L. Kuhn and Mary C. Stiner, 'The antiquity of
     hunter-gatherers', in Catherine Panter-Brick, Robert Layton and
     Peter Rowley-Conwy (eds.), *Hunter-Gatherers: An Interdisciplinary
     Perspective* (Cambridge University Press, 2001), pp. 106–7.

21   See Spinney, 'Cosy up with the Neanderthals'.

22   Jani Närhi, 'Beautiful reflections: the cognitive and evolutionary
     foundations of paradise representations', *Method and Theory in the*

Study of Religion, 20 (2008), p. 361. I tried this experiment with a group of postgraduate students in Myanmar, asking them, without any prompting, to draw pictures of paradise. They all drew an evolutionarily optimal landscape – except for one student, Lawoon Yan, a published poet, whose paradise consisted of piles of books, bottles of wine, an old record player and abundant snacks.

23 This example comes from Fran Barone's excellent blog, 'Home truths: an anthropology of house and home', published on Yale University's Human Relations Area Files site: https://hraf.yale.edu/home-truths-an-anthropology-of-house-and-home/.

24 Ibid.

25 In her book *Walking with Abel: Journeys with the Nomads of the African Savannah* (Penguin Books, 2015), Anna Badkhen gives the example of the West African Fulani herdsman Afo Bocoum, for whom settlement was a kind of homesickness and hopping on his motorbike twice a day to head out to the pasture to feed his cattle was a salve for his nostalgia and sense of loss (p. 17).

26 Steve Sheppard (ed.), *The Selected Writings of Edward Coke: Volume 1* (Liberty Fund, 2003), p. 137.

27 *The Reports of Sir Henry Yelverton . . . of Divers Special Cases in the Court of King's Bench, as Well in the Latter End of the Reign of Q. Elizabeth, as in the First Ten Years of K. James* (Court of the King's Bench of England, 1735), pp. 28–9. Coke was arguing against the use of general search warrants that could be issued by the state without any justification. Although he argued that the general search warrant was illegal, it continued to be used throughout the eighteenth century.

28 Quoted in Judith Flanders, *The Making of Home: The 500-year Story of How Our Houses Became Homes* (Atlantic Books, 2014), p. 96.

29 Setha Low, *Behind the Gates: Life, Security and the Pursuit of Happiness in Fortress America* (Routledge, 2003), p. 121.

30 The research on this is extensive. To take one example, see Jiayu Wu et al., 'Dismantling the fence for social justice? Evidence based on the inequity of urban green space accessibility in the central urban area of Beijing', *Environment and Planning B: Urban Analytics and City Science* (2018), pp. 1–19.

31 Setha Low, *Spatializing Culture: The Ethnography of Space and Place* (Routledge, 2017), p. 168.

32 Ibid., p. 166.

33 See Catherine Allerton, 'Making guests, making "liveliness": the transformative substances and sounds of Manggarai hospitality', *Journal of the Royal Anthropological Institute*, 18:S1 (2012), p. S50. The concern with being *ramai* is not limited to just this community, but is shared much more broadly across Indonesia. Even many thoroughly modern urbanites in Indonesia value this sense of lively, buzzy collectivity as an aspect of what being at home means.

34 Catherine Allerton, *Potent Landscapes: Place and Mobility in Eastern Indonesia* (University of Hawai'i Press, 2013), p. 50.

35 Ibid., p. 54. Allerton uses the Manggarai term *ramé*, but throughout I use the more widely understood Indonesian term *ramai*, to which it is equivalent.

36 See Will Buckingham, *Stealing with the Eyes: Imaginings and Incantations in Indonesia* (Haus Publishing, 2018), p. 151.

2 A Stranger at the Door

1 Bruce Chatwin, *The Anatomy of Restlessness* (Viking, 1996), p. 102.

2 John F. Hoffecker, 'Migration and innovation in palaeolithic Europe', in David Christian (ed.), *The Cambridge World History*, Volume I (Cambridge University Press, 2020), pp. 394–413.

3 The poem is 'The Call of the Deer' (*Lu ming*) from *The Minor Odes* (*Xiao ya*); the translation is my own.

4 Ovid, *Metamorphoses*, translated by A. D. Melville (Oxford World's Classics, 2009), p. 117.

5 Emily Wilson, 'Why I gave Homer a contemporary voice in the *Odyssey*', *Literary Hub* (19 December 2017): https://lithub.com/why-i-gave-homer-a-contemporary-voice-in-the-odyssey.

6 Homer, *The Odyssey*, translated by Emily Wilson (W. W. Norton, 2018), p. 23.

7 Ibid., p. 248.

8 Ibid., p. 24.

9 Martha Nussbaum, *Anger and Forgiveness: Resentment, Generosity, Justice* (Oxford University Press, 2016), p. 21.

10 Malcolm Gladwell, *Talking to Strangers* (Little, Brown and Company, 2019), p. 343.

11 Seneca, *Letters from a Stoic*, translated by Robin Campbell (Penguin Books, 2004), p. 66.

12 Onora O'Neill, *A Question of Trust: The BBC Reith Lectures 2002* (Cambridge University Press, 2002), p. 24.

13 See Jason Faulkner et al., 'Evolved disease-avoidance mechanisms and contemporary xenophobic attitudes', *Group Processes &*

Intergroup Relations, 7:4 (2004), pp. 333–53. And, of course, the arrow of causality can also go the other way, with the fear of contagion itself fuelling xenophobia: see Yasmeen Serhan and Timothy McLaughlin, 'The other problematic outbreak', *The Atlantic* (13 March 2020).

14 See 'The truth about migration: how evolution made us xenophobes', *New Scientist* (6 April 2016): https://www.new scientist.com/article/mg23030680-800-the-truth-about-migration-how-evolution-made-us-xenophobes/. Although these arguments are superficially plausible, it is not clear to me how they might be put to the test.

15 The research here is complex and still contentious. One piece that explores the arguments is Joseph Stromberg, 'Are babies bigoted?', *Smithsonian Magazine* (13 March 2013): https://www.smithsonianmag.com/science-nature/are-babies-bigoted-1980725/.

16 Judith Heerwagen and Gordon Orians, 'The ecological world of children', in Peter Kahn and Stephen Kellert (eds.), *Children and Nature: Psychological, Sociocultural, and Evolutionary Investigations* (MIT Press, 2002), pp. 29–64. The in-built nature of the fear of strangers (and snakes, spiders and heights) has been questioned by Vanessa LoBue and Karen Adolph in their paper 'Fear in infancy: lessons from snakes, spiders, heights, and strangers', *Developmental Psychology* 5:9 (2019), pp. 1889–907. LoBue and Adolph argue that the children's responses to each of these stimuli are a much more complex and context-dependent 'suite of behaviors'. In this more complex picture, context is all: infants seem more reliably scared of strangers when not at home than they are in their homes; they are more scared when they are

seated on the floor than when they are on their mothers' laps, and so on. It is the context, in other words, that sets the stage for the precise mix of xenophobia – fear, desire for withdrawal – and philoxenia – curiosity, fascination or desire to connect.

17   Jennifer Hanh-Holbrook, Colin Holbrook and Jesse Bering, 'Snakes, spiders, strangers: How the evolved fear of strangers may misdirect efforts to protect children from harm', in James Lampinen and Kathy Sexton-Radek (eds.), *Protecting Children from Violence: Evidence-based Interventions* (Psychology Press, 2010), pp. 263–89.

18   Gary Ngyuen, 'Teen combats Islamophobia by inviting strangers to dine with her Muslim family', *World Religion News* (22 May 2017).

19   See Mona Siddiqui, *Hospitality and Islam: Welcoming in God's Name* (Yale University Press, 2015), p. 100.

3 Come on in

1   Dendevin Badarc and Raymond A. Zilinskas (eds.), *Mongolia Today: Science, Culture, Environment and Development* (Routledge, 2015), pp. 11–14.

2   Caroline Humphrey, 'The host and the guest: one hundred rules of good behaviour in rural Mongolia', *Journal of the Anglo-Mongolian Society*, 10 (1987), pp. 43–54. This saying is puzzling, if entertaining. It may be that 'donkey' here is a mistranslation of 'mule'. As mules are incapable of breeding, then the implication is of making a whole lot of noise without any actual results.

3   I'm grateful to Caroline Humphrey and to Gregory Delaplace for

their insights into the continued contemporary relevance of the *yos* in Mongolia.

4   Caroline Humphrey, 'Hospitality and tone: holding patterns for strangeness in rural Mongolia', *Journal of the Royal Anthropological Institute* (2012), pp. S63–S75.

5   I owe this insight to the informative information on Mongolian hats in the Cambridge Museum of Archaeology and Anthropology.

6   Things ended badly for Simukov. In 1939, he fell victim to Stalin's purges. He was arrested by the NKVD, the People's Commissariat for Internal Affairs, and taken into custody in Ulaanbaatar. There he was accused of being a spy and shipped off to Siberia. Hardened by the rigours of life in Mongolia, during the sixteen months of his interrogation he consistently protested his innocence. To no avail. In 1941, he was sent to the Gulag, sentenced to eight years. Simukov died in prison in 1942. He was only forty years old. For a brief biography of Simukov, see 'In memory of Andrej Dmitrievich Simukov (1902–1942)', in Dendevin Badarch and Raymond Zilinskas (eds.), *Mongolia Today: Science, Culture, Environment and Development* (RoutledgeCurzon, 2003), pp. xi–xiii.

7   Cicero, *The Nature of the Gods*, translated by Horace C. P. McGregor (Penguin Books, 1972), p. 150.

8   Humphrey, 'Hospitality and tone', p. S67.

9   Alban Gautier, 'Hospitality in pre-Viking Anglo-Saxon England', *Early Medieval Europe*, 17:1 (2009), pp. 23–44.

10 In Howell D. Chickering Jr's translation, 'Now you may enter, in your battle-armor, / wearing war-masks, to see Hrothgar; / let shields stay here, tightened war-wood, / your battle-shafts wait /

the result of words': see *Beowulf: A Dual-Language Edition* (Anchor Books, 2006), pp. 71–3.

11 Homer, *The Odyssey*, translated by Emily Wilson (W. W. Norton, 2018), p. 109.

12 See Stephanie Strom, 'Starbucks seeks to keep guns out of its coffee shops', *New York Times* (18 September 2013).

13 The open letter is, at the time of writing, still published online: https://stories.starbucks.com/press/2013/open-letter-from-howard.

14 See Victor Turner, *The Ritual Process: Structure and Anti-Structure* (Cornell University Press, 1969), p. 95.

15 Turner writes that such liminal states are marked by a confusion of categories, by a combination of 'lowliness and sacredness' (ibid., p. 96). If this is true, then it should come as no surprise that two footsore beggars turning up at the door of Baucis and Philemon turn out to be gods in disguise (see p. 41–2).

16 Ritual, of course, is more apparent at these major turning points. Then it helps us navigate difficult transitions. As Roel Sterckx writes in *Chinese Thought: From Confucius to Cook Ding* (Pelican Books, 2019): 'Human psychology, not least in our emotional dispositions, functions better with a guide or road map' (p. 229). When we do not know how to navigate through the world, the formal pointers provided by ritual 'offer comfort and help us stay on our feet, both physically and mentally'.

17 See Catherine Bell, *Ritual: Perspectives and Dimensions* (Oxford University Press, 2009), p. 189. Bell also notes that at certain times in Chinese history Daoist philosophers, rival to the Confucian schools, put forward similar arguments.

18 There is a translation of this story in Mark Edward Lewis, *Writing*

and Authority in Early China (SUNY Press, 1999), p. 226.

19 The translation is my own.

20 The translation is my own.

21 Humphrey, 'Hospitality and tone', p. S66.

22 Adam B. Seligman et al., *Ritual and Its Consequences: An Essay on the Limits of Sincerity* (Oxford University Press, 2008), p. 133.

23 See ibid., p. 22, for the following example: '. . . when we ask our children to please feed the dog and they refuse, we may get angry and shout, "DAMN it, feed the dog now!" At this point we both leave the illusionary world of mutuality and respect for the one of brute power. We fall back into a world from which politeness had saved us.'

24 Ibid., p. 95. Seligman and his colleagues give a terrific example of this mixture of ritual and play, not in the context of welcoming guests, but in what might seem the most serious setting of all: a funeral. 'Funerals in northern Taiwan, for instance,' they write, 'include a period when a ritual specialist, dressed in Buddhist robes, performs elaborate and esoteric mudras to help the dead soul through the underworld. At the same time, he keeps up a steady monologue of jokes at the expense of both the dead person and the society around him – certainly not excluding visiting anthropologists.' While funerals elsewhere may not be so explicit in resorting to playfulness, I know many people who have attended funerals, expecting sombre ritual, only to find that the event is unexpectedly light-hearted, filled with life, fun and joking (the reverse is sometimes true for weddings).

25 Julian Pitt-Rivers, 'The law of hospitality', *HAU: Journal of Ethnographic Theory*, 2:1 (2012), p. 513. In his book *On Humour* (Routledge, 2002), Simon Critchley calls jokes 'anti-rites' that

'mock, parody or deride' the rituals of a given society (p. 5); but he draws the opposition between ritual and humour too firmly. Humour and ritual are not like matter and anti-matter, one cancelling the other out; instead they often coexist in a subtle, ticklish play of formality and joking that shifts the boundaries, without destroying them.

26 Daniela Antonacci, Ivan Norscia and Elisabetta Palagi, 'Stranger to familiar: wild strepsirhines manage xenophobia by playing', *PLoS One*, 5:10 (2010).

27 Mohamed El-Gomati, 'How to tackle the EDL', *Guardian* (31 May 2013): https://www.theguardian.com/commentisfree/2013/may/31/edl-english-defence-league-york-mosque.

28 Homer, *The Odyssey*, translated by Emily Wilson (W. W. Norton, 2018), p. 352.

29 See Melissa Mueller, 'Helen's hands: weaving for *kleos* in the *Odyssey*', *Helios* 37:1 (2010), pp. 1–21.

30 The word *kleos* is related to the word 'to hear': it is explicitly about one's standing in the eyes of others. For more on *kleos* in the *Odyssey*, see Charles Segal, '*Kleos* and its ironies in the *Odyssey*', *L'antiquité classique* 52 (1983), pp. 22–47.

31 Homer, *The Odyssey*, p. 203.

32 Ibid., p. 216.

33 Chickering Jr, *Beowulf*, p. 155.

34 Ibid., p. 157.

35 The risks are real. One particularly grim case was that of the Italian police officer, Dino Maglio, who in 2015 was convicted of drugging and raping female guests who came to stay with him: see Stephanie Kirkgaessner and Alessia Cerantola, 'Couchsurfing rapist Dino Maglio escaped investigation for months', *Guardian*

(29 May 2015). There are legitimate questions to be asked about safety here, as there are about the safety of other contexts in which strangers meet: hotels, inns, hotels and so on.

36 See Bryan Van Norden's translation, *The Essential Mengzi* (Hackett Publishing Company, 2009), p. 36.

37 Marcel Mauss, *The Gift: The Form and Reason for Exchange in Archaic Societies*, translated by W. D. Halls (Routledge, 1990).

38 Marcel Fournier, *Marcel Mauss: A Biography* (Princeton University Press, 2006), p. 280.

39 Mauss, *The Gift*, p. 17.

40 Ibid., p. 4.

41 As David Graeber complains in *Debt: The First 5000 Years* (Melville House, 2010): the 'logic of the marketplace has insinuated itself even into the thinking of those who are most explicitly opposed to it' (p. 90).

42 Roy Wagner, '"Luck in double focus": ritualised hospitality in Melanesia', *Journal of the Royal Anthropological Institute* (2012) p. S171. Wagner writes that 'the vast majority of the earth's peoples' know that what is important is not the return, but the 'indefinite postponement of return', not the accounting, but instead the social relationship that gift-giving forges.

43 Hla Pe, *Burma: Literature, Historiography, Scholarship, Language, Life, and Buddhism* (Institute of Southeast Asian Studies, 1985), pp. 159–60.

44 As Eric Mullis writes in his paper 'Toward a Confucian ethic of the gift', *Dao* 7 (2008): 'Our relationships with others demand that gifts be given in a generous spirit, for such relationships are themselves gifts that create a debt that can never be fully settled' (p. 193).

45 Susan McKinnon, *From a Shattered Sun: Hierarchy, Gender and Alliance in the Tanimbar Islands* (University of Wisconsin Press, 1991), p. 251.

46 Julian Pitt-Rivers, 'The place of grace in anthropology', *Hau: Journal of Ethnographic Theory*, 1:1 (2011), p. 437. Pitt-Rivers writes that Mauss 'makes no mention of grace, and the gratuity of the gift is, for him, a sociological delusion'; but then he goes on to say that, contrary to Mauss's view, this gratuity or grace is no delusion, but instead essential gift-giving.

47 Lewis Hyde, *The Gift* (Vintage, 2009).

4 Codes of Honour

1 I am grateful to Hasan Yakub Hasan for providing a written version of this tale, upon which my own retelling is based.

2 See Magnus Marsden, 'Fatal embrace: trading in hospitality on the frontiers of south and central Asia', *Journal of the Royal Anthropological Institute*, 18:S1 (2012), pp. S117–S130.

3 During the years of Taliban rule in Afghanistan, Sufism was repressed, although when I was over the border in Pakistan in the 1990s, large *degs* were still used at shrines to Sufi saints such as Lal Shahbaz Qalandar. Since the end of Taliban rule, Sufism has been seeing a resurgence in Afghanistan.

4 The force with which pressure cookers can explode means that they are also used for making bombs. See Michael Crowley, 'A short recent history of pressure-cooker bombs', *Time Magazine* (17 April 2013).

5 Martha Nussbaum, *Anger and Forgiveness: Resentment, Generosity,*

Justice (Oxford University Press, 2016), pp. 19–21.

6   Homer, *The Odyssey*, translated by Emily Wilson (W. W. Norton, 2018), p. 329.

7   Ibid. p. 110.

8   Ibid. p. 470.

9   Ibid. p. 486.

10 Julian Pitt-Rivers, 'The law of hospitality', *HAU: Journal of Ethnographic Theory*, 2:1 (2012), p. 517.

11 Caroline Humphrey, 'Hospitality and tone: holding patterns for strangeness in rural Mongolia', *Journal of the Royal Anthropological Institute* (2012), p. S72.

12 Lekë Dukagjini, *Kanuni i Lekë Dukagjinit: The Code of Lekë Dukagjini*, translated by Leonard Fox and compiled by Shtjefën Gjeçovi (Gjonlekaj Publishing Company, 1989), p. xvi.

13 Mirjona Sadiku, 'A tradition of honor, hospitality and blood feuds: exploring the Kanun customary law in contemporary Albania', *Balkan Social Science Review*, 3 (June 2014), pp. 93–115. In his unpublished PhD thesis, 'Not nearly so far: Three journeys in South East Europe' (University of Reading, 2013), the poet Tom Phillips writes: 'Besa is a quality, an obligation, a gift. It's your word of honour, an oath, a promise, but it can also mean truce, haven, protection, peace. It's none of these alone, and all of them at once, existing where they overlap or in the gaps between them. Even the village elders who codified Albania's complex traditions of honour, hospitality and vengeance in the kanun or bodies of customary law struggled to describe it in all its possible forms – or the numerous ways in which it can be kept or broken. It's a serious matter' (p. 55).

14 Ismail Kadare, *Broken April* (Vintage Classics, 2003), p. 27.

15 Edith Durham, *High Albania* (Edward Arnold, 1909), p. 31.

16 Marcus Tanner, *Albania's Mountain Queen: Edith Durham and the Balkans* (I.B. Tauris, 2014), p. 10.

17 Durham, *High Albania*, p. 192.

18 Ibid., p. 32.

19 Thanks go here to Rubina Bala, who answered many of my questions about Albanian hospitality.

20 See Jana Arsovska, 'Understanding a "culture of violence and crime": the Kanun of Lek Dukagjini and the rise of the Albanian sexual-slavery rackets', *European Journal of Crime, Criminal Law and Criminal Justice*, 14:2 (2006), p. 170.

21 See Roland Littlewood, 'Trauma and the Kanun: two responses to loss in Albania and Kosova', *International Journal of Social Psychiatry*, 48:2 (2002), p. 90.

22 Sadiku, 'A tradition of honor, hospitality and blood feuds', p. 97.

23 See Andrew Hosken and Albana Kasapi, 'The children trapped by Albania's blood feuds', *The World Tonight*, BBC Radio 4 (12 November 2017): https://www.bbc.com/news/world-europe–41901300.

24 See the report by the Commissioner General for Refugees and Stateless Persons, *Blood Feuds in Contemporary Albania: Characterisation, Prevalence and Response by the State* (CGRA, 2017): https://www.cgra.be/sites/default/files/rapporten/blood_feuds_in_contemporary_albania._characterisation_prevalence_and_response_by_the_state.pdf.

25 Durham, *High Albania*, p. 41.

26 Isabella Beeton, *Mrs Beeton's Book of Household Management*, edited by Nicola Humble (Oxford University Press, 2000), p. 368.

27 Ibid., pp. 21–4.

28   Jennifer Cash, 'Performing hospitality in Moldova: ambiguous, alternative, and undeveloped models of national identity', *History and Anthropology*, 24:1 (2013), p. 73.

29   Alain de Botton, *Status Anxiety* (Penguin, 2005), p. 302.

30   I have used a pseudonym here, for obvious reasons.

31   Andrew Shryock, 'Breaking hospitality apart: bad hosts, bad guests, and the problem of sovereignty', *Journal of the Royal Anthropological Institute*, 18:1 (2012), pp. S20–S33.

32   The quote comes from a conversation between Stallings and the Greek poet Adrianne Kalfopoulou about their volunteering with Syrian refugees in an anarchist squat in Athens in 2016. The conversation appears online in *Image Journal* #100: https:// imagejournal.org/article/28385/.

33   Pitt-Rivers, 'The law of hospitality', p. 517.

34   Homer, *The Odyssey*, p. 484.

35   Martha Nussbaum, *Anger and Forgiveness*, p. 28.

36   Seneca, *Anger, Mercy, Revenge*, translated by Robert A. Kaster and Martha Nussbaum (University of Chicago Press, 2010), p. 92.

5   Feasts

1   Jean Anthelme Brillat-Savarin, *The Physiology of Taste*, translated by M. F. K. Fisher (Vintage, 2001), p. 189–91.

2   Erica Boothby, Margaret Clark and John Bargh, 'Shared experiences are amplified', *Psychological Science*, 25:12 (2014).

3   Ryuzaburo Nakata and Noboyuki Kawai, 'The "social" facilitation of eating without the presence of others: self-reflection on eating makes food taste better and people eat more', *Physiology*

& Behavior, 179 (2017), pp. 23–9.

4   V. I. Clendenen, C. P. Herman and J. Polivy, 'Social facilitation
     of eating among friends and strangers', *Appetite*, 23:1 (1994),
     pp. 1–13.

5   Paula Michaels, 'An ethnohistorical journey through Kazakh
     hospitality', in Jeffrey Sahadeo and Russell Zanca (eds.), *Everyday
     Life in Central Asia: Past and Present* (Indiana University Press,
     2007), p. 149.

6   C. P. Herman, 'The social facilitation of eating: a review',
     Appetite, 86 (2015), pp. 61–73.

7   Brian Hayden, *The Power of Feasts: From Prehistory to the Present
     Day* (Cambridge University Press, 2014), p. 12.

8   Brian Hayden, 'A prolegomenon to the importance of feasting',
     in Michael Dietler and Brian Hayden (eds.), *Feasts: Archaeological
     and Ethnographic Perspectives on Food, Politics, and Power*
     (University of Alabama Press, 2001), pp. 23–64.

9   See Hayden, *The Power of Feasts*: 'feasting constitutes a new kind
     of human behaviour, one that probably first emerged in the Upper
     Palaeolithic in a few favourable locations and only became more
     widespread in the Mesolithic/Archaic and Neolithic periods'
     (p. 4).

10   Heather Pringle, 'Ancient sorcerer's "wake" was first feast for the
     dead?', *National Geographic* (31 August 2010): https://www.
     nationalgeographic.com/news/2010/8/100830-first-feast-
     science-proceedings-n-shaman-sorcerer-tortoise/.

11   Natalie D. Munro and Leore Grosman, 'Early evidence (ca.
     12,000 B.P.) for feasting at a burial cave in Israel', *Proceedings of
     the National Academy of Sciences of the United States of America*,
     107:35 (2010), pp. 15362–6.

12 For more on the ritual context, see Leore Grosman and Natalie D. Munro, 'A Natufian ritual event', *Current Anthropology*, 57:3 (June 2016), pp. 311–31.

13 Martin Jones, *Feast: Why Humans Share Food* (Oxford University Press, 2007), p. 130.

14 Hanne Nymann, 'Feasting on locusts and truffles in the second millennium BCE', in Susanne Kerner, Cynthia Chou and Marten Warmind (eds.), *Commensality: From Everyday Food to Feast* (Bloomsbury Academic, 2015), pp. 151–64.

15 Susan Sherratt, 'Feasting in the Homeric epic', *Hesperia*, 73 (2004), pp. 310–37. Interestingly, in the *Odyssey*, the Cyclops is depicted as a cheese-maker. The link between cheese-making and cannibalism is not entirely clear.

16 Michaels, 'An ethnohistorical journey through Kazakh hospitality', p. 147.

17 Ibid. p. 148.

18 Plato, *Republic* 573d, in John M. Cooper (ed.), *Plato: Complete Works* (Hackett Publishing Company, 1997), p. 1182.

19 Elizabeth Telfer, *Food for Thought: Philosophy and Food* (Routledge, 2002), p. 32.

20 Plato, *Phaedo* 64d, in Cooper (ed.), *Plato*, p. 56.

21 Plato, *Symposium* 220b, ibid., p. 501.

22 Plato, *Republic* 372d, ibid., pp. 1011–12.

23 Brad Inwood and L. P. Gerson (trans. and eds.), *The Epicurus Reader: Selected Writings and Testimonia* (Hackett Publishing Company, 1994), p. 32.

24 '*Hospes hic bene manebis, hic summum bonum voluptas est.*' The word '*hospes*' can mean 'guest', but also 'stranger'. See Seneca, *Letters on Ethics*, translated by Margaret Graver and A. A. Long

(University of Chicago Press, 2015), p. 77.

25 The quote comes from *The Life of Epicurus* by the not always reliable Diogenes Laertius: see Inwood and Gerson (trans. and eds.), *The Epicurus Reader*, p. 82.

26 Emmanuel Levinas, *Totality and Infinity: An Essay on Exteriority*, translated by Alphonso Lingis (Duquesne University Press, 2011), p. 201.

27 Immanuel Kant, *Toward Perpetual Peace and Other Writings on Politics, Peace, and History*, edited by Pauline Kleingeld and translated by David Colclasure (Yale University Press, 2006), p. 82.

28 The translation is my own.

29 Carolinne White, *The Rule of Benedict: Translated with an Introduction and Notes* (Penguin Books, 2008), p. 61.

30 Andrew Jotischky, *A Hermit's Cookbook: Monks, Food and Fasting in the Middle Ages* (Continuum, 2011), p. 150.

31 The translation is my own.

32 Sarah Mattice, 'Drinking to get drunk: pleasure, creativity, and social harmony in Greece and China', *Comparative and Continental Philosophy*, 3:2 (2011), p. 245.

33 The translation is my own.

34 Jones, *Feast*, p. 31.

35 There is a similar belief in the *langar* ceremonies at Sufi shrines discussed earlier, with the distribution of food also accruing spiritual benefit.

36 Michel Onfray, *Appetites for Thought* (Reaktion Books, 2015), p. 37.

37 Immanuel Kant, *Anthropology from a Pragmatic Point of View*, translated and edited by Robert B. Louden (Cambridge University Press, 2006), p. 64.

38 Ibid., p. 180.
39 Fuchsia Dunlop, 'Fuchsia Dunlop on the fiery charms of Sichuan hotpot', *Financial Times Magazine* (9 November 2018).

6 Leave-taking

1 Homer, *The Odyssey*, translated by Emily Wilson (W. W. Norton, 2018), p. 25.
2 Tiffany Watt Smith, *The Book of Human Emotions* (Profile Books, 2016), pp. 138–40.
3 Immanuel Kant, *Anthropology from a Pragmatic Point of View*, translated and edited by Robert B. Louden (Cambridge University Press, 2006), p. 71.
4 Alexander Loney, '*Pompē* in the *Odyssey*', in Thomas Biggs (ed.), *The Epic Journey in Greek and Roman Literature* (Cambridge University Press, 2019), pp. 31–58.
5 'Hostage to Hospitality', *Home Truths*, BBC Radio 4 (2006): https://www.bbc.co.uk/radio4/hometruths/0231kidnapped.shtml.
6 Stuart Lockwood, 'That's me in the picture: Stuart Lockwood with Saddam Hussein, 24 August 1990, Baghdad, Iraq', *Guardian* (5 June 2015).
7 'The MacNeil/Lehrer NewsHour, 1990-08-23', American Archive of Public Broadcasting (1990): http://americanarchive.org/catalog/cpb-aacip_507-bc3st7fg5q.
8 Adam Kosto, *Hostages in the Middle Ages* (Oxford University Press, 2012), p. 11. The word *obses* has the same root as 'obsess'. The connection begins in the sixteenth century, when 'to obsess'

is used for 'to haunt': so evil spirits would obsess, or sit beside, their hosts, and refuse to leave.

9   Adam Kosto, 'Hostages in the Carolingian world (714–840)', *Early Medieval Europe*, 11:2 (2002), pp. 123–47.

10 Homer, *The Odyssey*, p. 59.

11 Nawal Nasrallah, *Annals of the Caliphs' Kitchens: Ibn Sayyār al-Warrāq's Tenth-Century Baghdadi Cookbook* (Brill, 2007), p. 507.

12 Mary Douglas, *Purity and Danger* (Routledge, 2013).

13 Roland Eisenberg, *What the Rabbis Said: 250 Topics from the Talmud* (Praeger Publishers Inc., 2010), p. 74.

14 I am grateful to Ana Marija Grbić for her insights into the Serbian tradition of 'fuck off coffee'. There is a variant of this pattern in Alison Morrison and Conrad Lashley (eds.), *In Search of Hospitality: Theoretical Perspectives and Debates* (Routledge, 2011), p. 33, although in Serbian villages today, the serving of *slatko* is more common than coffee when welcoming guests, and the terms for 'welcome coffee' and 'talking coffee' that Morrison and Lashley refer to are not in common use.

15 Isabella Beeton, *Mrs Beeton's Book of Household Management*, edited by Nicola Humble (Oxford University Press, 2008), p. 18.

16 Amitai Touval, *An Anthropological Study of Hospitality: The Innkeeper and the Guest* (Palgrave Macmillan, 2017), p. 22.

17 Lyly's book labours under the arduous and not particularly witty sub-subtitle *The anatomy of wit very pleasant for all Gentlemen to read, and most necessary to remember: wherein are contained the delights that Wit followeth in his youth by the pleasantness of love, and the happiness he reapeth in age, by the perfectness of wisdom.*

18 Mona Siddiqui, *Hospitality and Islam: Welcoming in God's Name* (Yale University Press, 2015), p. 109.

19   Julie Kerr, '"Welcome the coming and speed the parting guest": hospitality in twelfth-century England', *Journal of Medieval History*, 33 (2007), pp. 142–3.

20   Finbar McCormick, 'Ritual feasting in Iron Age Ireland', in Gabriel Cooney et al., *Relics of Old Decency: Archaeological Studies in Later Prehistory. Festschrift for Barry Raftery* (Wordwell, 2009), pp. 405–12.

21   William Young, 'Arab hospitality as a rite of incorporation: the case of the Rashaayda Bedouin of eastern Sudan', *Anthropos*, 102:1 (2007), pp. 47–69. Young goes into fascinating detail about the precise rituals at every stage of this process.

22   Charles Stafford, *Separation and Reunion in Modern China* (Cambridge University Press, 2004), pp. 56–7.

23   Ibid., p. 58.

24   The translation is my own.

25   Torbjörn Lundmark, *Tales of Hi and Bye: Greeting and Parting Rituals Around the World* (Cambridge University Press, 2009), p. 114.

26   Kate Fox, *Watching the English* (Hachette, 2005), p. 59.

27   Andrew Shryock, 'Breaking hospitality apart: bad hosts, bad guests, and the problem of sovereignty', *Journal of the Royal Anthropological Institute*, 18:1 (2012), p. S23.

28   Tom Selwyn, 'An anthropology of hospitality', in Morrison and Lashley (eds.), *In Search of Hospitality*, p. 19.

29   Young, 'Arab hospitality as a rite of incorporation', p. 65.

30   Barbara Smuts, 'Reflections', in J. M. Coetzee et al., *The Lives of Animals* (Princeton University Press, 1999), pp. 109–13.

7 Ghosts

1 Emmanuel Levinas, *God, Death and Time* (Stanford University Press, 2000), p. 9.

2 Tiffanie Wen, 'Why do people believe in ghosts?', *The Atlantic* (5 September 2014).

3 Owen Davies, *The Haunted: A Social History of Ghosts* (Palgrave Macmillan, 2007), p. 241.

4 Jesse Bering, Katrina McLeod and Todd Shackelford, 'Reasoning about dead agents reveals possible adaptive trends', *Human Nature*, 16:4 (2005), pp. 376–7.

5 Henry Gehman, *Stories of the Departed: Minor Anthologies of the Pali Canon*, Volume IV (Pali Text Society, 1942), p. 10.

6 Ibid., p. 104.

7 Homer, *The Odyssey*, translated by Emily Wilson (W. W. Norton, 2018), p. 280.

8 Part of the genius of *Les Revenants* is that this burning hunger is never remarked upon, whether by the dead or the living. Instead it is just part of the background of their (after)lives.

9 Jane Ferguson, 'Terminally haunted: aviation ghosts, hybrid Buddhist practices, and disaster aversion strategies amongst airport workers in Myanmar and Thailand', *Asia Pacific Journal of Anthropology*, 15:1 (2014), pp. 47–64.

10 Patrice Ladwig, 'Visitors from Hell: transformative hospitality to ghosts in a Lao Buddhist festival', *Journal of the Royal Anthropological Institute*, 18:S1 (2012), pp. S90–S102. See also Ladwig's chapter 'Can things reach the dead? The ontological status of objects and the study of Lao Buddhist rituals for the

spirits of the deceased', in Kirsten W. Endre and Andrea Lauser (eds.), *Engaging the Spirit World: Popular Beliefs and Practices in Modern Southeast Asia* (Berghahn Books, 2011), pp. 19–41.

11 Heonik Kwon, *The Ghosts of the American War in Vietnam* (Cambridge University Press, 2008), pp. 37–40.

12 Ferguson, 'Terminally haunted', p. 60. Ferguson writes: 'Soe Naing was on tower communications duty when, on two separate occasions, Myanmar Airways pilots reported that the auto-start was already engaged, even though they had just entered the cockpit and hadn't touched the instruments. This was very disturbing for the Myanmar Airways pilots, but they were not allowed to leave the cockpit, or abort the flights. In both cases the flights went as planned and without incident. Soe Naing also mentioned having once seen a *tasay* [ghost] from the tower, but when I asked him to describe it in detail, he told me that the ghost flitted past too quickly on the concrete below for him to get a good look at it.'

13 Charlie Moore, 'M6 fatal crashes are due to ghosts including phantom lorries, vanishing hitchhikers and even Roman soldiers, says paranormal investigator', *Mail Online* (23 September 2018).

14 Aung Kyaw Min, 'The road of no return', *Myanmar Times* (25 January 2015).

15 For more context on the building of the new capital, see Dulyapak Preecharushh, *Naypyidaw: The New Capital of Burma* (White Lotus Books, 2014).

16 Bénédicte Brac de la Perrière, 'Possession and rebirth in Burma (Myanmar)', *Contemporary Buddhism*, 16:1 (2015), pp. 61–74.

17 For more on Burmese ghosts and what makes them so terrifying, see Melford Spiro, *Burmese Supernaturalism: A Study in the*

Explanation and Reduction of Suffering (Prentice Hall, 1967), p. 34.

18 Douglas Long, 'The ghost guide: 6 terrifying ghouls of Myanmar', *Myanmar Times* (30 October 2015).

19 Bruce Kapferer, *A Celebration of Demons: Exorcism and the Aesthetics of Healing in Sri Lanka* (Indiana University Press, 1983), p. 53.

20 The quote comes from Francis Young, who explores the contemporary revival of exorcism in his book *A History of Exorcism in the Catholic Church* (Palgrave Macmillan, 2016), p. 241.

21 Deborah Hyde, 'Exorcists are back – and people are getting hurt', *Guardian* (6 March 2018). See also 'Exorcism: Vatican course opens doors to 250 priests', *BBC News* (17 April 2018): https://www.bbc.co.uk/news/world-europe-43697573.

22 Pat Ashworth, 'Deliver us from evil', *Church Times* (17 February 2017).

23 Nicholas Hellen, 'Anglican priest exorcises "poltergeist" for Muslim family', *Sunday Times* (20 January 2019).

24 Aristotle, translated and edited by Robert Crisp, *Nicomachean Ethics* (Cambridge University Press, 2000), p. 19.

8 Pilgrims

1 Michael F. Fisher, *Migration: A World History* (Oxford University Press, 2014), p. 2. As Jan and Leo Lucassen and Patrick Manning write, 'Human migration history extends to the full scope of human history, some 150–200,000 years': see *Migration History in World History: Multidisciplinary Approaches* (Brill, 2010), p. 30.

2 See Lile Jia, E. R. Hirt and S. C. Karpen, 'Lessons from a faraway

land: the effect of spatial distance on creative cognition', *Journal of Experimental Social Psychology*, 45:5 (2009), pp. 1127–31.

3   Ken Smith, quoted in Clare Brown and Don Paterson (eds.), *Don't Ask Me What I Mean: Poets in Their Own Words* (Picador, 2003), p. 274.

4   John 14:6.

5   See Elsaid M. Badawi and Muhammad Abdel Haleem, *Arabic–English Dictionary of Qur'anic Usage* (Brill, 2008), pp. 419–20.

6   The translation is my own. For an alternative translation, see Brook Ziporyn, *Zhuangzi: The Essential Writings, with Selections from Traditional Commentaries* (Hackett Publishing Company, 2008), pp. 13–14.

7   St Augustine, *Confessions* (Oxford University Press, 1989), p. 118.

8   The idea of 'free and easy wandering' comes from the *Zhuangzi*: see Ziporyn, *Zhuangzi*, pp. 3–8. François Jullien writes that, in these metaphors of the 'way' or 'path', 'the essential quality of the way is that it is viable. It does not lead to any goal, but one can pass along it, one always can pass along it, so one can always move on (instead of becoming bogged down or finding one's path blocked)': see 'Did philosophers have to become fixated on truth?', *Critical Inquiry*, 28 (2002), p. 820.

9   Bruce Chatwin, *The Anatomy of Restlessness* (Penguin Books, 1997), p. 113.

10   M. A. Claussen, '*Peregrinatio* and *peregrini* in Augustine's *City of God*', *Traditio*, 46 (1991), p. 37.

11   Stephanie Hayes-Healy, 'Patterns of *peregrinatio* in the Early Middle Ages', in Stephanie Hayes-Healy (ed.), *Medieval Paradigms: Essays in Honor of Jeremy DuQuesnay Adams*, Volume 2 (Palgrave Macmillan, 2005), p. 16.

12   See Hadas Goldgeier, Natalie D. Munro and Leore Grosman,
      'Remembering a sacred place: the depositional history of Hilazon
      Tachtit, a Natufian burial cave', *Journal of Anthropological
      Archaeology*, 56 (2019), p. 101111.

13   Joy McCorriston, 'The Neolithic in Arabia: a view from the
      south', *Arabian Archaeology and Epigraphy*, 24 (2013), p. 70.

14   Joy McCorriston, 'Inter-cultural pilgrimage, identity, and the
      axial age in the ancient Near East', in Troels Myrup Kristensen
      and Wiebke Friese (eds.), *Excavating Pilgrimage: Archaeological
      Approaches to Sacred Travel and Movement in the Ancient World*
      (Routledge, 2017), p. 12.

15   Lionel Casson, *Travel in the Ancient World* (George Allen &
      Unwin, 1974), p. 32.

16   For religious travel in ancient Greece, see Inge Nielsen,
      'Collective mysteries and greek pilgrimage: The cases of Eleusis,
      Thebes and Andania', in Kristensen and Friese (eds.), *Excavating
      Pilgrimage*, pp. 28–46. For travel to sporting events in ancient
      Greece, see Fernando García Romero, 'Sports tourism in ancient
      Greece', *Journal of Tourism History*, 5:2 (2013), pp. 146–60.
      Kristensen and Friese (eds.), *Excavating Pilgrimage*, has a wealth
      of other information on pilgrimage in antiquity.

17   As a corrective to this, see 'The truth about migration: we are a
      stay-at-home species', *New Scientist* (6 April 2016).

18   Ewen Callaway, 'UK mapped out by genetic ancestry', *Nature*
      (18 March 2015): https://www.nature.com/news/british-isles-
      mapped-out-by-genetic-ancestry–1.17136.

19   Patrick Greenfield, 'Calls for 195-year-old Vagrancy Act to be
      scrapped in England and Wales', *Guardian* (19 June 2019):
      https://www.theguardian.com/society/2019/jun/19/calls-for-

195-year-old-vagrancy-act-scrapped-homeless.

20 Jiyin Cao, Adam D. Galinsky and William W. Maddux, 'Does
    travel broaden the mind? Breadth of foreign experiences increases
    generalized trust', *Social Psychological and Personality Science*, 5:5
    (2014), pp. 517–25. There is also evidence that we are more likely
    to be sincere and trustworthy when speaking a second language,
    or a language that isn't our mother tongue: see Yoella Bereby-
    Meyer et al., 'Honesty speaks a second language', *Topics in
    Cognitive Science*, 12:2 (2012), pp. 1–12.

21 Jessica de Bloom et al., 'Vacation from work: a "ticket to
    creativity"? The effects of recreational travel on cognitive
    flexibility and originality', *Tourism Management*, 44 (2014),
    pp. 164–71.

22 See David H. Cropley, Arthur J. Cropley, James C. Kaufman and
    Mark A. Runco (eds.), *The Dark Side of Creativity* (Cambridge
    University Press, 2010).

23 Jackson G. Lu et al., 'The dark side of going abroad: how broad
    foreign experiences increase immoral behavior', *Journal of
    Personality and Social Psychology*, 112:1 (2017), pp. 1–16.

24 See Denis Tolkach, Christine Yinghuan Zeng and Stephen Pratt,
    'Tourists behaving badly: how culture shapes conduct when we're
    on holiday', *The Conversation* (9 February 2017): https://
    theconversation.com/tourists-behaving-badly-how-culture-
    shapes-conduct-when-were-on-holiday-72285. The article draws
    upon their research published as 'Ethics of Chinese & Western
    tourists in Hong Kong', *Annals of Tourism Research*, 63 (2017).
    The idea that unethical behaviour might increase when people are
    severed from the bonds of reciprocity and the mutual moral
    surveillance of more settled populations is superficially plausible;

but it is hard, on the data there is, to draw too many general conclusions. In particular, when the data concerns relatively privileged groups such as college students (or travelling British kids with guitars in Barcelona), it would be risky to extrapolate and draw conclusions about less privileged mobile populations where the dynamics may be very different.

25 See Kevin O'Gorman, 'Dimensions of hospitality: Exploring ancient and classical origins', in Conrad Lashley (ed.), *Hospitality: A Social Lens* (Elsevier, 2006), p. 26. Incidentally, the name 'Xenophon' means, literally, 'the one with the voice of a stranger'.

26 See Bradley A. Ault, 'Housing the poor and homeless in ancient Greece', in Bradley Ault and Lisa Nevett (eds.), *Ancient Greek Houses and Households: Chronological, Regional, and Social Diversity* (University of Pennsylvania Press, 2015), pp. 150–55. The estimates for the number of guests the hostelry housed range from 140 to 420.

27 Carolinne White, *The Rule of Benedict: Translated with an Introduction and Notes* (Penguin Books, 2008), pp. 79 and 89. 'I was a stranger and you took me in' is from Matthew 25:35.

28 Kevin O'Gorman. 'Iranian hospitality: a hidden treasure', *International Journal of Contemporary Hospitality Management*, 9:1 (2007), pp. 31–6.

29 The translation is my own.

30 Ibn Battuta, *Travels in Asia and Africa, 1325–1354,* translated by H. A. R. Gibb (Routledge, 2004), p. 286.

31 Patrick Olivelle, *King, Governance, and Law in Ancient India* (Oxford University Press, 2016), p. 156.

32 David Graeber, *The Utopia of Rules: On Technology, Stupidity,*

and the Secret Joys of Bureaucracy (Melville House, 2015), p. 152.

33 Amitai Touval, *An Anthropological Study of Hospitality: The Innkeeper and the Guest* (Palgrave Macmillan, 2017), p. 60.

34 Graeber, *The Utopia of Rules*, p. 152.

35 Jill Hamilton, *Thomas Cook: The Holiday-Maker* (Sutton Publishing, 2005), p. 61.

36 Quoted ibid., p. 1.

37 Ibid.

38 Hamilton gives a fascinating account of Thomas Cook's radicalism.

39 Emmanuel Levinas, *Totality and Infinity: An Essay on Exteriority*, translated by Alphonso Lingis (Duquesne University Press, 2011), p. 33.

9 Who Goes There?

1 The figures here are from the UNHCR, on their useful dashboard: https://data2.unhcr.org/en/situations/mediterranean/location/5179.

2 Mary Harris, 'Bulgaria forces Greek train back over border on suspicion of refugee smuggling', *Greek Reporter* (23 June 2016).

3 Dina Nayeri, *The Ungrateful Refugee* (Canongate, 2019), p. 62.

4 Robert Garland, *Wandering Guests: The Ancient Greek Diaspora from the Age of Homer to the Death of Alexander the Great* (Princeton University Press, 2014), p. 115.

5 Livy, *The History of Rome: Books 1–5*, translated by Valerie M. Warrior (Hackett Publishing Company, 2006), p. 16. Livy clearly had a poor opinion of these refugees, referring to them as 'a host

of shady, low-born people'. Their low-born shadiness was subsequently, Livy says, managed by the appointment of a hundred patrician senators to oversee the growing state.

6   See *Greece: Inhumane Conditions at Land Border*, Human Rights Watch (27 July 2018): https://www.hrw.org/news/2018/07/27/greece-inhumane-conditions-land-border.

7   Gazmend Kapllani, *A Short Border Handbook* (Granta Books, 2017), p. 30.

8   Athena Farrokhzad, *White Blight*, translated by Jennifer Hayashida (Argos Books, 2015), p. 52.

9   See Alexander C. Diener and Joshua Hagen, *Borders: A Very Short Introduction* (Oxford University Press, 2012), p. 21.

10   Walls, as Ursula K. Le Guin reminds us, are ambiguous, two-faced – they both exclude and contain: see *The Dispossessed* (Hachette, 2015), p. 1.

11   Jerry D. Moore, *The Prehistory of Home* (University of California Press, 2012), p. 119.

12   *The Epic of Gilgamesh*, translated by Andrew George (Penguin Books, 1999), p. 2.

13   One example is the Pharaoh Senusret III, 'who erected stelae to designate Egypt's southern border with Nubia': see Diener and Hagen, *Borders*, p. 23.

14   Julia Lovell puts it well: 'The first great myth of the Great Wall is its singularity, that the term meaningfully refers to one ancient structure with a coherently chronicled past.' She argues that there is 'no single Great Wall, but instead many lesser walls': see *The Great Wall: China Against the World, 1000 BC–AD 2000* (Grove/Atlantic, 2007), p. 15.

15   In his study of the archaeology of borders, Bryan Feuer writes,

'Even boundaries designed and built to represent considerable barriers such as Hadrian's Wall, the Great Wall of China and the Berlin Wall were not totally impermeable, and in the first two instances, were not meant to be': see *Boundaries, Borders and Frontiers in Archaeology: A Study of Spatial Relationships* (McFarland and Company, 2016), p. 60.

16 In his fascinating history of the idea of foreignness in North America, the legal historian Kunal M. Parker writes about how the idea of foreignness has been used to deny the rights of citizenship to those considered outsiders: black and Native American communities, women and the poor. Parker writes: 'A "foreigner" might come from across the ocean, from relatively nearby, or from nowhere at all': see *Making Foreigners: Immigration and Citizenship Law in America, 1600–2000* (Cambridge University Press, 2015), p. 25.

17 John C. Torpey, *The Invention of the Passport: Surveillance, Citizenship and the State* (Cambridge University Press, 2018), p. 12.

18 I have not been able to corroborate this and it may be a local myth. But even if it is, the myth says something about the way that we imaginatively divide up the world.

19 Benedict Anderson, *Imagined Communities* (Verso Books, 2006), pp. 6–7.

20 For a thorough survey of relationships between ancient Greeks and non-Greeks, see Erik Jensen, *Barbarians in the Greek and Roman World* (Hackett Publishing Company, 2018).

21 See Magnus Fiskesjö, 'On the "raw" and the "cooked" barbarians of imperial China', *Inner Asia*, 1:2 (1999), pp. 139–68. The metaphors of 'raw' and 'cooked' have a complicated relationship

with ideas of state power. The implication of 'raw' is 'not yet cooked': in other words, not yet transformed by the fires of culture and statehood. Fiskesjö writes: 'The translation "Raw and Cooked" . . . highlights that the barbarians are transformed, made to accept "civilisation", under the guidance of the benevolent, virtuous emperor (he is the chief "cook", the virtuoso!). The people on the peripheries are identified, appropriated, and, when ready ("Cooked"), "ingested" into the body of the state.' While all Han Chinese were considered 'cooked', there was a distinction between those barbarians who remained in their raw state, and didn't pay taxes ('raw barbarians' or *shengfan*), and those who were at least lightly braised, and paid their taxes ('cooked barbarians' or *shufan*): see James Stuart Olson, *An Ethnohistorical Dictionary of China* (Greenwood Publishing Group, 1998), p. 95.

22 The translation is my own.

23 Diener and Hagen, *Borders*, p. 42.

24 Elina Troscenko, 'With a border fence in the backyard: Materialization of the border in the landscape and the social lives of border people', in Tone Bringa and Hege Toje (eds.), *Eurasian Borderlands: Spatializing Borders in the Aftermath of State Collapse* (Palgrave Macmillan, 2016), pp. 87–106.

25 Kapka Kassabova, *Border* (Granta Books, 2017), p. 320.

26 Patrick Olivelle, *King, Governance, and Law in Ancient India* (Oxford University Press, 2016), p. 172.

27 Chun-shu Chang, *The Rise of the Chinese Empire: Frontier, Immigration, and Empire in Han China, 130 BC–AD 157* (Michigan University Press, 2007), p. 137.

28 The connection between borders and taxes in the medieval Islamic world is complex: see Ralph W. Brauer, 'Boundaries and frontiers

in medieval Muslim geography', *Transactions of the American Philosophical Society*, 85:6 (1995), pp. 1–73. Drawing on the accounts of medieval travellers in the Islamic world, Brauer argues that sea borders were relatively well defined and very systematically taxed. But inland borders were much less clearly defined, and on land the mechanisms of taxation, and their use in controlling human movement, were much more complex.

29 Torpey, *The Invention of the Passport*, pp. 157–8.

30 Francis Fukuyama, *The End of History and the Last Man* (The Free Press, 1992).

31 Tim Marshall, *Divided: Why We're Living in an Age of Walls* (Elliott and Thompson, 2018), p. 1.

32 Daniel Trilling, *Lights in the Distance* (Verso Books, 2018), p. xi.

33 See, for example, 'Turkey claims migrant killed in Greek border clash', *BBC News* (4 March 2020): https://www.bbc.com/news/world-europe-51735715.

34 The directive is the Carrier Sanctions Directive 2001/51/EC and it fines airlines for carrying those without proper documentation. Thus those seeking asylum are unable to even board a plane. The directive reads, in part: 'In order to combat illegal immigration effectively, it is essential that all the Member States introduce provisions laying down the obligations of carriers transporting foreign nationals into the territory of the Member States . . . the maximum amount of the penalty imposed as a lump sum for each infringement is not less that EUR 500,000 or equivalent national currency at the rate of exchange published in the Official Journal on 10 August 2001, irrespective of the number of persons carried': https://eur-lex.europa.eu/legal-content/EN/TXT/PDF/?uri=CELEX:32001L0051&from=EN.

35 Helena Smith, 'Refugee crisis: how Greeks opened their hearts to strangers', *Guardian* (12 March 2016).

10 Crowds

1 The excellent Language Log website, curated by Victor Mair, has an entertaining discussion on the difficulty of translating *lao wai*: https://languagelog.ldc.upenn.edu/nll/?p=11626. One debate is how much the term applies to all foreigners and how much to white foreigners only. China scholar and long-standing *lao wai* Brendan O'Kane traces the term to an edict written by the Kangxi Emperor in response to a papal ban on Confucian rites, giving weight to the argument that the term has always been associated, to some degree, with skin colour.

2 United Nations, *World Urbanization Prospects: The 2018 Revision* (United Nations, 2018): https://www.un.org/development/desa/publications/2018-revision-of-world-urbanization-prospects.html.

3 Douglas P. Fry, *Beyond War: The Human Potential for Peace* (Oxford University Press, 2007), p. 203. Fry also writes: 'We high-tech folks of the twenty-first century rarely pause to consider the immense plasticity in the nature of our species that allows a hunter-gatherer primate to live in this Internet world of strangers, stock exchanges, and cruise missiles. A macroscopic anthropological perspective highlights the human capacity for creating and adjusting to immense social and institutional changes' (p. 204).

4 The anthropologists used to call this 'fictive kinship', a term that

has fallen out of favour over the previous few decades. In his anthropological classic *A Critique of the Study of Kinship* (University of Michigan Press, 1984), David M. Schneider asks: 'Why should adoption and other forms of "fictive" kinship be so clearly differentiated from true kinship – always for anthropologists, and allegedly for all societies?' (p. 176). He takes adoption as a test case that helps blur the distinction, writing: 'If the bond between the parent and the natural child and the adopted child were equally strong, of essentially the same quality or significance, then there would be no reason why the distinction between adoptive, putative, fictive relationship and "true" or "real" relationship should be so consistently drawn, as it has for the past hundred years or more' (p. 99).

5   One day, when I took a trip away from the city, I stayed in a small family hotel. I got to know the owner and her daughter, who was five. One evening we were chatting, and the girl referred to me as 'uncle' or *shushu*, only to be reprimanded by her mother, who thought I was youthful enough to be referred to instead as 'older brother' or *gege*. The girl was having nothing of it. 'But he drinks beer,' she protested. 'That makes him an uncle.' For the rest of my stay, I was 'uncle', not 'older brother'.

6   Florence Weber, for example, writes about 'everyday kinship', which is 'not rooted in filiation or alliance, but in help with no expectations in return, pursuing a common cause, and sharing resources': quoted in T. Pfirsch and C. Araos, 'Urban kinships', *Articulo: Journal of Urban Research*, 20 (2017), p. 3.

7   Christopher Dell, 'Megacity', in Kristin Feireiss (ed.), *City and Structure: Photo-essays by H. G. Esch* (Hatje Cantz, 2008), p. 41.

8   For more on urbanisation and epidemics, see James C. Scott,

Against the Grain: A Deep History of the Earliest States (Yale University Press, 2017), p. 101.

9   Jo Ann Scurlock and Burton Andersen, *Diagnoses in Assyrian and Babylonian Medicine: Ancient Sources, Translations, and Modern Medical Analyses* (University of Illinois Press, 2010).

10   See Markham J. Geller, *Ancient Babylonian Medicine: Theory and Practice* (Wiley-Blackwell, 2010). In *Diagnoses in Assyrian and Babylonian Medicine*, Scurlock and Andersen also give an example of quarantine measures put in place to manage a woman who has an infectious fever. One preserved letter says: 'give stern orders that nobody is to drink from the cup from which she drinks; nobody is to sit on the seat on which she sits and nobody is to lie on the bed on which she lies' (p. 17).

11   John Aberth, *Plagues in World History* (Rowman & Littlefield, 2011), p. 4.

12   John F. Nunn, *Ancient Egyptian Medicine* (University of Oklahoma Press, 2002). Interestingly, there is no evidence in Egypt, either textual or in the human remains of mummies, of bubonic plague.

13   Thucydides, *The Peloponnesian War*, translated by Martin Hammond (Oxford University Press, 2009), p. 99.

14   Ibid., pp. 102–3.

15   Boccaccio, *The Decameron*, translated by G. H. McWilliam (Penguin Books, 1972), p. 50.

16   P. D. Smith, *City: A Guidebook for the Urban Age* (Bloomsbury, 2012), pp. 54–5.

17   Dick Whittington was a historical figure, although, unlike the figure in the popular tale, he was not born into poverty; nor is there any evidence that he had much to do with cats. In the story,

Whittington moves to London with his cat and lives in poverty. But the cat ends up heading aboard the good ship *Unicorn* to the Barbary coast, or present-day North Africa, where the Moorish king is having a problem with rats, his court at risk of plague. Whittington's cat, who is pregnant, kills the rodents and has kittens. When the ship returns to London, Whittington is rewarded handsomely (though he never sees the cat again).

18　For this argument, see Scott, *Against the Grain*. Scott's view is that for most of history nobody in their right mind (other than the very privileged) would want to live in an urban centre. For his more detailed exploration of how the tension between state and non-state power has played out in South-East Asian history, see his wonderful *The Art of Not Being Governed: An Anarchist History of Upland Southeast Asia* (Yale University Press, 2009).

19　Sometimes this is talked about as 'eusociality'. For ultrasociality, see Peter Turchin, 'The Puzzle of Ultrasociality', in Peter Richerson and Morten Christiansen (eds.), *Cultural Evolution: Society, Technology, Language, and Religion* (MIT Press, 2013), pp. 61–73. For eusociality, see Edward Wilson, *The Social Conquest of the Earth* (W. W. Norton, 2012), p. 16.

20　Frans de Waal, *Primates and Philosophers* (Princeton University Press, 2006), p. 4.

21　Matthew Lieberman, *Social: Why Our Brains Are Wired to Connect* (Oxford University Press, 2013), p. 9.

22　L. A. Maher and Margaret Conkey, 'Homes for hunters? Exploring the concept of home at hunter-gatherer sites in Upper Paleolithic Europe and Epipaleolithic Southwest Asia', *Current Anthropology*, 60:1 (2019), pp. 91–137.

23　Smith, *City*, p. xi.

24 Once – in a Chinese temple dedicated to the sea goddess Mazu in the Burmese city of Yangon – I watched as the HR department from a local Chinese firm turned up with a stack of CVs, elbowed their way to the front and went through the documents systematically, clattering the moon blocks, asking the goddess her advice. There are worse ways to recruit.

25 See Di Wang, *Street Culture in Chengdu: Public Space, Urban Commoners, and Local Politics, 1870–1930* (Stanford University Press, 2003), p. 68.

26 See Judith Farquhar and Qicheng Zhang's wonderful account of Chinese practices for 'nourishing life' in *Ten Thousand Things: Nurturing Life in Contemporary Beijing* (Zone Books, 2012), p. 57.

27 For a discussion of this *renao* city culture when it comes to night markets, see Shuenn-Der Yu, 'Hot and noisy: Taiwan's night market culture', in David K. Jordan, Andrew D. Morris and Marc L. Moskowitz (eds.), *The Minor Arts of Daily Life: Popular Culture in Taiwan* (University of Hawai'i Press), pp. 129–49.

28 Barbara Ehrenreich, *Dancing in the Streets: A History of Collective Joy* (Granta Books, 2007), p. 253.

29 Ibid., p. 248.

30 Valerie Hansen, The Beijing Qingming scroll and its significance for the study of Chinese history (*Journal of Sung-Yuan Studies*, 1996). Although the scroll is often associated with the Qingming (tomb-sweeping) spring festival, Hansen argues that the word *qingming* should be translated as 'peaceful and orderly', so that the painting represents an ideal mode of urban life. She develops this idea in 'The mystery of the Qingming scroll and its subject: the case against Kaifeng', *Journal of Sung-Yuan Studies*, 26 (1996), pp. 183–200. Another reason why Hansen argues that this is a

fantasy of a city, rather than a depiction of an actual city, is the absence of women ('where are all the women?' she asks).

31 This comes from chapter 15 of the *Jin Ping Mei*. The translation is my own. The term for 'dense crowds' is literally 'human smoke': an agglomeration so thick and changeable that it is impossible to pick out any single individual, any one particle. An alternative translation of the passage can be found in David Tod Roy (ed. and trans.), *The Plum in the Golden Vase, or, Chin P'ing Mei, Volume One: The Gathering* (Princeton University Press, 1993), p. 300. There are earlier references to the term 'hot and noisy' in Wu Cheng-en's *The Journey to the West*, which dates to the century before the *Jin Ping Mei*. Here is the section from chapter 88, where the pilgrims, on the way to India to collect scriptures, come to the Jade Flower City: 'they entered the city gates, and thereupon they saw a great street filled with wine-stores and song-houses, abundantly hot and noisy'; the translation is my own.

32 Smith, *City*, p. 35.

33 For multicultural Chang'an, see Sanping Chen, *Multicultural China in the Early Middle Ages* (University of Pennsylvania Press, 2012), and Edward H. Schafer's wonderful *The Golden Peaches of Samarkand: A Study of T'ang Exotics* (University of California Press, 1963).

34 Michael Harris, *Solitude: In Pursuit of a Singular Life in a Crowded World* (St Martin's Press, 2017), p. 27.

11 Trouble with the Neighbours

1   The greeting in Burmese is *Sa pi bi la?* Similarly, over in China, you can greet people with a friendly *Ni chi le ma*, or 'Have you eaten?' In both places, you might also greet people with other everyday questions, like 'Where are you going?' One of my favourites in Chinese is the simple, 'What are you up to?'

2   Keith Wrightson, 'The "decline of neighbourliness" revisited', in Norman Jones and Daniel Woolf (eds.), *Local Identities in Late Medieval and Early Modern England* (Palgrave Macmillan, 2007), p. 23.

3   Richard D. Lewis tells the following story: 'I once asked a Finnish peasant how much personal space he felt he had a right to. He was a man who took such questions seriously, so he thought about it for a full minute. Then he took his *puukko* (woodman's knife) out of its sheath and stretched his right arm out in front of him, holding the *puukko* with the blade parallel to the ground. "That distance," he replied': see *Finland: Cultural Lone Wolf* (Intercultural Press, 2005), p. 151.

4   Wrightson, 'The "decline of neighbourliness" revisited', p. 24.

5   Richard Hoggart, *Everyday Language and Everyday Life* (Routledge, 2018), pp. 75–6.

6   Quoted in Emily Cockayne, *Cheek by Jowl: A History of Neighbours* (The Bodley Head, 2012), p. 22.

7   M. E. J. Richardson, *Hammurabi's Laws: Text, Translation and Glossary* (Continuum, 2000). For the matrimonial gossip case see p. 91. The situation, as far as it is possible to make sense of the text, is this. Somebody goes to his future bride's house to

negotiate and pay a bride price. If the future husband's neighbour then gossips about them, causing the wedding to be cancelled, the neighbour must pay double the bride price to the man as recompense. The neighbour is also not permitted to go and marry the woman in question.

8   John Muir, *Life and Letters in the Ancient Greek World* (Routledge, 2009), p. 54.

9   Here 'outlandish' means 'foreign', but it is not clear where Herbert got this aphorism from. The authorship of the collection of proverbs is still debated by scholars.

10 W. Mieder, '"Good fences make good neighbours": history and significance of an ambiguous proverb', *Folklore*, 114:2 (2003), pp. 155–79.

11 See Igor Khristoforov, 'Blurred lines: land surveying and the creation of landed property in nineteenth-century Russia', *Cahiers du monde russe*, 57:1 (2016), pp. 31–54. Khristoforov writes: 'In northern Russia, initiation rites accompanied the ploughing of boundary furrows: children were brought here and beaten in order to remind them of the borders of their father's plot of land; from here comes the Novgorod saying "Don't try to teach or tell me; I was flogged at the boundary ditch" (*Ty menia ne uchi, ty mne ne rasskazivai, ia na mezhevoi iame sechen*)' (p. 34).

12 Some examples can be found in Matthew R. Christ, *The Bad Citizen in Classical Athens* (Cambridge University Press, 2006).

13 Aristotle, translated and edited by Robert Crisp, *Nicomachean Ethics* (Cambridge University Press, 2000), p. 19. The passage reads as follows: 'But bad people cannot be in concord, except to a small extent, just as they can be friends only to a small extent; for

they try to get more than their share of advantages, while falling
short in difficult jobs and public services. And since each wishes
this for himself, he keeps a sharp eye on his neighbour and holds
him back, because if people do not look out for the common
interest, it is destroyed' (1167b10, p. 172).

14 See Slavoj Žižek, *Against the Double Blackmail* (Penguin Books,
2016). Žižek attributes this insight to Adam Kotsko in his book
Creepiness (John Hunt Publishing, 2015). But Kotsko actually
makes the more modest claim that 'creepiness has often been close
at hand in the form of the creepy neighbour' (p. 25).

15 For a good overview of Yangon's rush to development, see
Maaike Matelski and Marion Sabrié, 'Challenges and resilience in
Myanmar's urbanization: a special issue on Yangon', *Moussons*, 33
(2019).

16 See http://www.futurecities.nl/en/cities/yangon-en/.

17 In *Colonial Policy and Practice: A Comparative Study of Burma and
Netherlands India* (Cambridge University Press, 1948), Furnivall
wrote that in Yangon, 'There is a plural society, with different
sections of the community living side by side, but separately,
within the same political unit' (p. 304). For a fascinating
discussion of Yangon's 'plural society', see Richard Cockett,
Blood, Dreams and Gold: The Changing Face of Burma (Yale
University Press, 2015).

18 Miri Rubin, *Cities of Strangers: Making Lives in Medieval Europe*
(Cambridge University Press, 2020), p. 2.

19 Robert Hard, *Diogenes the Cynic: Sayings and Anecdotes, with
Other Popular Moralists* (Oxford World's Classics, 2012), p. 16.

20 Melford Spiro, *Burmese Supernaturalism* (Prentice-Hall, 1967),
p. 28.

21   Kwame Anthony Appiah, *Cosmopolitanism* (W. W. Norton, 2006), p. 144.

22   Zon Pann Pwint, 'Nirvana market', *Myanmar Times* (15 November 2019). There is a recognition that many of those who flock to the nirvana markets are not just local members of the community, but those who are poor and needy from elsewhere. One woman interviewed by the *Myanmar Times* said, 'The ritual has been deeply rooted in Yangon for years. It's a kind of charity. People share food with others less fortunate, regardless of their religion and status.' The nirvana market functions, in this way, as a kind of food bank; but it does so also under the guise of a carnival or a festival. As for the householders and shops who donate, their gift-giving helps them accrue spiritual merit, useful – as the Buddhists say – in both this life and the next.

23   For the full speech, see the *Telegraph* (5 October 2016).

24   Kwame Anthony Appiah, '"Mrs May, we are all citizens of the world," says philosopher', BBC Online (12 October 2016): https://www.bbc.com/news/uk-politics-37788717.

25   Jon Bloomfield, *Our City: Migrants and the Making of Modern Birmingham* (Unbound, 2019), p. 19.

26   Quoted in Rubin, *Cities of Strangers*, p. 9. In practice, Isidore was more interested in 'holding the lives' of his fellow Christian believers than those of other communities, in particular the Jewish communities.

27   Bloomfield, *Our City*, lists some of my old Birmingham haunts: the revamped library, the Bull Ring (which is regrettably private land, but which at least functions, in the main, as public space), the Midlands Arts Centre and Cannon Hill Park.

28   See Matelski and Sabrié, 'Challenges and resilience in Myanmar's

urbanization': 'While the city presents unique opportunities to Myanmar's people, it also increasingly faces problems of marginalisation, congestion, and gentrification that contribute to rising inequalities rather than inclusive development' (p. 12).

12 Loneliness

1 'Letter Sent to Zi'an' by Yu Xuanji: the translation is my own.

2 Fay Bound Alberti, in her terrific cultural history of loneliness, writes: 'Choosing to be alone for artistic purposes . . . was an educated middle-class activity, requiring physical space as well as time away from economic activities. It was also traditionally white, male, and privileged; the same conventions have not been applied to black writers and women have long been identified through family structures rather than in terms of their own individual accomplishments': see *A Biography of Loneliness: The History of an Emotion* (Oxford University Press, 2019), p. 24.

3 Rebecca Solnit, *A Field Guide to Getting Lost* (Canongate, 2006), p. 131.

4 The lentils were in honour of the Tibetan hermit-sage Jetsun Milarepa, who lived in the eleventh century. According to later accounts, Milarepa used nettles as substitutes for meat, for barley flour, for seasoning and for salt. In paintings of the sage, he is often tinged with green due to his nettle-based diet. It became clear, over the years, that Milarepa was always going to outdo me: however many nettles I ate on those solitary retreats, it was never enough to turn myself green.

5 The figure of 5 per cent for 'chronic loneliness' is the same as

pre-lockdown figures, but the report found a significant increase in the 'lockdown lonely'. It concludes that 14.3 per cent of the UK population suffered from this lockdown loneliness. See 'Coronavirus and loneliness, Great Britain: 3 April to 3 May 2020' (Office of National Statistics 2020): https://www.ons.gov.uk/peoplepopulationandcommunity/wellbeing/bulletins/coronaviru sandlonelinessgreatbritain/3aprilto3may2020.

6   Moya Sarner, 'Feeling lonely? You're not on your own', *New Scientist* (19 July 2017).

7   See Louise C. Hawkley and John T. Cacioppo, 'Loneliness matters: a theoretical and empirical review of consequences and mechanisms', *Annals of Behavioural Medicine*, 40:2 (2010).

8   The claim is based on a paper by Julianne Holt-Lunstad, Timothy B. Smith and J. Bradley Layton, 'Social relationships and mortality risk: a meta-analytic review', *PLoS Medicine*, 7:7 (2010).

9   See Vivek H. Murthy, *Together: Loneliness, Health and What Happens When We Find Connection* (Profile Books, 2020), pp. 13–14.

10   Alberti, *A Biography of Loneliness*, p. 5.

11   Famously, Robin Dunbar has argued that human language arose out of gossip, which he sees as a form of social grooming: see *Grooming, Gossip, and the Evolution of Language* (Harvard University Press, 1996).

12   'Gentle touch soothes the pain of social rejection', *UCL News* (18 October 2017): https://www.ucl.ac.uk/news/2017/oct/gentle-touch-soothes-pain-social-rejection.

13   Maria Konnikova, 'The power of touch', *New Yorker* (4 March 2015).

14   David J. Linden, *Touch: The Science of the Sense That Makes Us Human* (Penguin Books, 2015), p. 4.

15   Paula Cocozza, 'No hugging: are we living through a crisis of touch?', *Guardian* (7 March 2018).

16   Alberti, *A Biography of Loneliness*, p. ix.

17   See the article by Laura Mol, 'Loneliness and touch starvation in times of the coronavirus', *Studium Generale* (14 April 2020): https://www.sg.uu.nl/artikelen/2020/04/loneliness-and-touch-starvation-times-coronavirus.

18   Frans de Waal, *Primates and Philosophers* (Princeton University Press, 2006), p. 4.

19   Lars Svendsen, *A Philosophy of Loneliness* (Reaktion Books, 2017), p. 20.

20   Patricia Joy Huntington, *Loneliness and Lament: A Journey to Receptivity* (Indiana University Press, 2009), p. 7.

21   Bertrand Russell, *Autobiography* (Routledge, 2009), p. 160.

22   The question of hunter-gatherer leisure time has been debated ever since the anthropologist Marshall Sahlins, in 1966, called hunter-gatherer society 'the original affluent society'. Although Sahlins downplays the significant drawbacks of life in such societies, recent evidence suggests that the transition to agriculture does lead to a diminution of free time: see Victoria Reyes-García, 'Did foragers enjoy more free time?', *Nature Human Behaviour*, 3 (2019), pp. 772–3.

23   Jared Diamond, *The World Until Yesterday* (Penguin Books, 2013), p. 457.

24   John and Stephanie Cacioppo, 'Loneliness is a modern epidemic in need of treatment', *New Scientist* (30 December 2014).

25   In *Together*, Murthy writes: 'loneliness serves a vital function by

warning us when something essential for our survival – social connection – is lacking' (p. 23).

26 Jill Lepore, 'The history of loneliness', *New Yorker* (6 April 2020).

27 Olivia Laing, *The Lonely City: Adventures in the Art of Being Alone* (Canongate, 2016), pp. 3–4.

28 Zhenzhu Yue, Cong Feng et al., 'Lonely in a crowd: Population density contributes to perceived loneliness in China', in Sarah J. Bevinn (ed.), *Psychology of Loneliness* (Nova Science Publishers, 2011), pp. 137–49.

29 See Svendsen, *A Philosophy of Loneliness*, chapter 4, for an interesting exploration of what the data about loneliness and trust say.

30 Ken J. Rotenberg, 'Loneliness and interpersonal trust', *Journal of Social and Clinical Psychology*, 13:2 (1994), pp. 152–73.

31 Rotenberg writes: 'Loneliness was negatively associated with: (a) generalised beliefs in reliability of others; (b) reliability trust behaviour towards unfamiliar others; (c) reliability trust in close peers; (d) emotional trust in close peers; and (e) ratings of trusting of relationships with close peers' (p. 170).

32 Zhaobao Jia and Wenhua Tian, 'Loneliness of left-behind children: a cross-sectional survey in a sample of rural China', *Child: Care, Health and Development*, 36:6 (2010), pp. 812–17.

33 See Guoying Wang et al., 'Loneliness among the rural older people in Anhui, China: prevalence and associated factors', *Geriatric Psychiatry*, 26:11 (2011), and Zhen-Qiang Wu et al., 'Correlation between loneliness and social relationship among empty nest elderly in Anhui rural area, China', *Aging & Mental Health*, 14:1 (2010), pp. 108–12.

34 See https://ideasfactorybg.org/en/baba-residence/.

35 See the news item on the Euromontana website (23 February 2018): https://www.euromontana.org/en/baba-residence-initiative-attract-young-people-depopulated-villages-bulgaria/.

36 Anelia Chalakova, 'Baba Residence brings life back to the depopulated Bulgarian villages!', *Bulgarka* (11 June 2017): https://www.bulgarkamagazine.com/en/резиденция-баба-връща-живота-на-об/.

37 Yanina Taneva, personal communication.

38 Biljana Sikimic and Anne-Marie Sorescu, 'The concept of loneliness and death among Vlachs in north-eastern Serbia', *Symposia: Journal for Studies in Ethnology and Anthropology* (2004), p. 165.

39 See, for example, Leng Leng Thang, 'Before we give them fuzzy robots, let's try solving elderly loneliness with people', *Quartz* (12 December 2018): https://qz.com/1490605/before-we-give-them-fuzzy-robots-lets-try-solving-elderly-loneliness-with-people/.

40 For more on giving and its relationship with loneliness, see Jenny de Jong Gierveld and Pearl A. Dykstra, 'Virtue is its own reward? Support-giving in the family and loneliness in middle and old age', *Ageing & Society*, 28:2 (2008), pp. 271–87.

41 Michelle Anne Parsons, 'Being unneeded in post-Soviet Russia: lessons for an anthropology of loneliness', *Transcultural Psychiatry* (2020), pp. 1–14.

42 Ibid., p. 7.

43 James Fowler and Nicholas Christakis, 'Cooperative behavior cascades in human social networks', *Proceedings of the National Academy of Sciences*, 107:12 (2010), pp. 5334–8.

Epilogue

1   Helen Dunmore, 'My Life's Stem Was Cut', *Counting Backwards: Poems 1975–2017* (Bloodaxe Books, 2019).

2   Elee didn't get to finish the book and so I completed it on her behalf after her death. It was published as Elee Kirk and Will Buckingham, *Snapshots of Museum Experience* (Routledge, 2018).